Journey to Alternity

Transformational Healing Through Stories and Metaphors

Judith Simon Prager, Ph.D.

Writers Club Press
San Jose New York Lincoln Shanghai

Journey to Alternity
Transformational Healing Through Stories and Metaphors

Published by Writers Club Press
an imprint of iUniverse.com, Inc.

For information address:
iUniverse.com, Inc.
620 North 48th Street
Suite 201
Lincoln, NE 68504-3467
www.iuniverse.com

ISBN: 0-595-09560-7

Printed in the United States of America

This book is dedicated to Harry Youtt, lunatic, lover, poet, soul mate. Even more than it has infused this book, his spirit has illuminated every page of all my lives.

To Dr Sowmya & Panchanathan
Best wishes in your Journey!
TM Srinivasan, Nov, 2004.

Contents

Preface

How to Read this Book/Author's Note:

This is a book made up mostly of stories and they are meant to illustrate Alternity, alternate realities, for you.

In addition, there are six Interchapters. These are hard to read, full of scientific facts and provided for those who need verification of the mechanisms behind the miracles and mysteries reported in this book. *Feel free to skip them if they slow you down on your way.*

All of the stories are meaningful and true, but my favorites are "Beth and the Angel," "The Hardest Thing of All," "The Story of a Playwright and the Tale of Her Cat," "Not Enough," "Annie Oakley" and "Liz' Wild Ride," because they whisper and shout, all at the same time, how magically the tragic may be transformed.

The final chapters, "The New Wisdom?" and "Getting Unstuck Without Coming Unglued," take my ideas into the future.

You may be stimulated to come back to the Interchapters after you see how the process works, to find out **why** it does. As often as possible, the ideas are cross-referenced, so you can sort of "click" yourself around in this book as if it were a multi-media CD, while lying comfortably in bed or wherever you like best to read.

Exercises are woven about in the text and you can find most of them at the end of the book, where you can try the techniques for your own personal transformation.

Acknowledgements

Thanks to our "family," for their support, inspiration and love:
Our wonderful children, in order of appearance, Daniele Prager, Jennifer Youtt Hatzmann, Jonathan and Julie Sparling Youtt and Brad Prager. And our grandson, Jack Thomas Mullally.

Our "adopted children" and sustaining friends: Sarah Sheer, Nancy Sullivan, Jo-Anne Henry, Mark and Cindy Brown, John and Inger Lanese, Judith Acosta and a special thanks to Deanna Hare, who graciously proofread this manuscript and whose story is included within.

Our sisters and brothers in life and in-law: Jeff and Shelle McKenzie, Alan and Stephanie Mittman, and Stan and Nancy Youtt. And my cousin Marilyn Simon.

Thanks to everyone I've ever met, good and bad examples, my teachers, all. And especially to: Dr. Ronald Wong Jue, Gil Boyne, David Quigley, Linda McCallum, Richard Farr, Don Jacobs, Mala Spotted Eagle, Marcus Hong, Garnet and Annie Dupuis, Timothy Trujillo, Annika and Dr. Hans Gruenn and Anita Meier, "sister" and teacher.

Thanks to all of my clients, whether or not I've used their real names and their stories, and to all who allowed me to be part of their transformation.

Introduction

Into the Magic

"Our lives are a path to ourselves."
—*Herman Hesse*

"There's no use running if you're on the wrong road."
—*Country & Western Song*

You pick up the newspaper and you're reading about String Theory and the latest belief that Time and Space (your old standbys) are likely to become obsolete. Scientists explain that time and space are "an illusion...primitive notions that will be replaced by something more sophisticated."

You turn on the television, and there's *Touched by an Angel* or *The X-Files* or a program in which people slide through time or are morphed into something else entirely.

Whatever the biologists are cloning, you're not certain you want to know, and as for genetically engineered food, it's likely dangerous and perhaps catastrophic.

And the pace of it! You almost feel like looking for a lamppost to hold onto as the winds of change threaten to sweep your feet down unknown roads to the future. Feeling foolish to discuss it and desperate to understand it.

Well, if String Theory is correct, there may be no "out there," out there. (See Interchapter 6 on "reality.") Einstein said it a half century ago and we're still digesting it like a half-baked sausage: *Reality is relative to the observer.* YOU are in the experiment, and everything counts. Maybe the Strings (unimaginably small elements which, in vibrating, configure to produce different harmonic chords giving rise to particles) are affected by our thoughts as well as our presence. The way the string vibrates determines each particle's properties within 11-dimensional space…and the point of this obscure tangent is that probably nothing is as we thought it was.

Even consciousness. Every once in a while, there is an article in *Time Magazine* or *Newsweek* about where exactly in the brain "consciousness" is located. Those who study the nature of consciousness from a non-local perspective believe that looking for consciousness in the brain is like looking for Dan Rather in the television set. It's not there, but everywhere. In the "out there" that may not be out there. They feel, and I tend to agree, that our brain is the receiver. It's the software, and the universe is the hardware.

At a recent conference, scientist Peter Russell, author of *The Global Brain*, said, "One moment you don't have the idea, and the next, there it is. The Ah-ha!, and it's not individual consciousness. You say, 'It came to me; I was inspired.'"

As a hypnotherapist, I work with unexplored territory in the mind. Sometimes that means the parts responsible for transformative healing, for spontaneous remissions…for that visionary "Ah-ha!"

In the late '80s and '90s when greed was good and high-pressure jobs were a measure of importance, I used to be in the decidedly glamorous business of advertising. I created commercials, ads and direct marketing for American Express, Sears, Timex and other icons of our lives. I worked on the famed Madison Avenue, bounced around between high-status agencies including Grey and Ogilvy & Mather and rose to the position of Vice President, Creative Director, helping the world appreciate the benefits of Candies' shoes and AT&T services.

I was also a "best-selling" novelist and a writer of soap operas for television (*General Hospital*, right before Luke raped Laura, for those who mark the passage of time in media moments).

Today I work in the "healing arts." This is not what I had in mind. In some ways, I stand outside of society, now. People who hear of my work eye me strangely. I "forget" to charge critically ill clients. And miracles sometimes happen.

At the risk of putting you off this early on in my story, I'll confess that my clients have been "cured" by angels, made love to by ghosts, they've numbed toothaches for weeks by self-hypnotic trances, even cured phobias talking to a fruit bowl. Lives have been changed, call these events what you will.

I've studied with people who would heal you by marching you through every second of your past. I've studied with people who would heal you through altering your perception of your past and your future. I've studied with those who would help you transform everything in this moment. I've studied with others who would heal you through your energy fields. I've seen all of it work, some of the time.

I don't have a "grid" (See Interchapter 5—Grids and Gestalts) or a formula for helping people heal. It doesn't have to be "my way." I just have the awesome belief that when I sit near people, in absolute presence, turning my full love and attention on them, we connect somewhere else and they have permission to be or feel or see everything differently. Metaphorically, rather than literally. Transpersonally. That means beyond their singular person. They "get it" that they're not their name or their disease, but part of something magnificent, and, imagining that field, they create other possibilities, including the possibility of wholeness.

This business I'm now in—it's not a career path, it's a calling. How it happened to me, the "powers" which appeared, the longings to be of use which overwhelmed mundane reason, and the strange healings I've alluded to, are all part of this story.

The other part is that I firmly believe it could happen to you. As the changes inherent in the new paradigms rushing toward us in these extraordinary times awaken us, people will increasingly hear the call, open the doors of perception and find themselves rich in new dimensions they never anticipated.

* * *

Why Metaphors, Stories and Creativity

Example is not the main thing in influencing others. It is the only thing.

—*Albert Schweitzer*

My husband and I also teach in the Writers' Program at UCLA. We teach "creativity," which has proven to be the "String" in my theory. Through creativity we all can create *Alternities*: alternate realities which are as real as your last thought. As real as yesterday and tomorrow (which do not literally exist at all). Stories and pictures that can be held in your body as experience and transform your world.

Dwell for a moment on this: *illness exists in three-dimensional reality.* If reality is all there is, if it is solid and immutable, then we are stuck with it and in it. But if we can function on other planes as well, we can soar into realms rich in answers and an infinite abundance of possibilities.

Carolyn Myss, Ph.D., has said that if you believe it takes chemotherapy and five years to "beat" cancer, it does. But if you believe it can be gone "in the wink of an eye," that can be your truth. As you will see in some of these stories, healing—which happens in both the mind and the body—is not connected with time (see Interchapter 3: Time and Synchronicity), but more likely with belief system.

Your brain does not recognize the difference between something imagined and something real. (See Interchapter 1: The Mind/Body Connection and the Placebo Effect.) That is why you go through the wringer at a scary movie or wake up with a palpitating heart and sweaty hands from a frightening dream. Your body has reacted as if those events were real. The implications for healing are enormous.

That is why this book is about metaphors. How we picture something affects its outcome.

That is why sports teams are named after courageous animals. We shout, "Go get 'em, Tigers!" and that fierce image drives the plays. The team that called itself "The Chickens" wouldn't even make it onto the field. (Even Disney's "Ducks" have to be "Mighty.")

Joseph Campbell said we need a new story for the whole world. Each of us, too, could use a new story, one that connects us to everything, everyone and meaning. Many of my clients you'll encounter in this book (all of whom are real, but some of whose names have been changed to protect their privacy) have benefited by the experience of creating or even discovering a story that existed just beyond their sight.

The great psychiatrist and hypnotherapist, Milton Erickson, M.D., used healing stories and metaphors to invite his patients to consider alternative responses to their problems. For the part of the brain involved in healing, a picture is truly worth 1,000 words, and stories are pictures rather than facts or arguments.

In their book, *The Sacred*, authors Peggy V. Beck and Anna L. Waters report on the way the Navaho views stories. "When Yellowman (a storyteller) says that the stories are important because they allow us to envision the possibility of things not ordinarily seen or experienced, he means too that we have the ability to use our imagination—the intangible part of our thinking mind. This ability to seek for possibilities beyond the ordinary is at the root of Learning the Way. For this reason, storytelling and stories are an essential part of The People's lives."

Listening on a different level is typical of Native American training. They quote a Papago woman, Maria Chona, on the hypnotic effect of stories. "My father went on talking to me in a low voice. This is how people always talk to their children, so low and quiet, the child thinks he is dreaming. But he never forgets."

Luther Standing Bear recalled the education of Lakota children this way. "Training began with children who were taught to sit still and enjoy it. They were taught to use their organs of smell, to look when there was apparently nothing to see, and to listen intently when all seemingly was quiet. A child that cannot sit still is a half-developed child."

"You don't ask questions when you [are growing up]. You watch and listen and wait, and the answer will come to you. It's yours then, not like learning in school," a Keres Native American man explained.

"Learning the Way" often means that the answers are "coded" in stories. "The 'coding' of knowledge in stories is like not asking 'why,' because you have to listen more closely. Then you also have more of a chance to suddenly discover meanings, concepts and ideas by yourself," Beck and Walters write.

When we use words to paint a picture, we're using a left-brained tool in a right-brained capacity. Poet T.S. Eliot explained how it worked in this way: "The only way of expressing emotion in the form of art is by finding an 'objective correlative,' in other words, a set of objects, a situation, a chain of events which shall be the formula of that particular emotion, such that when the external facts, which must terminate in sensory experience, are given, the emotion is immediately evoked."

That is, if I want to make you sad, I can't command you to feel sad, I have to paint you a sad picture and have it resonate with you. And the picture may be of an abandoned child, which is one kind of sadness, or a scene of injustice, which may, in your case lead to anger, rather than sadness, which is why the metaphor must be chosen correctly, as it serves as an "objective correlative," a metaphor for the emotion.

We often evoke personal historical scenes to resonate with the metaphor. And good actors call on those historical moments to plug into a sad scene in the present. But, like actors, we can change the present scene by using different metaphors. And these metaphors may come from anywhere, not just our own personal history. That is why "past life regression" works. It doesn't matter where they come from—if they evoke a feeling that changes how we feel about the present, they can be healing.

As speaker Barbara Gluck puts it, we sit in classrooms staring out the window and are chastised for daydreaming, when we are really going to what she identifies as our right brain, our inspiration, our imagination, our connection with the infinite. We are expected, instead, to concentrate on the material, the literal, the "real." Ultimately, she says, in a thought that is both surprising and challenging: "Stress is mostly being unable to get to the right side of the brain."

* * *

The Method of this Book: Stories, Exercises and The Science Behind It All

Journey to Alternity is a book of healing stories that can point the way to using your creativity, wisdom and higher powers to enrich your life and strengthen your body.

Woven through the tales of healing and also at the end of this book you will find experiential exercises designed to help you examine your own readiness for using metaphors and symbols to transform your life.

The "transpersonal" part is important, too. Because when we move beyond our "self" to what Larry Dossey, M.D., in his book *Reinventing Medicine*, calls "non-local" experience, we realize that our mind is not our brain, and that we can move freely through space and time. "[Non-local] expressions include sharing of thoughts and feelings at a distance, gaining information and wisdom through dreams and visions, knowing the future, radical breakthroughs in creativity and discovery and many more. And this part of your mind can be used today in healing illness and disease in what I call Era III healing," Dossey writes.

Throughout, too, there are optional INTERCHAPTERS—sections for the skeptics or readers wanting or needing plausible explanations from scientists, physicists, physicians and others, of the phenomena described in this book—those who can help us bridge the gap between the concrete and the envisioned. Because they are so fact-packed, they are slower reading, so feel free to skip them if you're excited by the magic of the stories and your belief system tells you to trust the material without the "proof."

As much as possible, ideas are cross-referenced, so if you are reading something provocative to your imagination, you can jump around and find out the science behind it or a story that illustrates it or an exercise that lets you experience it.

I believe that we are on the verge of ascending a new rung on the evolutionary ladder, that we can invoke conscious human evolution. Even if you believe that we were created whole, you probably agree that human nature has a way to go to be closer to the models provided by our spiritual leaders such as Jesus, Mohammad, Confucius, Buddha and those others who showed us our potential. As we move along from ape to angel, from bestial to spiritual beings, we also become more joyful. Some people believe we can move from *homo sapiens* to *homo noeticus,* the "knowing" humans, who go beyond their five senses to a sixth, understanding each other's feelings and sharing in the "one mind." The next step centers at the heart. Reading this book with your heart as well as your mind might set up the resonance for your own shift.

Kierkegaard said, "Life can only be understood backwards, but it must be lived forwards." I believe it can also be understood—and changed—when you step outside of it and see it differently.

And, as I explain in Interchapter 5:

I'm using the metaphor of metaphor to explode the prison of limits that has characterized three-dimensional life.

I'm using the illusion of allusion to melt hard forms and make them malleable.

I'm offering you Alternity—the domain of endless possibilities—and inviting you to move in.

Chapter One

Crossing the Boundaries of Time

"I am certain that I have been here as I am now a thousand times before,
and I hope to return a thousand times…
Man is the dialogue between nature and God….
What is lacking is Self-Knowledge. After that, all the rest will follow."

—*J.W. von Goethe*

While my mother lay dying, suddenly and unexpectedly critically ill in a hospital in Encino, California, and my sisters and I took turns visiting her, I found myself one of those sad afternoons sitting in the waiting room with a gnome-like woman who quietly explained to me how things really worked. In my sadness, I was not inclined to have a conversation with a stranger, and yet, as the saying goes, "when the pupil is ready, the teacher appears."

I suppose I was so dazed with my mother's unexpected condition, I was not surprised that my mentor appeared in this form. A small, ordinary-looking middle-aged woman with soft, doughy features and a New York accent, she was finishing up her studies for a medical degree, having already garnered a Ph.D. in something to do with brain chemistry. But she chose to discuss none of that with me. Instead, she presented me

1

with a thought, as if she pulled it from her conventional handbag, a thought that has stuck with me on my journey ever since:

"If something is broken here," she gestured in front of herself, "the mechanic fixes it here." She gestured in the same place. "If it's broken here," she gestured in the same place, looking intently at me, "the magician," she said, studying me to see if I was paying close attention, "the *magician* fixes it *here*," and she gestured somewhere else entirely.

* * *

In the other room, they were trying to fix my mother's heart in her body, but it was broken *somewhere else*. Just hours before, looking less like my mother than like a sweet and confused child who had danced around her loneliness long enough, danced until she thought she saw a clearing, she had said to me, "I was thinking..." She glanced shyly at me, knowing I was her metaphysical daughter, knowing at least that I wouldn't be shocked, her pretty face both embarrassed and defensive, "I've been thinking that it's been six years since Daddy died. And I thought, if I joined him now, we could be the right age for each other and, you know...go 'round again...together."

"Mom!" I had said desperately, "he's in *eternity*. He'll wait for you."

But she'd made her decision. And then she left to find the only man she'd loved her whole life through.

* * *

My "magician's journey" had actually begun two years before with two invitations, one from my husband Harry and one from sources unknown.

The mysterious impulse came on the wind: something or someone had seemed to tap me on the shoulder and whisper, "Don't ask any questions. Just follow me."

I like to think my summoner was Albert Einstein, because nowadays much of what he said resonates with me as if it were the national anthem of a country of the soul. "The most beautiful thing we can experience is the mysterious," he said. "It is the source of all true art and science. He to whom this emotion is a stranger, who no longer pauses to wonder and stand rapt in awe is as good as dead."

The other invitation was a more literal tap on my other shoulder, as Harry asked me if I'd like to go with him to a hypnosis conference.

He had long been interested in the art of hypnosis, in part because of what I came to call the Youtt (rhymes with boot) family secret. Apocryphal or not, it had its historic place in the lore of the family into which I had married. It seems grandfather Harry Youtt the first, for whom my Harry was named, had some abilities to reckon with in the field of mesmerism. A charmer, an inventor, he was also a character. The legend (which the family has quietly suppressed) has it that hypnosis had gotten the old man into trouble. So much trouble that he had been escorted, at least figuratively, across the border, asked or invited to vacate the small Vermont village in which he lived. Seems he had hypnotized the mayor in a barbershop and convinced the man to wear his jacket inside out and walk backwards down the main street of the town.

While such a story might horrify the domesticated, it obviously only served to inspire my Harry. So, when he heard about a four-day seminar on hypnosis, hypnotherapy and the various techniques and uses of the same, he indulged his lifelong curiosity and enrolled.

Three days into it, his mind aswirl at having seen its own boundlessness, he approached me with this offer: "Tomorrow they're doing past life regressions," he said. "Come with me," he said, meaning only to the seminar, little knowing the paths of the mysterious.

I went. All the way.

The four-day seminar was held in a large hotel in Anaheim, California, which is, we must remember, also the home of Disneyland. These annual conferences, I later found out, were assembled by Gil Boyne, a self-promoting but very influential hypnotherapist known far and wide for his astonishingly effective "Sleep now!" command to put people into immediate trances. He was able to bring together some of the more visible and innovative people in this field, including medical doctors, therapists, and famous hypnotists. Three or four programs on a variety of subjects in the field ran concurrently in a line of ballroom-sized conference rooms.

In one of these arenas, filled to capacity with assembled prospective time travelers, Harry and I sat on hard, folding chairs—the kind called bridge chairs, an irony doubtless lost on most, although we were to accomplish these regressions through what is called the "bridge" technique. An attractive hypnotherapist named Holly Holmes from Northern California gave a short lecture and then invited us to "get comfortable" (something, oddly, we don't seem to do automatically and naturally in modern times. This usually involves a great deal of shifting and fussing. Give it a try. If I said to you "get comfortable," would you have to move?). She invited us to allow our gaze to rest on a large icon in the front of the room. It was, if I remember correctly, the logo of the Hypnosis Training Institute, a sort of medical Caduceus complete with a single eye in the center. Holmes then began what was called an "induction" for a room full of people, mostly credentialed people in the field there for continuing education and enlightenment.

(I relate this to give you an overview and not as a manual for doing it yourself. It should be done only with the aid of a therapist; I'm painfully serious about this. What is revealed must be processed. If you opened to your conscious mind the secrets which your unconscious mind has been protecting you from by concealing them without having an experienced person there to help you understand these often painful revelations, it would be like pulling the stitches out of a wound without having the means to repair the exposed flesh and nerves.)

Holmes then described the "affect bridge technique." We were to think of a feeling we'd had, which we felt strongly or often in this life. (It was not to be too emotionally charged, as she was not in a position to see each of us individually through an abreaction or any trauma this process might open.) We were to feel where in our bodies we experienced this feeling. We were to remember the last time we had this feeling. Then we were to relax, holding onto the feeling, as she took us down into a trance. When she said, "in your mind's eye, look at your feet," we would be there. Wherever there was.

There is a discussion of what I imagine "past lives" might be in Interchapter 2. Suffice it to say at this early point that "real" or otherwise, whatever it is, it can promote wisdom and healing and therefore it is a useful tool in exploring our outer and inner limits.

* * *

I turned to Harry and was about to say. "Let's find out where we last knew each other." But I decided against it. After all, everyone was entitled to his own trip and his own past.

The room got quiet and we began. We were reminded to revisit a feeling we encountered often. Harry later told me that he had decided he'd just be an observer, not really participate. He was certain he could play along and maintain his distance; as an observer it might be interesting to simply pretend and see where it took him.

Of course, I didn't learn about what was going on in his mind, what he was seeing and feeling as he sat next to me in that room, until later. I'm telling you up front, so you'll understand how it must have struck him when I told him about my vision. But unbeknownst to me, and much to his surprise, this, he told me later, was how his journey went.

He thought about how he felt about having been a lawyer, which made him uncomfortable these days. Where in his body? In his stomach. When did he last have that feeling? When he last read through the *American Bar Association Journal* to which he still subscribed, although he had left his practice in New York and was not even admitted to the bar in California. Now the trance induction happened, and when he looked down at his feet in his mind's eye, he was wearing army boots, foreign army boots. And he knew, instinctively, because he certainly did not know it objectively, that they were the style the French wore in the First World War. Suddenly, his commanding officer was telling him he had to go into the trenches in the morning and kill the enemy. He refused, it made no sense, it was a futile war, it had nothing to do with him or even with the men he might kill. His commanding officer was not cruel, in fact Harry respected him, but the officer insisted that if Harry did not comply the next day, the officer would have to kill him. Harry despaired, feeling helpless, and in the morning he left with his troop, weapon in hand, to charge the enemy on orders. Immediately, he found himself impaled on the end of an enemy soldier's fixed bayonet. He was stabbed to death. In the stomach.

Coming up from the trance, which could have taken one second or an hour, all he needed to know about this feeling that had plagued him all his life was revealed to him in the way often called "knowing." Without words and long explanations, he understood the meaning of his distaste for authority, of his abhorrence of blindly following rules, of the visceral feelings in his stomach when he represented "the law," or when "the law," unjustly punished his clients.

He looked at me and I was frowning, lost in my own contemplation. We got up and started walking out, past others moving slowly, digesting what had just happened to them, what had been revealed. We'd all been in that room physically together, but we'd been invited to move up and out of chronos time, the linear time along which we walk the straight and narrow, in blinders.

Harry and I stumbled over our words as we began to talk about what we had just experienced as we headed for the exit of the cavernous room. "Where'd you go?" I asked him.

As I said, he didn't tell me about what he'd seen and done just then. "Nowhere," he said. "I didn't do it. I just observed." He hesitated. "Where'd you go?"

"Well, when she said bring up a feeling I often had, I thought about loving you."

"You nut. It's supposed to be a bad feeling, a problem."

"Well, it was my trip, and that's what I wanted to know about. Loving you."

"So?"

"So, then she said, where in your body do you feel it and I thought in my heart, but it kept going to my groin. So I let it. Then she asked when was the last time I felt it and I thought about the last time we made love."

"You are a nut."

"And then, when I looked down at my feet, they were bare."

Harry tells me he thought to himself then: *Sure, I die in the First World War and she gets to be an Indian princess.*

But I said, "It was in a barn, somewhere in Europe. I think it was France. I had bicycled all the way from Paris and you were there, too. You looked like Douglas Fairbanks or John Barrymore, but it was you, somehow I could tell."

"France," he said. "*I* was in–" Harry started to say, but he stopped himself.

"We were in a hay loft, making love. I had come all this way to make love with you. You were a soldier. You didn't look like you, but I knew it was you. And you were wearing a French World War I uniform—"

He stopped walking, saw an empty folding chair placed beside the door, and simply sat down, while I finished my story,

"—and I was saying to you, 'Don't go. You don't have to go. If you go you'll be killed….'"

Chapter Two

Sailing Away

"Yearning and letting go:
Yearning is pointing yourself in the direction of your desire.
Letting go is trusting that you will get there."

—*JSP*

Of course I became a hypnotherapist after that. I wanted to know everything, past, present and future.

For Albert Einstein, those lines blurred. "To those of us who believe in physics," he said, "the separation between past, present and future is only an illusion."

How was it that I could almost understand that? I now desperately wanted to experience the fluidity, the elasticity, the stunning un-concreteness of it all.

I was not raised in an especially mystical tradition, except perhaps for my mother's well-known telepathic skills. If she wanted my grandmother or my father to call her, she had only to speak her desire aloud. Once she would utter the words: "I wish your father would call," her three daughters would turn into a small-town version of The Supremes, singing "One...two...three!" and gesturing in unison to the phone, which would obligingly ring.

My mother apparently could send mental messages to my father and my grandmother. With me, she received. This was in the days before cellular phones and occasionally proved itself invaluable. Once in a junior high school art class, the tool I was using to carve a balsa wood bunny rabbit jumped from my right hand and sliced into my left. Oozing blood from the wound, I was rushed to the school nurse, who tried calling my mother at home. There was no answer.

"We'll have to take you to the hospital and have you sewn up without her if we can't reach your mother soon," the nurse said, giving every evidence that she wished I would have the decency to bleed to death in the girl's room alone and spare her the paperwork, the trip to the hospital, the trouble.

Oh, Mom, I thought, so loud I knew she'd hear it, *I need you.*

Another student entered the office. Florence Nightingale took his temperature with cynicism and disdain. "You're perfectly fine. Go back to class and take the test."

"How did you know there was a test?"

The nurse pointed to the door, watched the hapless student exit, and then dialed my home again, to no avail. She picked up her purse and said, officiously, "Let's go."

Mom! I thought, even louder than before. I wasn't going to the operating room without her. "Try once more," I said to the nurse.

Handbag still on her arm, she sighed, complied, dialed. Still no answer. "Sorry, we tried. I've got to get you to the hospital. We'll call your mother from there." Just as she suspected, she would have to be responsible for this wayward child whose clumsiness threatened to endanger the Art Department Sculpture Program with the wrath of the Board of Education should word of art lessons with X-Acto knives leak out.

I tried once more, too. *Mom, I need you,* I thought, almost resigned.

Brushing brusquely past me, the nurse was on her way out the door when she nearly collided with my mother who came walking in with a frown on her face, crossed over to me and without missing a beat said, "What's wrong?"

Maybe you've have had incidents like that, yourself. Or known people who have. So, although I would send my mother Halloween cards addressed to "my favorite witch," my childhood was not excessively filled with the paranormal.

I wasn't part of the drug-infested '60s, either, having married at 18 a scientist I met at Cornell University, a Spock-like man of great logic who judged me harshly and found me too much a free spirit for his liking. I tried to behave. We lived first in California where he helped put men on the moon, then moved to New York City, where we parented two brilliant, beautiful children and I wrote a fairly successful novel. And, after years of painful miscommunication, as soon as I could support myself and the children with a job as an advertising copywriter, we divorced.

Time passed, as they say in cheap novels, either when nothing much happened, or the author is loath to go into the details. One event of great significance occurred at this time, and I actually "forgot" it in the first draft of this book and have had to stop, recognize its significance, and revise the manuscript acknowledging the fact of it.

I had a nervous breakdown.

It was very grim and seemed to focus on germs. I washed my hands all day long in Clorox and ammonia. If a magazine came into the house with the words "New Cure for Cancer" on the cover, I wouldn't even touch it, but insisted my husband carry it out to the incinerator. I tell you this information, not because we live in a tell-all age and "sharing is bonding," but because, when I found myself a few short years later holding the hands of strangers dying of cancer, it constituted a transformation of the kind that fills this book.

Engaged in the healing process, I got out of frightened little "me" in those moments and became something larger, something "non-local," something much more everything. (See Interchapter 4.)

In 1982 I remarried, and you've already met Harry. Turns out that, irony being a theme I can relate to, although Harry was a lawyer of significant reputation when I married him, he was more a free spirit than

I was. After five years of marriage, I had grown pretty content, with ever-better jobs in advertising, a rented, luxurious house on a lake in the country and the comings and goings of our four combined teen-aged children rivaling the antics of the Brady Bunch.

If our lives were a little short on purpose, they was open-hearted, romantic, and pretty much what one could expect of a happy existence in the late 20th Century.

But, as Carl Jung insisted, "Man cannot stand a meaningless life."

So, one day Harry came home from lawyering and said, "Judeet!" (He calls me "Judeet," as if we were French. "Judeet. *Ma* Judeet. *My* love." In this case he needed all of those endearments.)

"Judeet, my love," he came home and said. "If I continue being a lawyer, I will shortly be dead. And our children won't have a father and you won't have a husband. So, instead of that, I want to give away everything we own and go out to California to build a boat and sail around the world on it. What do you say?"

Me? I said, yes. I felt: *what?!* but I said yes.

I was younger, then, not bitten by the bug of larger meaning, not having yet heard the clarion call of healing. I held youthful, perhaps even nihilistic notions.

I thought, for example, that positioning oneself somewhere inevitable and inviting lightning to strike would be the finest form of voluntary death.

Death by lightning—more than romantic, more than dramatic—absolutely divine. A summoning, unequivocal, instantaneous, from the god Zeus. To come, now, to his side. An omnipotent finger pointed from parted heavens, deliberate in its choice, transporting my spirit to the other world. Irresistible. So gorgeously quick, that it is less to die than to combust. To conflagrate orgasmically.

Having been born on the Summer Solstice, the first day of summer, I had an affinity to lightning. The frequent electrical storms on my birthday were a salute, my personal celestial fireworks—and an annual reminder of the opportunity to arrange such a rendezvous with Zeus. Should the time seem right.

By the time of this incident, however, my adolescent suicidal tendencies had abated, even dissolved, so that, when Harry and I clung to each other, naked, in the hot August night, in the lake outside the door of our country home north of New York City, I had accumulated much that was too wonderful to lose. I did not welcome the suggestive thunderclaps, the jolts of electricity threatening us not many miles away.

In the four years we lived in the house in Croton-on-Hudson, we had often taken the canoe around the lake's perimeters, but we never chose to submerge our bodies in what had always become by August an algaefied flora soup, catalyzed and encouraged as it was by the runoff of fertilizer from nearby landscapes. Lake Turtles-breath, our mocking name for Lake Woodrock, was alive then with snakes and fish and turtles and a carpet of mud-slime that gave way to ooze underfoot. Beautiful on the surface, it did not invite any closer intimacy.

But this season had been scorchingly hot. The air clung like Saran Wrap. I had begun to sink into that malaise of indecision that typically precedes an impending, life-changing decision. It had in fact become a full-blown lethargy, and it defined my not yet having arrived at a position of total acceptance of what was inevitably to come. A Harry invitation.

It was a hot summer night of the kind that generate an electricity that begins lightly, delicately—with the hum of cicadas. On nights like this one, the Second Movement brings the lightning, a still-crisp volatility, crackling thin and dry through the humidity. And it is only the thunder that follows somewhat later, in answer, that resonates against the saturated air and bears its own weight.

Taunted by the cloying air, dense as steam and nearly as torpid, we tore off our clothes and dove into the lake, feeling the languid, algid growths reaching out their swaying branches to stroke us as we glided by.

Harry, ever impulsive, dove in first, waiting for me to join him in the night-black water, illuminated as it was by the bolts of electricity from the darkest reaches above us. I hesitated and then slipped into the lake, skimming through the water to glide into his arms.

Catching me, Harry then swam away again, to find a rock on the bottom large enough for him to stand upon. Blindly, I followed. Clouds hid the moon, and all was black.

He called to me and I found his outstretched arm. A foot shorter than he, I clung to him like a child, like a monkey, legs wrapped around his waist, feeling his nakedness, his protectiveness.

A jolt of lightning. A jarring clack of thunder challenged us as Zeus moved closer…laughing.

"This is how Viking chieftains are conceived," Harry said, and I kissed his wet and craggy face. Fish, or the branches of plants, brushed by us, and the currents under the water ran alternately cool and warm.

We were about to give up the life we knew, to toss it all—jobs, home, possessions, everything. Because, if ever we had once believed in them, we had stopped believing in THINGS. Because we were looking for what it was we were supposed to do—really do—with our lives before they ended and we stood surrounded by cars and VCRs and no explanations.

It was Harry's idea at the beginning. He figured that if, like Noah, he built a boat and we just sailed off, self-sufficiently, listening quietly to the universe, we might be able to come so close to God or to meaning, or even to ourselves, that we would not only be saved, but we could bring the message back. Rich as our life together had become, when we looked at it closely we could only see ourselves parked beside a dead-end sign (in our case at the hub of a fancy cul-de-sac). And all the luxuries in the world could not tune out the small voice inside us that asked the eternal questions.

I agreed in theory, but, as the time for departure drew near, I hesitated. As I let go of familiar life-lines—all those customs that defined me—as the time grew ever nearer—what had seemed wisely, if bravely inevitable began to loom also vast and insurmountable.

And suddenly, here and now, not because of the ominous electrical storm, but in its presence, I became afraid.

"Are we doing the right thing? Does it make sense?" I said.

And it was then that he delivered the answer that clinched the deal, that opened the doors to trust and pushed us on our inevitable way.

"Everybody dies," he said, holding me close, running his hands through my hair, stroking my back as the troubled air swirled around us, occupied by creatures, waiting, too, for his reply.

"Everybody dies," he repeated quietly, "but not everybody lives."

It became silent, but for the soft gurgle of the water we had disturbed. Even Zeus paused.

But the silence was only a respite that invited a premature confidence. Then the sky ignited again, only more boldly. And the thunder boomed.

Applause? Laughter? Concurrence? Disdain? My affinity for lightning made me see it as confirmation.

So we gave away the cars, the washing machine, whatever else wouldn't fit into boxes in one little self-storage room in Fishkill, and Harry moved out to California while I stayed to help our youngest with his college applications.

Then I quit my job at Ogilvy & Mather, where I had been writing Sears radio and television commercials for savings on washing machines and Craftsman tools.

This plan, which had an urgency of its own, did not include strategies on finances. By the time I came to join Harry, we were pretty much out of money, and he was living in the factory on the half-finished boat.

Time passed. The details are not pretty, so we'll just move ahead. Most difficult for me was the fact that the factory smelled of chemicals. Because my father, whom I had adored, had recently died of lung disease initiated by his work in factories as a young man, my nerves were becoming shattered.

It looked like we'd come to the end of our nautical rope: the only escape on the horizon was the wide blue sea, and since I'd never sailed, questions remained about my sea-legs, my sea stomach, and my sanity.

In panic, I found another advertising/marketing job creating nationwide zoo and save-the-animal promotions for Kal Kan pet food. And, lo and behold! Harry decided he didn't have to set sail after all—something about having received permission to pursue his dream having freed him from actually having to live it.

So we moved to Hermosa Beach where my new job was located and life looked like it was going to be a down-scale model of our earlier, more typical start.

But then the cosmic plan activated quickly.

We now lived in a dreary basement apartment, began teaching in the Writers Program at UCLA, Harry took me to the past-life hypnosis conference and I began studying and practicing hypnotherapy. I met the woman in the waiting room. She introduced me to Transpersonal psychologists working in altered states, and suddenly, doors mysteriously opened, people began to call me, and I began to put it all together.

But it's not as if suddenly one day you step outside and find a magic wand on the porch. It's as if suddenly, every day, it wafts across your face like a silk scarf of a breeze, and you smile and it's gone, but you're changed. A little bit. Cell by cell and breath by breath. It can happen to you too, if you want it, believe it, and listen and remember. The Ayervedic scholars say we don't have to learn anything more. We just have to remember.

Within a period of five short years, I went from being a hot-shot advertising executive to being virtually homeless to becoming a "healer," working with some of the people in the most progressive fields of transpersonal and mind/body work.

Who we are and what we are is *that* mutable. For you, too. Life is about change, and our responses to it. And about engaging the magic.

As soon as we let go of our preconceptions, our labels, our limits, we are boundless. Everything lives in potential, in possibilities. All we have to bring to it is our trust.

Of course, to some, change is threatening and not everyone is willing to reconsider his or her preconceptions about reality and the nature of consciousness. "We would rather be ruined than change," the poet W. H. Auden said. "We would rather die in our dread than climb the cross of the moment and let our illusions die."

But you are reading this book, so maybe he didn't write that about you.

Stories About Mind/Body Healing and Beyond

In a letter to the journal, *Alternative Therapies*, Dr. Bernie Siegel, author of *Love, Medicine and Miracles*, wrote: "Over 70 years ago, Carl Jung interpreted a dream presented to him at a conference and made an accurate diagnosis of a brain tumor. I have yet to meet a medical student who was taught that [skill] while attending medical school. Our minds and bodies communicate via images…. I could write many pages about my patients' specific dreams relating to their health, ranging from a white cat named Miracle appearing in a dream and telling the dreamer how to treat her cancer, which proved correct, to visualizing one's malignancy and finding the surgeon's description of his findings to be exactly what the patient saw in her dream." [See Chapter Five, The Story of a Playwright and the Tale of Her Cat, for a similar story.]

"The last point I would leave you with," he wrote, "is a bit mystical. Who or what creates the dream and who or what is observing it? I have had a near death experience and continued to see while out of my body. Recently I watched a program on the subject in which people blind from birth had the same experience and could see while they were out of their bodies. When they were resuscitated they were blind again. Putting that together with the memories carried by all of our bodies' cells, as demonstrated by transplant recipients knowing elements of the donor's life history, makes us rather interesting and mystical organisms." (January 2000.)

As the game of "peek-a-boo" mystifies a baby who thinks your reappearance from behind the wall is magic, so these healing stories may seem magical because the mechanisms which make them possible are incompletely understood.

Knowing they really happened helps model them for the creative answers you can find within yourself.

Chapter Three

Beth and the Angel

A Vision and a Spontaneous Remission

"Miracles happen, not in opposition to Nature,
but in opposition to what we know of Nature"

—*St. Augustine*

The first time we saw Beth, she was waiting in the hall outside our class-room, draped Elvira-like in flowing black robes with a short, tight hel-met of black hair around her intelligent, open, very white face, bracketed on either side by giant hoop earrings.

What were we to think? She was our very first student in the first cre-ative writing course Harry and I taught together in the UCLA Writers Program and we wondered if we were ready for this class.

It turned out that Beth was a producer of the popular daytime tele-vision program, Judge Wopner's "People's Court." She had decided she wanted to reach deeper and find her meaning through her writing. In that first class she had begun a thinly-disguised autobiography about a very independent, free-spirited woman in the '60s named Rocky with whom she had much in common.

We hadn't seen her in a while and when I heard her voice on the phone a week before we were to begin teaching an advanced writing course, I started my usual animated babbling about how good it was to hear from her, anticipating that she was calling to let us know she'd be joining our new class. Instead she said, "I just wanted to tell you that I'd really like to take your new course," and she paused, "but I can't."

Not one to pry I said, "Oh, I'm sorry."

"I can't do anything right now. I've got cancer."

"Beth!"

"Inoperable pelvic cancer." Her voice was filled with that familiar odd irony that seemed like a cross between petulance and humor.

Since I am telling you all—that which is conventionally believable and otherwise—I will relate how Beth found out about her condition.

For her birthday, a friend of hers had given her the gift of a visit to a psychic named Todd. (Having subsequently seen him myself I can tell you more about my visit with him, which was also remarkable, in Chapter Twenty-Five.)

For now, I'll describe him as probably in his late 20's, lanky, upbeat, and very chatty. He has an androgynous style and he lives in a little shack behind his mother's bigger shack on a shady block in Los Angeles. Religious icons decorated the room consistent with his beginning with a prayer for our highest good, and candles burning when he is working.

When I asked him about his powers, he confided that he'd always heard voices and that he had at one time been a Born-Again Christian. "And if you are psychic with them," he said, his eyes rolling, "you had better be right. Or else you'll be labeled a false prophet." So he had learned to be painfully, vitally careful about the information he received and dispensed.

Todd is also able to see into the body, which is what he had done that day for Beth.

"You're supposed to live a long time," he had told her. "But if you don't take care of what's wrong with you, you won't."

"What's wrong with me?"

"There are black spots on your pelvis," he had said.

So she went the next day to the gynecologist and the second opinion had a medical name.

"Oh my God," I said to Beth on the phone, or something else equally clumsy. *Inoperable* is not a promising concept, it's just a negative response to what ought to be done. "What...what can they do for you? What's the treatment?"

"Not a lot. Well, there is this radiation treatment, they stick a radioactive kind of tampon up inside me and I have to lie completely still for two days, but that's about all they can do," she said sadly.

I had just begun my work as a hypnotherapist and I so fully believed in the mind/body connection, I offered to work with her if she'd let me try out my techniques on her.

"I'll try anything," Beth said. "Sure. I'd like that."

You might say it was a bargain made in heaven.

Every other Saturday for a period of months, I traveled up to Beth's house in the San Fernando Valley and, well, we experimented. I certainly can't claim that I knew what I was doing back then. We locked her barking dogs away, turned off the phones, turned on the air conditioning to drown out the street sounds, pulled the blinds and began.

I regressed her to her childhood and then accidentally (before I'd studied it) regressed her further ("go further back, before that time, to find out the meaning of your illness") and she found herself being stoned to death on a cobblestone street, looking up at the spires of buildings above her. As I said, don't try this yourself. It does no good. I didn't know then what to do with that information and it didn't help her. Thank goodness it also didn't hurt her.

I helped her rescue her inner child and find new inner parents, a technique I'd learned from David Quigley's Alchemical Hypnotherapy school which I will tell you about in Chapter Twenty-Two, "Into the Conference Room with Morning Light."

Many healers work with the concept of light as a vibration higher than our solid bodies. I suggested to Beth that she envision light moving through her body, but, even in trance, she had difficulty moving it through her pelvis. It could enter her and unfold through her head and chest and waist, but to her mind's eye the part of her body in which there was disease was a black pit and nothing could penetrate it.

Then, just before she was going in for her treatment, I decided that what might be most profitable would be to find an inner guide and have him or her help Beth create a visualization of the way her treatment would help her heal. (See Interchapter 1 on Mind/Body medicine, Interchapter 6 on the Holographic Universe, as well as Chapter Twenty-Four on Grandpapa and White Eagle and the Exercise at the end on Finding Guides.)

One of the very few benefits of my not having asked for society's sanction over my work is my vast freedom to follow methods unproveable in the prison of three dimensions. So, having studied both guides and visualizations, and knowing Beth, I figured it was time to call upon the universe for some of its abundant wisdom.

On this day, she lay on the bed as she had every other Saturday and I put her into trance. Blinds closed, air conditioner on, dogs out of earshot. She closed her eyes and I looked at her sweet face and began the induction, which, after we had worked together so often, was a very simple whisper about breaths and letting go.

Then we took an imaginary walk on a beach in search of her guide. After a few false starts (with practice, you can tell when it's not the right guide or not a true guide), she suddenly saw what she called "A Russian Monk." He was robed and flying through the sky.

"Ask him his name," I said, feeling through her excitement that he was the one. She hesitated. "It's Gregor," she said, frowning. Her husband's name is Greg and I knew she was feeling that she wasn't being "creative" if she made up a guide with the same name.

"Ask him if he is from the light," I said, a precaution well taken, as not all visitors are guides available for our highest good.

She did, he was. Then we asked him for a visualization of how the treatment would work to heal her.

"He says I should picture my insides as a tree with green and brown leaves, picture the cancer as the brown and drying and dying leaves. I should see the radiation as a wind blowing the dead leaves off the tree, and then green buds begin to grow in their place, healthy green buds, healthy white cells."

"Very nice," I said. "Tell him thank you." She thanked him and I began to take her through the visualization, which I embellished with sensual memories, important to effective stimulation of the cells' intelligence: the sounds of the crackling dry leaves, the smell of the soil, the colors, the textures.

When we got to the wind, her body on the bed began to shake. I could almost see the wind blowing through her. And I felt something resonate in me, as well. It was the first time I realized I could share the trance experience with my clients.

When she came up from the trance, she sat up slowly, waking like a cat fat and logy from a meal.

"The light went all the way through," she said almost inaudibly.

* * *

Three days later she called me to report that she still felt the light streaming through her.

This is a story about the magic, so you know that when Beth went back to her doctor, a Slavic man who must have been absent from medical school during the class in professional bedside manner, he burst into tears and hugged her. She was fine. Fine! He hadn't really dared hope, it didn't seem likely she would pull through—this was simply amazing. She was fine!

But this experience had been too drastic, too ultimate for Beth to accept its ending this easily. So she made another appointment with Todd.

"Stand up against the wall," he said, examining her body with his whatever-ray vision. "Well, they're gone. The black spots are gone. You're okay."

Her body untensed, and she was about to move away from the wall when he said to her, "You know, there's an angel standing right next to you. A tall angel. Actually, a very tall—have you ever seen an angel?"

"Well, once, in hypnosis, I saw—I thought he was a Russian Monk, but he was flying and I guess he could have been—"

"Do you know his name?"

"Gregor," she said, frowning again.

He picked up a book of angels and looked it up. "Ah," he said, "you're pronouncing it wrong. His name is Grigor." He looked up from the book. "And he's one of the tallest angels."

* * *

Later that day, she called to tell me all about it. "I *really saw him*," she said. He'd really come to her. It's always different from how we thought it would be. That's why we have to abandon trying to control things. We do our best. We do our best with the clearest, purest integrity and the universe responds.

Chapter Four

Joe the Mailman

Pain Relief in a Postal Truck

*"For there was never yet philosopher
that could endure the toothache patiently".*

—*Shakespeare, Much Ado About Nothing*

You may recall that we moved to California so that Harry could build a boat on which he planned to sail around the world. While Harry and I were building the boat, we spent some time living on it in the factory. That's a whole other story, but when I had lived that way for as long as I could stand it, I found a job at a marketing agency promoting the sale of Kal Kan pet food and creating events in partnership with zoos across the country. The income allowed me to insist that we move to the relative comfort of an apartment, on the land, from which we could safely just look at the water.

Harry found us a little dive in Hermosa Beach, a sleepy town populated by surfer dudes and old hippies. It had The Bijou, a second-run, run-down, down-town movie theater that played only foreign films, which suited us grandly. The town also featured loud, single men in boxer shorts who thought farting was clever, beer was water, music was only as good as it was loud, and if one found the perfect wave, there was nothing to then do but die.

It would have been sheer flattery to call our little dwelling a beach shack. It had been created, clumsily, around the stilts that held up the main house, so that whoever lived upstairs could enjoy the view of the Pacific. Our place had a view of the alley. We'd gone from living in a factory to living in the equivalent of an old refrigerator box on the street.

As the floor above was not insulated, we barely survived a successive series of apparently nomadic bachelor party dudes in the house above us whose stereo speakers rested on our ceiling, but only when not in use. When activated, the speakers virtually thumped around the floor filling our dark little dwelling with the bass line of some of the greatest acid rock hits of our time. It was like living in a disco from which you cannot go home.

Our landlord had been a cop in town and was known, if not loved, by the locals. His wealth was never explained but it had the effect of contributing to the endless string of rumors and epithets which followed him everywhere. And being rich never saved him from being considered a low-life. With a booming voice and the ragged appearance of an old salt who had spent most of his time under the rum barrel, he had still managed to buy up a considerable amount of beachfront property and turn over a nice profit, from legitimate dwellings as well as illegal fabrications such as ours.

We were somewhat anomalous, there, by age, by vocabulary, by, let's face it, taste in music. By the hours we kept, or would like to have kept if it had been quiet enough to sleep before dawn. In all the five years we lived there, we never met people with whom we seemed to have anything in common. Every time we went to The Bijou, reading subtitles in seats behind us were interesting-looking couples who drifted through in silence, like the specters in the library in *Wings of Desire*, but we never exchanged a word.

One of the few people whose name we even actually knew was Joe the Mailman (that being, for all we also knew, the way it appeared on his birth certificate). A throwback from the great postmen of small town America, Joe knew trivia about the neighborhood, kept tabs on the kids, made even the common complaints which pass for conversation seem sunny.

A week before Christmas in 1992, I was looking for Joe to give him his holiday envelope. I enlisted Harry, too, to look for Joe. He was late that day and when I finally saw him, across the street and down the alley, Harry and I both walked toward him.

After a round of "hey's"" and "hi's!" I handed him the envelope marked "Joe," and said, "Would you please deliver this for me?" He looked at it and thanked me, but he seemed a little glum. Harry stayed behind to talk to him as I walked back toward home.

It didn't take Harry long to find out that Joe had just lost the crown on a tooth, that he was in considerable pain, and that his dental plan would not kick in until after the new year.

There is hardly anything you can say to Harry that will wince him up faster than the simple word "tooth-ache." His fear of dentistry is legend, finally justified when a dentist in New York confirmed that his root system rivaled the schematic of the London underground, and actually drew a map of this convoluted network for future dentists to work by. So, Joe's plight did not fall on unsympathetic ears.

"You should let Judith hypnotize you," Harry said. "She can make the pain go away."

Joe's eyes lit up, Harry told me later. I wasn't there to see it, only to follow it through. Because when Harry came home, he recounted the conversation. "Thanks a lot," I thought. "Thanks for volunteering me." I'd never done hypnotic anesthesia, although I had studied it.

I went out to look for Joe, trepidation dogging my steps. It's very hard to put a person in pain in a trance. The pain is all they can think about, unless you can distract them.

He was coming out of a building down the block when he saw me. "Would you?" he said. "I saw Pat Collins on television. I'd really appreciate it if you would."

"Sure," I said, bravado dripping from my every pore. "Get into your truck."

He was desperate, the only thing I had going for me, there in a mail truck in the middle of the block in the middle of the day. Desperate people tend to be in an altered state already, and they can be very susceptible to suggestion. I had him sit in the driver's seat, take off his hat, and get into a comfortable position. I did a quick induction and it seemed to me he slipped easily into trance.

He was relaxed; I was cooking, I knew what I had to do next. Then, out of the quiet of this afternoon, from right beside the truck, a screaming din began as construction workers in the building against which we were parked began drilling and sawing and raising an ear-bending ruckus. Luckily, hypnosis can accommodate all sorts of surprises. You can incorporate them. You say, "Just as that construction you hear is done with machines, so your mind is a machine and you can control it. Go now to your control room in your mind. See the buttons and switches in front of you..."

Or something like that. The control room is a place in which you can regulate pain. I had him find the "pain" rheostat and I asked him to notice that his tooth pain could be read as going from one, which was lowest, to ten, which was the greatest pain he could endure. Then I had him turn it up to five and signal when he had. He grimaced and signaled. Then I asked him to turn the pain up to nine. He hesitated, then grimaced further and signaled again. Then I had him turn it down to zero. His face relaxed completely.

"How did you do that?" I asked, rhetorically. "You controlled the pain. You turned it up, and you saw that you could turn it down whenever you wanted to, whenever you needed to." I taught him how to return to this trance state whenever he had to turn the pain down, and explained that he now knew that he could. And then I brought him up from the trance.

He looked at me, surprised as almost everyone is after being hypnotized, and said, as almost everyone then says, "I don't know if I was hypnotized or not. I heard every word you said." He paused, adding with a smile, "But my cheek feels numb."

I gave him a small kiss on his other cheek, said, "Merry Christmas," and walked away heading home.

I was so relieved, I hardly noticed when he started his engine. By the time I turned around to watch him go, I just caught a glimpse of him driving away, raising his fist out the window and shouting "Ya-HOO!"

I was somewhat afraid to learn what had happened after that. We moved away shortly thereafter, and I'd forgotten all about the incident when Harry came home one afternoon in May and told me he'd just bumped into Joe.

"And?" I said, knowing he'd guess what I needed to know.

"And...he had an exceptionally normal holiday. Whenever the toothache threatened, he knew what to do, so he wasn't in pain at all!"

I was thrilled. Man, I thought, this is lovely magic.

Too bad it even has to be thought of as magic, it's so natural and easy. Joe's only frustration about the whole business, he'd told Harry, was that no one would believe he'd gone from abject pain to master of his own destiny because some lady had hypnotized him in the middle of the afternoon in his mail truck.

Chapter Five

Story of a Playwright and Tale of a Cat

Knowing She Can Write Her Own Future

"You can't solve a problem with the same kind of thinking that created it."

—*Albert Einstein*

Virginia is a small, Southern firebrand with flowing red hair and a flare for the dramatic ("You think *I'm* dramatic—we call mother Scarlet O'Hara!"). While the rest of us either live Thoreau's "lives of quiet desperation" or simply exist through days and nights punctuated by events of different sizes and shapes, only the largest or worst or most colorful events bothered to happen to Virginia.

A playwright, she used that Tennessee Williams influence to call forth comedies and tragedies which had graced small theaters in Texas and New York.

She had tried her hand at fiction in our classes, returning often and always ready with a new story, and like many of our other former students, she kept in touch.

So we were not surprised to hear her voice on the phone one evening, just checking in, we thought, or reporting about another play which had been optioned, until we realized she was calling to say *goodbye*.

She had been diagnosed with tumors on her liver and ovaries and her doctor had pronounced that in the blood test her CH125 level "indicates ovarian cancer." This diagnosis had come at a time shortly after her younger, beloved and mentally-challenged brother (did we suggest drama?) had been told he needed a heart operation for a defect that ran in the family and for which she might also be a candidate.

The old Virginia spunk had sputtered. The hands-on-hips little spitfire had resigned under one too many serious medical prognoses. They had overwhelmed her spirit and she was willing to check out. So she was, as understatedly as everything else had been grandiose, calling to say goodbye.

Harry took the call. "Hold on," he said. "Hold on, just a minute. Stop it right there. Do you remember what Judith does?"

"She's my writing teacher at UCLA. Just like you."

Harry explained my other avocation.

Virginia was not, however, necessarily inclined to be healed. She was angry and hurt and a plethora of other adjectives, but she was, at this moment, beyond soothing.

"When's your operation?" Harry also has his stubborn side.

"Next Wednesday."

"Fine. Judith will be there Saturday. Give me directions to your apartment."

As you can imagine, it's hard enough working with someone who is attuned to the idea of being healed. On Saturday our little Tasmanian devil was in a mood to take on God *mano a mano*. She had a few, actually many, choice words for a Deity who would hurt her lovely, slow brother and then throw this mess at her heart, her liver and her ovaries.

Her apartment was a trove of framed photographs of good friends and family, multiple-pillowed couches, Southern charm. Reigning imperiously in this domain was her cat, Leander, about whom she had written many stories for our class.

"You know," I said, sinking slowly into a marshmallo-inspired maroon chair, "it's sometimes hard for us initially to understand the meaning in the things that happen to us. But it might just be that we can't see the whole picture from here and that, somewhere else, on some other level, there's a point to it all."

I will not write Virginia's next words, the essence of which was that any Being that would come up with this cruelty for any purpose and then try to justify it would have to be a low-life so-and-so, only much worse.

Virginia had settled into a long, pillowed sofa and I had pulled up a foot stool to sit by her side. Leander moved closer.

"Did you have Leander altered?" I asked.

"Yes." She was momentarily stunned by the apparent non sequitur interrupting her diatribe.

"The cat of a friend of mine," I said, "swallowed a shoelace the other day and they had to take him to the vet and have his stomach cut open to remove it."

She looked at me, puzzled. The change of subject did defuse her, somewhat, but she still wasn't anywhere near mellow.

"So probably, they wanted to tell this cat, whose name was Rover, I think—a fact which could, by itself, give a cat a complex—but I imagine they wanted to explain to Rover that they were cutting open his stomach and causing him endless amounts of pain for his own good. But he wasn't in a position to understand the words or the concept."

She frowned.

"So, probably, when Leander was in the cat hospital, licking the place where his balls used to be and wondering why any (I used the same epithets on her) would do such a thing to him, and when Rover was licking the stitches up and down his stomach, wondering what kind of a master would do this 'for his own good,' maybe our situations could be like that. That we're not in a position to understand the larger thinking behind it."

She wasn't in the mood to agree. But she didn't argue.

Now that her flagrant hostility was tempered somewhat, we talked about trance. She told me later that it was only because she had such an abiding trust in Harry and me (our way of working with writers is always and without exception supportive—see Exercise: Finding Your Own Strength) that she even considered allowing this to happen. At this time, however, she wasn't balking, and that was good enough.

I began by doing a procedure I had learned from the nurses at the Medical Center in Prescott, Arizona. It was part of "healing hands," which the doctors recognized had a salutary effect on the patients, even if no one completely understood how or why.

I did an "auric cleansing," smoothing out her aura to relax and clear her for about five minutes as she lay on the couch with her eyes closed. Virginia later labeled it a "psychic tranquilizer."

Leander leapt up, hovering close to her left side where the trouble was, but I urged him down, telling him I understood their affinity for each other, since I'd heard the stories about him in class. Much to Virginia's surprise, he parked himself between the two of us at my feet.

Then I put my hands over her left side, let them build up some heat and light and directed a healing at the place where the tumors had been noted.

I put Virginia into a trance and had her go inside and examine the area, reporting what she saw. She was stunned to find a "huge, translucent/opaque white ball."

"Ask it what it's doing there," I said.

"My father's in it. He says he wants to kill me. And it's laughing. It says it wants to take away my creativity."

"Do you want to find out what this is about, to talk to it, or your father?"

"No!"

I waited in case she wanted to reconsider. People often want to reconcile, they just don't know where to begin.

"No," she said, again. "But it's laughing at me."

"I promise you, Virginia," I said, and to this day I don't know what made me say it, "that you'll have the last laugh."

Then I took her for a walk along the beach to find a safe place and a guide who might have wisdom for us about what we are to do. Guides are often useful because they seem not to have a vested interest in anything but the truth and therefore their perception is accepted by the unconscious as well as the conscious mind. They may also be a direct conduit to the unconscious, telling us about bodily circumstances of which our conscious mind is not aware. (See Chapter Twenty-Four and also Exercise on Finding Guides as well as Interchapter 1 on Mind/Body Medicine) We took a "walk" on the beach and for a while, no one was there, and then she saw a beautiful horse.

"Ask him if he will take you to your guide."

"He will." They rode along the cliffs by the ocean and then, at the end of the beach they came to a cave. She entered. No one was there. But there she found "milk and honey," she said. "And almonds."

"It's for you?"

"Yes."

"Well, then, enjoy it."

About this time, Leander jumped up and landed on her stomach, where he cleaned himself with an "I dare you" gleam in his eye. We both chose to ignore him.

The guide then came along and it was as unique as Virginia, neither a him nor a her, neither big nor little, neither male nor female, but all of those. She sat on "their" lap.

"Are they an angel?"

"We are not an angel," they said. "We do not flap wings."

I asked her to ask them if they could show her a movie of her future so that she could see her life after the operation.

"They don't know what a movie is, but they have a book."

"Look at it."

It was beautiful, she loved the texture of the pages, and it was very large. But the pages were blank.

"Of course," I said. "*You're* the playwright. You have to write it. There's lots more to come."

I assured her again in trance that she would have the last laugh and said "Won't the doctors be surprised when there's nothing wrong."

When she came up from trance, we hugged, I left and, as always, just trusted in the process. She did let me know that, right after our session, she found herself calm, up through the operation and sleeping better than she had in a month.

Virginia had obtained another doctor, in fact the head of oncology at Cedars-Sinai, and had her operation on Wednesday. Her sister called Harry right after the surgery to report that she was fine, everything was benign.

They did a laparoscopy and gave her a souvenir Polaroid photo of her innards. There, right in the middle, was a huge, translucent/opaque white ball, "dead accurately corresponding to what I saw," she told me.

With busy lives, people sometimes elude you for months or even years. We hadn't spoken in some time when I decided to write this chapter and I called her for an update. This is what she told me.

First she said, "Had I not had that session with you, I firmly believe I'd have had cancer."

I wasn't sure I understood her, so I asked her to explain and she said, "I truly believe that I had cancer when you walked into my house and I know that I did not when you left. After my operation, I told the doctor about your work and I asked him if he thought I'd had cancer, and he hesitated and said he didn't know, but that I don't have it now.

"But there's something even more amazing you have to know.

"Remember when you talked to me about how it would be if I couldn't explain to Leander why I was hurting him if I had to for his own good? And I didn't quite understand? Well, remarkable as this seems, Leander has taken the cancer for me! He now has liver cancer. And I

have to go through the chemotherapy with him. And he's frightened
and hurting, and I can't explain to him why I am putting him through
this. So now, maybe, a little, I understand that we can't always see the
full picture.

"And I did want you to know that, even though I still don't understand the reason, these near tragedies have made my family a lot closer,
even though every one of us has lost our faith.

"Oh, and you know what else I did? I did the 'healing hands' with
him. And my hands get hot like yours, and he just lays there so calm and
lets me do whatever I think I'm doing to try and heal him.

"I'm the better caretaker, you see. I can do the shopping and take him
to the vet for chemo, and cook for him, all of which he couldn't do for
me, so if one of us had to have it, I guess it made sense that he does.
Although I'm going to love him well," she said. "I know I can."

Anything's possible. Virginia proved that. So, girl, prove it again.
Therein lies another tale.

Interchapter 1:

The Mind/Body Connection and Beyond

"Health is the proper relationship between the microcosm, which is man, and the macrocosm, which is the universe. Disease is the disruption of this relationship."

—*Dr. Yeshe Donden, physician to the Dalai Lama*

Here's some of the philosophy and background science. If you prefer the stories, feel free to move on to A Bittersweet Healing.

We can think something and heal ourselves, and maybe even, according to Dr. Larry Dossey, think something and heal others. Consciousness may be shared.

There's a wonderful Irish movie called *Into the West*. It is a fable about two boys and a magic white horse. At one point, the grandfather tells a tale about the horse: how a beautiful princess from the land where no one grows old happened to fall in love with a handsome man and wanted him, too, to live forever. So she took him to her land so he could be spared the inevitability of aging. He stayed with her for 1,000 years, but missed his people so much, he asked to return home.

"You will stay young if you remain on the horse," the beautiful princess told him, and he headed for home on the horse. All went well, until, excited to see his people, he dismounted and immediately disintegrated.

"What's 'disintegrated?'" one of the boys asks the grandfather.

"Dissolved into a pile of dust," the grandfather says.

"And the beautiful princess," asks the other boy, "What did she look like?"

"Close your eyes," says grandpa. "Do you see a princess?"

"Yes," says the boy.

"Is she beautiful?"

"Yes," says the boy.

"That's her!"

* * *

Perhaps that story makes you smile because you hadn't given any credence to the possibility that we can share the same consciousness. In one of my sessions with a mother and a daughter (see story in Chapter Seven) behind closed eyes they opened my eyes to this very notion. (And for more on transpersonal, shared consciousness, see Interchapter 4.)

Visualizing has been helping people get well as long as people had imaginations. Whether in the Greek healing tradition where dreams were called upon for diagnosis and healing, or in journeys with medicine men and Shamans, or just in stories from grandparents, wisdom has been called upon through the imagination. The Simonton's were the first to scientifically document how imagining white blood cells eating up cancer cells produced healing. The point is, people visualize things and get well. Something shifts when they think in a new way and the body responds.

How can it be?

Some doctors and physicists have answers and I'm compiling them, just because it makes even more amazing the healings I've been privileged to attend.

Some years ago, I went to a conference put on by Harvard Medical School's Mind/Body Institute on the subject of "Spirituality and Healing." It was not really about either. It was about data. It was about the "medical model." When asked by someone in the audience how doctors could learn "healing language," the answer was something like "studies show that when people attend church twice a week their blood pressure is lowered." They didn't quite "get it" that healing happens off the page.

There were a few good papers. I put the notes from Dr. Larry Dossey in the Interchapter 3 on Time and Synchronicity because he believes we have to go beyond mind/body into Era III healing, which is "non-local."

Here are some notes about why visualization works—very medical model. From a paper by Stephen M. Kosslyn, Ph.D.

From a series of experiments he concluded that, "Visual mental imagery activates even the first visual areas in the brain...[and] spatial properties of images have a direct and systematic relation to the neural activity in these areas."

He later says, "Imaged objects may stand in for actual objects. Thus, imagery may engender bodily responses that are appropriate in the corresponding perceived situation."

Seems to me that means picturing something can make your body think it's happened!

* * *

A brief overview of the anatomy involved

The *nervous system* is divided into the *central nervous system* (CNS—the brain and the spinal cord) and the *peripheral nervous system* (PNS—made up of the somatic nervous system and the autonomic nervous system). The part of our brain that responds to visual images and vivid, emotionally-laden verbal descriptions is *the autonomic nervous system*. The ANS regulates heart rate, respiratory rate, digestion, hormonal production and balance and more. These functions used to be considered beyond our ability to consciously control, but it has been learned through biofeedback, that we can affect their reactions. Dr. Michael Samuels, author of *Healing With the Mind's Eye*, considers the autonomic nervous system key in mind/body interconnectivity.

There are two parts of the ANS: the sympathetic and the parasympathetic. When we feel threatened, the sympathetic system takes over and orders adrenalin to be dispersed, initiating a fight-or-flight readiness. This causes such responses as rapid heartbeat, increased respiration, and pupil dilation. Dr. Bruce Lipton, among many other researchers, has demonstrated how, at the cellular level, the over-activation of this system that so taxes the body and works to lower immunity, facilitates disease. Surely, you have heard it said, "the stress is making me sick." While the surge of energy from the sympathetic nervous system allowed us escape threats such as tigers in the wild, it was meant to have an "all clear" when the tiger went away. The unending surge of adrenalin due to problematic modern life, where there is never an "all clear,"—we have constant traffic, bills to pay, crime, the stock market to worry about and earthquakes to avoid—is a health hazard it itself. The stress is continuous and it costs us dearly in vital energy.

When the body is relaxed and peaceful, the parasympathetic system "creates balance, homeostasis and healing," as Samuels notes. This includes moderating the heart and respiratory rate and regulating blood pressure.

What is more, the cerebral cortex is made up of what we commonly call the right and left brains—the left for linear, logical thinking (and, some say, for dealing with the outside world), the right for images and non-verbal thought (and the inner world). The right brain is also connected with the limbic system (our emotional life), the hypothalamus (regulating the immune system and body chemistry) and the pituitary (managing metabolic process).

So this is how visualization can actually make a physical difference:

"When a person has a perception, either from the outer or inner world, neurons fire in the cerebral cortex and images form in the anterior right brain, which in turn stimulates the limbic system, and then the hypothalamus, and the pituitary gland," says Samuels. "Depending upon whether the person's perception is interpreted as peaceful or upsetting, the parasympathetic or sympathetic nervous system will be activated, and the reaction will be sustained by the hormones of the adrenals. **The hormones and nerve cells that are stimulated will cause changes in literally every cell in the body.**" (Emphasis, mine)

It is important to note that when we are not imagining something positive, we may be imagining a dire future, and that, too, obviously, has an effect.

If you want to read more about this subject, here are some references for doctors who are talking about mind/body work aloud: Larry Dossey, who has gone into what he calls "Era III" Medicine, beyond mind/body into "non-local," healing at a distance with this book *Reinventing Medicine* (earlier books, *Space, Time and Medicine, Recovering the Soul, Healing Words*) and Michael Samuels (*Healing with the Mind's Eye*), Joan Borysenko and the ubiquitous Deepak Chopra.

They are saying things like:

a) Our bodies are mutable, not nearly as solid and unforgiving as we thought (which bodes well for healing and "spontaneous remissions"). Our bodies are changing every moment, with every breath, not a single cell the same as it was the year before.

b) Every thought we have provokes a physical reaction.

c) The body's cells are intelligent, communicating with each other as if the entire body network were a "brain," and we can, and do, unknowingly, communicate with it all. For good or ill. (For more, see Chapter Twenty-Three on hypnosis in medical emergencies and how the right words said in an emergency can aid healing on the spot into stories.)

* * *

So, how mutable are our bodies? You'll be surprised

It took my breath away to read the studies being done on individuals with Multiple Personality Disorder (MPD). These are people who used to be called "split personalities," like the characters in *The Three Faces of Eve* or *Sybil*. One minute they're talking as if they were a sensible business person, the next as if they were an infant, the next as if they were a seductress.

In *The Holographic Universe*, Michael Talbot provides specific details of this phenomenon. Stunning proof that our bodies are not nearly as stuck in the rigid form we perceive as we have been led to believe.

Here's the overview, examples of physical conditions he discusses which can appear in the body of *some* of the personalities and be absent in the *very same body* when another personality has charge of it.

One personality could have allergies, another not.

One personality could have an acute reaction to drugs, such as swelling up, and as soon as another personality takes over the body, the reaction immediately disappears.

As one personality, the individual could be left-handed, and in an instant become right-handed as another personality emerged.

Eyesight, even color-blindness, varies drastically in different personalities of the same person.

They could be physically, diagnosably drunk and then, as fast as they can change personalities, be completely sober.

One personality can have a scar, burn marks, cysts, even tumors, and these solid physical traces can be *completely absent* on the other personalities of the same person.

Brain waves and voice patterns can be measurably different from personality to personality in the same person.

Even diabetes and epilepsy can appear and disappear in the same apparent body manifesting different personalities!

One multiple suffered three menstrual periods a month, because her personalities were each on their own cycles.

Imagine being a physician working with someone who so completely "becomes" someone else she can lose or regain a scar on her skin in an instant!

MPD is a terrible curse, but it's also a "proof" of our unlimitedness. Talbot says, "Once a multiple has undergone therapy and in some way becomes whole again, he or she can still make these switches at will. This suggests that somewhere in our psyches we all have the ability to control these things."

* * *

The mind can affect the body, as opposed to the belief that only the body can affect the mind. In physics, such interactions always go both ways. Nobel-winning physicist Eugene Wigner, discussing the relationship between human consciousness and the physical world, suggests that there are no examples of one-way interactions in modern physics. If the mind could be affected by the physical world, but not affect it, he suggests, it would be the only case of one-way interaction known in modern physics to occur.

* * *

Nothing is ever really lost, nor can be lost. Walt Whitman

What are these bodies that can change in the wink of an eye like a scene from a Dr. Jeckell/Mr. Hyde movie?

According to Chopra and Dossey, our bodies are essentially stardust and information systems. Every bit of our chemistry and physical make up is recycled from elements that have been here from space as long as there has been an earth. In fact, many of the molecules in our body are older than the sun. We know that because the formation of elements like iron required higher heat than is generated by our relatively modest, mid-sized sun. The iron in our blood was likely formed by a supernova before our sun was born. The calcium in our bones could be from the White Cliffs of Dover, the iron in our blood could be from the earliest stages of our galaxy's creation.

Chemicals enter and leave our bodies at such a rate that Dossey reports a conclusion by Aebersold that 98 percent atoms of the body are replaced annually. The lining of the stomach renews itself in a week; the skeletal system has a dynamic turnover; the skin is entirely replaced in a month; the liver is regenerated in six weeks.

In what he calls the "biodance," he shows how elements from the stars, from space and galaxies are shared by each of us, by trees and animals.

I picture it this way: a fish absorbs the calcium in the White Cliffs of Dover, a bird eats the fish, the bird is eaten by an animal who dies on the land and the calcium becomes grass which is eaten by cows whose milk we drink. The calcium will return again to the earth and recycle as everything in nature does. And the dance of life goes on.

What that means is that there is nothing new in us or unique to us but the organization of the information.

But even our DNA isn't really ours. A single DNA molecule "lives" for only a few months. Like the rest of us, they constantly renew themselves with matter from everyone and everywhere else. The actual physical part of them is totally renewed every year. The information system, the pattern, is what seems consistently to be considered "me," but we are learning that even the uniqueness of "me" and my DNA may be an illusion. First of all, our DNA is made of patterns that can be traced back since life began. Secondly, in studying viruses, Harvard biologist Bernard Davis suggests that virus' purposes may be to act as systems that transfer blocks of nucleic acid between organisms. He says, "It is not inconceivable that all DNA in the living world may be a part of an unbroken chain of low frequency contacts."

In such a mutable body, why should we rule out the possibility of "miraculous" cures?

What would it take to change the direction of illness and make it wellness again?

It might be consciousness. Dr. Candace Pert, former Chief of Brain Chemistry of the National Institute of Health studied neuropeptides, calling them the body's way of communicating between cells. She concludes that all of the body might function as does the brain, generating "thoughts" and making chemicals which respond to those thoughts.

There's that "gut" feeling—the intelligence in our intestine is responding to stimuli. Some people say that that response is more valid than an intellectual one because there is no censor, as there is in the mind, to stop it, to doubt, to rationalize.

So feeling nervous or queasy about something is a clue to stop and listen to your "gut." It is only our brain which will try to talk us into something we "knew" we shouldn't have gotten involved in. Maybe the brain is really spread out all over the body.

* * *

Body Language/Organ Language

Wise doctors take it seriously when someone whose "heart has been broken" then dies of heart failure. (My mother's heart disease manifested as difficulty breathing and her doctor treated her for sinus trouble. But my father had fairly recently died and she seemed to me literally to have had a broken heart.)

Someone who has found life to be a "pain in the ass" develops colon cancer. Someone who feels smothered suffers from asthma. A friend of mine whose marriage was on the rocks hurt in the area of his rib cage, until he told his wife how he felt and "got it off his chest." Another friend, pissed off by life, developed bladder cancer.

The French have an expression, *contre-coeur*,—going against the heart. You feel that something is the right or wrong thing to do, but your brain tells you otherwise and you marry the wrong person or you don't help when you should. And later, you say I "knew" it, but I didn't listen. You went against your heart. The mind has a lot of defenses, but the body, responding to the emotions, is very pure and is talking to you, as well.

There is an Ayervedic saying that connects the mind and body in a linear way: If you want to know what you were thinking ten years ago, look at your body now. If you want to know what your body will be like in ten years, look at your thoughts now.

Thoughts provoke physical reactions in the body. Every thought we think, every emotion we feel sends messages, waves of chemicals throughout our body. Our body is a pharmacopoeia, producing chemicals that cure or harm us. As Deepak Chopra explains it, two people could be riding the same roller coaster. One could feel frightened, anxious, upset and could be creating adrenalin and cortisol, a known carcinogen. At the same time, another person on the same ride could be feeling exhilarated, thrilled, full of life. And his or her body might be generating Interluken II, the chemical scientists are attempting to fabricate in labs across the country because it is an anti-carcinogen. Same ride, different emotions, different chemicals in the body. Different health. Those who were having fun were helping themselves to a healing experience. So, clearly, our lives are not about what happens to us so much as what we make of what happens to us. So hold on, find a metaphor that works, and enjoy the ride.

So much in life depends not upon what happens to us, but upon how we take it.

If I were to say something embarrassing to you, for example that your fly was open when you were addressing a group last week, blood would flood the capillaries of your cheeks and you would blush. That's a physical reaction to a thought. If you were to give an adolescent boy a Playboy magazine, he would quickly feel the effect of a thought on his body. And if you were to have a dream of being pursued by a stalker, you would awaken with sweaty palms, your heart rate accelerated perhaps so much you could feel it pounding against your rib cage, your breath coming in faster and shorter spurts.

Those physical effects are the result of thoughts and visions. That is the theory behind visualization for healing. If you can picture it, you can tell the body to do it. It may be that the cells which have been shown to communicate with each other throughout our body as a flowing mind do not communicate in words, as does our brain, but in images, which would explain why visualizing an occurrence may cause it to happen, rather than just wishing it. Make more T-cells, find and destroy cancer cells, lower the blood pressure, the temperature, slow down the heart, make a rash or a wart go away, the list and the practical demonstrations have been endless.

Even the most cynical types in the medical establishment have long been aware of the success reported by Doctors like O. Carl Simonton (*Getting Well Again, A Healing Journey*) in demonstrating the power of the mind when used for visualization in healing against cancer.

Consider it mind over matter, if you like, although it may be that mind and matter are all just waves and particles, and yours and mine are all much more shared than we know. In *The Seven Mysteries of Life,* G. Murchie does the calculations to prove that the exchange of the atoms of our breath is "repeated twenty thousand times a day" by the entire population of the planet, which means that every breath you inhale "must contain a quadrillion atoms breathed by the rest of mankind within the past few weeks and more than a million atoms breathed personally sometime by each and any person on Earth." Maybe the atoms in your next breath were also exhaled by Jesus Christ or Gandhi or Cleopatra…or me.

* * *

"I Sing the Body Electric." Walt Whitman

I believe that it is the awareness of this connectedness that will ultimately heal us. "The assumption of being an individual is our greatest
limitation," Pir Vilayat Kahn wrote.

Barbara Brennan, former NASA scientist and healer, author of the
seminal *Hands of Light*, put it this way, "All suffering is caused by the
illusion of separateness, which generates fear and self-hatred, which
eventually causes illness."

It is through connectedness with Universal Divinity through love that
we are made whole, she and nearly everyone in the healing field agrees.

Add to the list of medical seers: Brennan and Dr. Richard Gerber.
They both approach healing through the energy fields around us.
Brennan works with what she calls the Human Energy Field, our auric
bodies, while Gerber (*Vibrational Medicine*) relies on our understanding
that, at the particle level, all matter is really waves and particles of energy
(or it may be strings. See Interchapter 6 on Holographic Universe).

Gerber demonstrates that as beings of energy, it follows that we can
be affected by energy. And, in fact, we often use energy these days for
healing, including radiation, MRI, sound and light. Work done on
measuring electrical fields around baby salamanders showed that their
fields were those of *the adults they would become.* Stranger still, when
the energy fields around sprouts were measured, they turned out to be
not sprout-shaped, but shaped in the configuration of the adult plant.
The energy field seems to be, then, a template for growth, maybe even
the reason why we can start out with one single cell and turn into a
being with legs and arms, bones and blood; because the cells are following the energy pattern prescribed around them and differentiate to
the signals.

* * *

Placebo Is Good Medicine

Some doubters after hearing of miraculous cures are quick to assert that the problem was "just in the mind in the first place." An odd accusation.

Even if that were so, isn't the goal to help the person heal in any case? Dr. Bernie S. Siegel, *Love, Medicine & Miracles* writes about what is known as "the placebo effect," that it is true that about one-forth to one-third of patients respond by getting better if they are given a pill they believe to be effective, even if it really has no effective ingredients in it. Ah-ha! you say. See, just in their mind.

But it affects their bodies. Brendan O'Regan's paper on spontaneous remissions and miracles discusses actual physical effects of the placebo phenomenon. In an experiment, half of a study was given chemotherapy, the other half an inert substance. Because it is widely known that chemotherapy causes hair loss, 30 percent of those in the control group, thinking they were having chemotherapy, lost their hair. Apparently, their body made the chemicals that made that happen.

It turns out that the placebo effect is not simply a "let's pretend it doesn't hurt," response. Studies show that if a person responds positively to a placebo (a "sugar pill") painkiller, and then he or she is given a pill that *inhibits* pain control, without his/her knowledge, an amazing thing happens. The placebo won't work.

What does that mean? It suggests that in some of the people who respond to the placebo as if it were a chemical, their bodies may actually be *making* a pain-killing chemical, themselves. Remember, the body is a pharmacy. The inhibitor then neutralizes the very real drug their bodies have created. If that is so, then they haven't just "thought" themselves out of pain, they've thought themselves into painkillers and out of pain.

* * *

And what about Spontaneous Remissions?

These days, doctors have begun whispering among themselves about things like "spontaneous remissions" and odd experiments which prove the unspeakable: what some people would call miracles.

Doctors don't like "spontaneous remissions" for a lot of reasons, some of them understandable, some of them foolish. Obviously, if healing insists on happening without medical intervention, then the physicians might be out of business. But they are less concerned with that eventuality than with their inability to "control" the healing process if it happens all by itself. They like the consistency of prescribing an antibiotic and having it kill bacteria. Take this little pill and, there, now you're well. And we know how and why. They like the ease (to them) of surgery, the ability to cut out the offending growth and send you home lighter and apparently less threatened.

How, they ask, can they diagnose and treat an ailment by saying "Go home and visualize yourself well. Allow love into your heart. Pray. And maybe you'll get well by yourself."

And yet such things happen. They can be—have been—documented. They just are not predictable. For years, scientists in Japan have been studying this phenomenon, but our medical profession seems reticent to touch it.

There's the paper by Brendon O'Reagan, of the Institute of Noetic Sciences on "Healing, Remission, and Miracle Cures" compiling some 4,000 cases, but don't look for the medical establishment to think they have to move in that direction any faster than they've moved in the direction of realizing that what we eat affects us. (Note how long has it taken for even one fourth of the country's medical schools to put nutrition on the curriculum as a serious subject.)

And what about the body's natural healing mechanism? Norman Cousins has written that we had neglected **two bodily systems** in our map of the anatomy of humans. One was the **natural healing system** and the other was the **belief system**. Both of them come into play in the realm of spontaneous remissions.

The natural healing mechanism is generally overlooked as field of study by modern medicine. Our immune system regularly destroys invading viruses, bacteria and cancer cells. When we cut ourselves, burn ourselves, break our bones, our body regenerates with healthy tissue. Yet, as Dr. Michael Samuels points out in *Healing With the Mind's Eye*, "research on healing mechanisms does not even appear in medical textbooks."

So we won't hear a lot about spontaneous remissions from the medical profession, which considers these "anomalies," these "aberrations" to be unnatural.

But remember the Saint Augustine quote: "Miracles happen, not in opposition to Nature, but in opposition to what we know of Nature." Maybe miracles are the most natural thing of all.

Chapter Six

A Bittersweet Healing

A Mysterious Growth Comes and Goes With the Right Words

"Always do what you are afraid to do".

—*Ralph Waldo Emerson*

This story is somehow about money. Money is not, has never been, my best subject. To the world, it's a symbolic concept of value and exchange which has become concretized into a tangible measure of worth for which we sometimes kill each other and often, inadvertently, ourselves.

There are people who instinctively know how to make it, some have the Midas touch and may or may not see the paralyzing Midas effects on those around them. There are people for whom there is never enough. They focus on fears of future scarcity, which makes them live in as painful a present as any dreadful future they can imagine.

And then there are people like Harry and me who find the whole subject of money deeply confusing, giving it not a lot of thought and having it regard us with mild disdain in return.

Because I viewed the healing work as divinely inspired, it was hard for me to figure out how to charge for it, although my office cost me $300 a month whether or not my patients paid.

Somehow, the idea of saying, "Well it's $75 a session but if you want a miracle it'll be $125," didn't work for me, as if I had any say in the appearance of such a fortuitous event. I also don't work on a clock, time being a realm of its own and healing knowing nothing of it, so my sessions take as long as they take, making me even less "efficient" in the money-earning realm.

So I kept my job at the marketing agency in exchange for the freedom to offer my services as I chose. In the meantime, I was hoping my advertising efforts in the service of Mitsubishi Motors were ineffective in generating sales for that company because it hurt my conscience to support a corporation well-known in environmental circles as the enemy for burning down rainforests.

Impracticably and even mildly idealistically, every once in a while, Harry and I made an effort to develop a money-making plan we felt we could live with. In one of our pushes to offer a service for which corporations might reach into their deep pockets, we developed a series of creativity/brainstorming seminars. We had hoped we could light-fingeredly slip in the concept of soul or doing good or values as we inspired businesses to find creative solutions to their business problems. We presented to such capitalist strongholds as the International House of Pancakes and Saban Entertainment (the Mighty Morphin Power Rangers, Captain Kangaroo, the Louie Anderson show) and had helped them come up with unique and profitable business solutions.

Valuing joy over money, we had also given away our seminars to enthusiastic gatherings such the local chapter of the Institute of Noetic Sciences, a national group dedicated to the study of the nature of consciousness.

Our latest presentation to them had been very well received. We had regressed grown people to their earliest creative states, and set them to coloring and transforming the meanings of memories in light of newer wisdom. One older gentleman, a scholar from Harvard, broke down in tears upon experiencing a major realization as he wielded the crayons— gaining a new perspective on the childhood loss of his father. Looking at his primitive drawing of a very little boy and a stooping, sad grown man, he understood what had eluded him for 75 years—that he had been truly loved by his father, not carelessly abandoned, as he had always perceived.

At the next month's meeting, my work at the last session was publicly acknowledged and a woman named Evie, sat up in her seat and became convinced at that moment that I was the one meant to save her.

At lunch she asked to sit with me and told me her problem.

"I have a growth on my tongue which both my dentist and my doctor feel is very dangerous, might even be fatal," she said. Her pretty face was tight with care. "They have me with one foot in the grave!" Her eyes met mine intently. "I have to have an operation next week and it is supposed to be incredibly painful. And I'm very frightened. I know you're the person who I came here to meet. I'm not even a member. My friend brought me because her husband was busy. So you see, I'm just here to meet you so that you can help me."

Evie was in the not-enough-money, living-in-fear category. She told me she had developed this growth after someone who had promised her a lucrative job had reneged and she had become so angry she could think of almost nothing else. She had turned her life upside down to accommodate this potential position and then, without so much as an excuse me, he had betrayed her and it failed to materialize. And she was furious. What's more, her current job was not sufficient to pay the bills, they were mounting up and she was overwhelmed by concerns and bill collectors.

I recognize that the prevalent therapy often selects a course of confronting and dealing with the sources of anger. In hypnotherapy, we have lots of choices. We could deal with her problem literally, working simply on the tongue; we could talk to the part and examine the emotions locked in there; we could go somewhere else again, a childhood pattern, even a "past life" to find answers.

I told Evie I would see her that week. She was elated.

That elation ebbed when she came to my office and realized that I am a hypnotherapist. She had heard the word "healer," not hypnotherapist, and took two steps back. Oh, once someone had hypnotized her and it was not a good experience, and she wasn't sure…

We talked for a while, as I like to do, listening intently until I hear the clues that send me in the healing direction that is in harmony with the person's belief system. She repeated that the doctors and dentist were very concerned. That the pain would be excruciating. "The dentist had this operation himself and he said it was the worst pain he'd ever had in his life for at least a week. Every breath would be agony." She talked of her fears. Of money. Of jobs.

Shortly, I could feel her relax and I knew before she said it that she would trust me to help her.

Evie had done her own meditations in the past and already had an inner guide, who, while nameless, wore a purple robe or gown.

She went easily into trance and we initially "took her tongue out and put it on a counter or table." Then I asked her what she would have to do to fix it, file the growth down, cut it out, whatever seemed to make sense.

"Pour sugar on it," she said, remaining in trance.

"If you pour sugar on it three times a day in your imagination, will it heal itself?"

"Oh, yes," she said.

We asked her guide and he presented her with a gorgeous saber, the handle of which was embedded with rubies and emeralds. It spoke to her of her own powers, that she was totally complete, had all she needed to heal herself.

I asked her in trance if there was anything more she needed to know and she said, "What about the pain? How will I be able to stand the pain?"

"There will not be pain," I said, hardly aware of where this idea came from, "if you do not tense yourself up into a tight knot. If you completely relax, you will not have pain. And won't the doctors be surprised when they examine you and find nothing there!" Again these words appeared with a life of their own.

Evie came up from trance, hugged me and was gone. On the way home, I understood why she wanted to pour sugar on her tongue, so I called her and explained: "The growth on your tongue was born in bitterness at the person who promised you the job. It has to be healed with sweetness."

She laughed and agreed.

After the operation, I called her to find out what had happened. "First of all," she said, "I felt wonderful after I left you. The next morning, I meditated and Jesus came into me for a complete Christ healing. He looked up into my mouth through my tongue and saw that my tongue was completely healed and so was my life. Then I went in for the operation and guess what! It was nothing. This 'thing' that was going to be the cause of my demise. Nothing. 'Non-specific' nothing, they said. And the pain? There was none. I took one Alieve and didn't even need that!"

Some time later, Evie came back for another session with me. In her first healing, when I had mentioned the word "unconscious," she had seen a little boy, straight out of Our Gang Comedies with a cowlick like Alfalfa, whose name was Tommy. We decided to call Tommy back to find out what he knew about her life.

Tommy "was" her unconscious, and he led her down the stairs and pointed the way down a dark hall. She was afraid to go.

"You can bring Arnold Schwartzenegger or the Green Berets or anyone you want with you," I said. She took the guide in purple, now named Waldo, and her dog Feisty. It was still dark and scary, so I suggested a flashlight. Flashlight in hand, she proceeded down the hall. There were many doors to choose from. She opened one and it was a library.

"Ask Tommy what he wants to show you," I said.

"He's showing me a painting of a man turned away."

"Can you get into the painting?"

She did, and found that the man was her father and she was a little girl of about eight (who looked, surprisingly, a little like Tommy, who seemed always to want to get into the act). Moving along in that life, we found that her name was Elizabeth and she married someone wealthy, but her life was not happy.

"But you have lots of money," I said, pointedly.

"The money doesn't really matter, because my life is sad with this man."

At the end of this life, she died in bed and her last thought was that she was glad it was over.

We went back to the library where she saw a compact which, when opened, showed a fan with feathers in the shape of a heart. She couldn't see who was holding it, but when she looked down at her shoes, they were from another century. Then she saw the man who was to be her husband. He was wonderful. His name was Bruce and hers was Annie. Annie had a happy life and was self-assured and loving.

Annie knew how to live, how to love, what to value. Her life was whole and Evie could feel how it felt to be as content as Annie. We they rich? Not really, but that didn't matter. I asked her to take that experience with her as a "felt sense" back to the library, knowing that when she could fully incorporate Annie into her inner life, all of life will have to change on the outside.

She brought Annie with her and came up radiant, knowing how it feels to be complete, joyful and satisfied. She looked completely different and felt she could maintain this feeling into her real life.

Shortly thereafter, she took another job and became more adventurous, allowing herself the courage of Annie's confidence.

No Boundaries

Often when I speak publicly, I talk about the aspen trees in Colorado. They provide a metaphor that makes concrete a difficult concept: that of interconnectedness. Looking at the miles of forest, we see individual trees, each standing strong and alone. When we discover that the aspen is one of the largest organisms on the planet—ONE organism, a root system, and the trees are merely sprouts sent up to nourish the whole— we can begin to imagine the hidden interconnectedness among all of us. And we can then understand how each of our thoughts and feelings and words and deeds affect others, nourish or harm the whole.

Another metaphor is that of islands. Under the oceans, we are all one earth, with water obscuring some of the connected land masses. In the same way it has been said that we are all cells in the body of God. Knowing that, it would make no sense for the liver to attack the kidney. Like the aspen, would should be nourishing the whole, knowing that what happens to any of us, happens to all of us.

Chapter Seven

Healing Across the Language Barrier

A Daughter Translates a Trance

"Consciousness is a singular of which the plural is unknown."

—*Edwin Schrodinger*

The woman on the phone spoke with a slight Latina accent. She said her name was Maria and that her mother had had ovarian cancer which might now be in remission. Now the doctors wanted to do more surgery on her mother to make sure she was well, but she didn't want to undergo any more operations. Maria had heard I was a healer, would I help her?

In the medical circles in which I travel, my work is referred to as "complementary" or "integrative" rather than "alternative." I do take that literally and never suggest that my approach and efforts take the place of conventional medical practices. So I wasn't certain in which way she thought I could help.

As we spoke, something else began to concern me and I quickly asked, "Does your mother speak English?"

"No," Maria said, casually.

"I'm sorry," I said, "I'm a hypnotherapist. I use language to hypnotize her to communicate with her unconscious and my Spanish is not very good, so it wouldn't work. I couldn't do it."

"You have to help her," she said. "They said you were a healer."

I hesitated, then suggested, "What if I hypnotized you and you translated and put your mother in trance?"

"Could we do that?"

"Why not?" I said and we set a date.

Rosa and Maria showed up on time and a little tentative. I, on the other hand, was a lot tentative, but I had heard a talk by a man named Jack Mason, who worked in hospitals in South America and had helped in the delivery of breached-positioned babies without anesthesia by putting the suffering mother into an altered state through an untrained translator. ("I would say, 'Sleep deeeeeper, deeeeeeper, deeeeeper,'" Jack said in a soothing voice, "and she would translate, 'deeper/deeper/deeper' in a high little twirp." And still it worked.)

Actually, Maria proved to be a very graceful translator, eloquent and soft-spoken. I heard my words float through her and out of her again, into the ears of her mother in fluid Spanish and dulcet tones.

When I felt both of them were in an altered state, I decided it would be wise if Rosa found a "guide" who could act as the conduit for her own inner wisdom or that of higher powers. Because I knew she was Catholic, I though she might look for an angel or a saint to help her. So I took her for an imaginary walk along the beach, through a woods, looking for the guide. Finally, she saw a house, but it was locked. I asked her to go in through the window, but that, too, was locked. We looked for another house, and that one she entered.

"Is there a note for you there?"

"No."

"Is there a phone?"

"No."

"A television or a radio?"

"No," again, and "No," again from Maria.

"Is there a book, perhaps on the shelf, perhaps open on a table?"

"No."

"Is anyone in the back yard?"

"No."

"Is there a mirror in the house in which you can look at yourself?"

"No."

It has been my experience that the unconscious mind is not eager to appear just because we call it and that it tests us and tests the safety of doing so before it agrees to cooperate.

At about this time, as my ideas waned, out of my mouth came the question, "Is there a trap door?"

"A what?" Maria said before translating.

"A trap door. It's a door in the floor that leads down into the basement."

"Okay," she said and asked her mother in Spanish if there was a trap door.

"Of course," Rosa said.

And she proceeded to go "deeper, deeper, deeper," herself, seeing herself descending a rope staircase for several long, quiet minutes. When she said she was at the bottom of the rope, she looked around and discovered a pristine pool of water, never used by another person.

"Would you like to swim in it?" I asked.

She did, and could magically see inside herself. Checking her ovaries, she found them healthy. Would she promise to return every day to bathe and picture her ovaries healthy? She would.

When she was complete with this process, I brought her up.

Rosa was very excited about what she'd seen and had to exclaim about how beautiful the pool was and how she felt as she swam in it. I was quick to point out to Maria that this was not a diagnosis, this was good, solid mind/body visualization, which can send healing biochemicals to her ovaries to heal. But I emphasized that Rosa should have herself checked out, anyway. Maria agreed.

We had been sitting almost in a circle, the three of us, as if holding hands psychically. I felt that we had been experiencing and sharing the One Mind that day.

As I wondered if the others had felt what I'd felt, the absence of any barrier between us, Maria surprised me by making a remark that took my thoughts one step further.

"I couldn't figure out why my mother couldn't see the guide," she said, smiling. "He was right there! I wanted to say to her, there's your guide, Mama. Just look behind the tree!"

Chapter Eight

The Hardest Thing of All

Losing a Son and Gaining the World

"The telling question is, are you related to the infinite?"

—*Carl Jung*

Near midnight in a parking lot in the Denver airport, a handsome young man who had just bought a ticket home to Los Angeles was murdered by a hit-and-run driver. He happened to be the cherished, only son of a woman named Maggie, half-Cherokee Indian, half Irish, beautiful, delicate, and now broken. She had raised him as a single mother, they had bonded in their search for spirituality and meaning and now he was gone.

I had never met Maggie when my sister, Shelle, called and said, "There's a woman I work with who needs your help. Her son was killed and she can't get out of her depression. It's not enough for me to say I'm here for her. She really needs help."

I have only one strong requirement, I told Shelle. I couldn't call her and offer her my services; she has to call me herself. For her to seek me out infuses the connection with her commitment to it.

Maggie called me the next day in my advertising office in Orange County. I liked her voice, not a ounce of complaint in it, brave and friendly. She didn't tell me much about the story, only said how wonderful my sister was, how she touched lives and changed people, which I was glad to hear. Our father's legacy.

Because I thought Harry and I were leaving town the next day for a long weekend, I told her I would come up to work with her that night.

It's a long trip from Orange County to the San Fernando Valley where she lived. Hours. I had lots of time to talk to my guides. How do you help a person who has lost someone she loved, so suddenly, so senselessly, so mysteriously? Despite the fact that I seemed to have contacted Dirk to return to Sabra (Chapter Eleven, Not Just In The Movies, about Ghost), I am not a psychic like Todd who can converse with spirits beyond the veil. If she wanted to know what had happened to her son those last moments, I didn't imagine I could help her.

I had suggested on the phone that we do a past-life regression and find out where she had known Jim before. Connecting with a lost spirit allows us to experience having known the people who are important to us in the past and helps us to imagine that we will find them again. She had been thrilled at the prospect.

Driving the long road that evening, I couldn't help thinking, "What if I fail? What if I can't help her. She just wants her son back, and I can't make that happen. What if I fail?" This happened to be an exceptionally useless mantra and yet my mind fastened onto it like a Doberman on duty and shook it until it rattled. "What if I fail?" I chanted until my guides made me laugh by stopping me short. *Oh,* I heard them say, *you think this is about you? We thought it was about Maggie. We thought you just wanted to go and help the woman.* "I do, I said. *So just go and help her.*

So without much of a plan, I drove to her house and rang the bell. After I identified myself, the door opened and I was immediately nearly knocked over by a giant dog, I think it must have been a Bouvier de Flanders, black and furry, drooly and friendly. His name was Morgan and he was quickly banished from the evening's festivities.

Maggie was small and delicate with wild hair and large eyes. "You're so pretty," she said to me, which completely confused me, since my guides had succeeded in taking the emphasis off me. "So are you," I said, stupidly.

In the living room was a poster-sized photograph that was obviously Jim. She led me into a small den with two chairs and more pictures of Jim and we spoke for a while about him. At his funeral on a Native American Reservation, she had handed out a booklet she had printed up which contained the picture and excerpts from his diaries. There were intense, passionate poems and his writings about freeing himself from his ego and helping others. You could see his character in lines like: "If you help people, they may resent you and feel dependent, but do it anyway." And I was especially moved by, "Aches tear the soul. Soul comes through the cracks…"

She told me stories of people calling her up from ashrams and schools he had attended, telling her how important he had been to them.

Clearly, she was absorbed in his life and his loss.

Her heart hurt, she told me. Of course, I thought. She told me she wasn't sure she wanted to go on.

In her bedroom she lit two candles, one out in the open air, the other inside a glass globe. Then she put on a sleep mask and lay down on the bed. I performed a magnetic cleansing to clear her aura, which is part of the healing hands work I had studied in Arizona, and began to relax her with my words, to put her into an altered state. By the time I lifted one of her hands to test how deeply in trance she was, it dropped beside her like a rag doll and I knew we could begin.

I silently prayed for God to help and asked Jim if he were around to help, too. Down the river of time, she found herself in a gray uniform in a war. She was just standing by, not firing cannons, and she was clearly of limited intelligence or wit. She said her name was Joe, that she was "not white," and that she had a "paper," which I guessed was a letter of emancipation, but Joe couldn't read it or tell me about it. I was completely unable to relate this life to anything that would help us so I asked Joe to move ahead in time to his death. He was bailing hay in a barn and a white man impaled him with a pitchfork and dumped his body into the hay wagon. When I asked Maggie's guides to explain the meaning of this life to us, they say it was to learn "humility."

Because these apparently inapplicable lives often appear at the start, I hypothesize that our subconscious skirts the real issue to test the waters and picks a relatively safe life to practice on before we get to the business at hand.

But since this particular life was not advancing our cause, I was feeling somewhat humbled, myself, at this dead-end. How could I help this woman feel better about the loss of her beloved son? How could anyone help anyone feel better about this tragedy? I began to doubt that help could come in any form short of bringing Jim back.

When we went again down the river of time, this time I more emphatically asked her subconscious to take us to a time when she and the spirit we know as Jim made a bond or knew each other.

She smiled. "I'm at a picnic."

"Look at your feet. What are you wearing?"

"Shiny patent leather shoes."

"Are you a little girl?"

"I'm 16."

Her name was Mary and she lived in a small town and she was on a picnic with…"It's Jim. I know it's Jim."

"What's his name?" I asked, trying to get a context.

"Herb," she said, frowning. "He's wearing a beautiful white shirt. It's so white." She laughed. "He works at the newspaper."

There was such delight, I figured maybe we'd arrived at a life that would provide understanding. "You love Herb, don't you?" I said.

"Yes," she said. "My heart is soft."

"Do you marry Herb in this life? Go ahead to about the time you are eighteen."

"Oh, oh, no! There's a fire at the newspaper," she said and she began to moan. "There's a fire."

"A fire. What's happening."

"Herb is hurt. Oh, oh my God, oh, mmmmm, mmmm, mmmm…."
She was reduced to moans and a sort of rocking.

Hoping he recovered, and concerned to go farther on, I listened to
her moaning and finally asked, "And then what happens?"

Pause. Long pause. "He's gone."

Damn. I was so incredibly frustrated. I had her go ahead to the end
of that life and she died as a white haired old woman, still remembering Herb. I asked her to go to the Interlife and tell me what she had
learned and she said "love."

I was stumped. "Do you want to spend some more time at the picnic, Mary? You and Herb are so happy there."

"His shirt is so white," she said, smiling again. "He works at the
newspaper."

I let her re-live those happy moments for a minute or two and then,
desperate to give her something, I decided to take her for a walk on the
beach to find a guide. At least, I thought, she'll have some inner wisdom
to call on when she comes up from the trance.

"Somewhere behind the dunes on the beach," I told her, "there is a
guide waiting for you who can help you understand." I described in
great detail the sound of the seagulls, the feel of the sand under her feet,
the breeze on her face, the salt water in the air, the sun on her skin.
"When you see a guide," I said, using the hypnotic finger-signal technique called ideomotor to help her get deeper inside, "move this finger."

She was quiet for some time. Then she moved the finger I had gently
indicated. "Who do you see?"

"A man."

"Ask him if he is from the light."

"He's very light."

"Yes, but ask if he is from the light. He has to tell the truth. If he's
from the light, he might be your guide."

"He says yes."

"What's his name."

"George."

"Ask him if he will be your guide."

He didn't answer. At this point I was vibrating quite a lot, as I tend to do when I work intensely at this level. I almost felt the walls of the small room begin to palpitate. I was kneeling against the bed and I placed my two hands with the palms turned toward her face, generating energy toward her.

"Does he have a gift for you?"

"Yes."

"What is it?"

"A jewel box."

I hesitated. Sometimes people see a gift in trance and then they discover it manifested in their life sometime later by synchronicity. They see a ring and the next day someone gives them a ring or they find one in a Cracker Jacks box. That's the way it works. But it seemed not good enough for her needs. I was afraid to find out what was in the box, but my angels made me ask.

"What's in the box?"

She paused just a second. "Oh, my God. Oh, my God. It's so beautiful. It's a light. Oh, it's so beautiful. It's red and white and so bright. Oh, my God, it's going into my heart. Oh, it's in my heart. It's so bright. It's so beautiful…."

She almost levitated off the bed, such was her joy.

"Oh, it's in my heart. It's so bright. It's so beautiful."

"You can take that back with you and have that feeling forever. Whenever you want it, whenever you need it."

"It's so beautiful. I can feel it in my heart. It's filling my heart!"

I left her to that experience for a few moments. Then I realized that we still had not come to the meaning. And it is meaning that we are here about. Significance. It took all of my courage in the midst of this incredible moment to ask another question. I wondered if she would lose the majesty of the moment if I asked the meaning of it? Could I let this gift of light be enough? I have never in my life felt so frightened, nor so brave.

"Ask George or any other of your guides or higher wisdom why it is that you lost Jim and Herb so soon. Ask them what is the meaning of your losing Jim and Herb so…early."

She lay on the bed, the light in her chest still there, I could feel it, quiet. Minutes passed. I had no idea what would happen, whether the light would be enough, whether her inner wisdom would provide for her.

There was no breath in the room. The stillness was palpable. The candlelight flickered. My body vibrated as if I had touched a forbidden outlet.

Then she spoke. "I understand," she whispered. "Oh, I understand."

Again I was afraid, afraid to make her put it into words. Maybe it was good enough that she felt she understood. Maybe I shouldn't make her express it. But my guides insisted that I persist.

"What do you understand, Maggie?"

Then she said something which I hope *you* understand. It is the most profound concept in the universe, but it only makes sense if you understand it at an ultimate level. She said, "I understand…*that it isn't the person. It's the love.*"

What she meant was that Jim and Herb and all those of that spirit whom she had loved were in all her lives to show her the true meaning of love—the love that put the bright white and red light in her heart. The ultimate love which is between our souls and God or the One or the Universe.

And the reason we have love in these incarnations, in these three-dimensional bodies and lives is to *remind* us of that blinding, powerful, great and gorgeous and glorious love which is our connectedness to the universe.

It is so hard to explain, it's unique to each of us and our experiences. We seek romantic love for the burst of the feeling in a moment, for the nectar which explodes as an echo of the love we will feel again when we are reunited with God or the One or the Universe, as we always are between these lives.

I have no idea whether Maggie had this philosophy going in. Certainly in her great pain for the loss of Jim, she could not have had this as a conscious thought. It does not work on the conscious level. Here and now, she misses Jim and wants him back.

But in a transcendental moment of revelation, she was granted the ability to see something much larger than the *play* that is this life, or the play in which she lived as Mary loving Herb. She saw that it is "not the person, but the love," that we are about.

She also grasped joy. For that brief moment of true awareness, although she couldn't have the externally caused happiness of Jim in her life, she could have and always remember what joy feels like.

When she came up from trance, she was weak and shaken. She removed her eye shade and said, "The light's still in my heart. Do you feel this, can you feel it?" and put her hand to my heart.

"I don't know," I said honestly, "I'm vibrating so much, I guess so. I'm sure you feel it."

She sat up and put her hand to her right ear. "I hear a high-pitched sound in my ear," she said.

"Oh, that's just me. I always hear it when I'm vibrating."

"If you're vibrating and I'm hearing it," she laughed, "they're going to take us both away!"

She stood up slowly and came over to hug me. "I'll remember this until the day I die," she said.

As I picked up my purse to leave, I noticed that one of the candles was out. Improbably, it was the one protected by the globe. I'll always suspect that Jim was there and trying to tell us so.

She walked me to my car. Her saying she'd remember this until the day she died reminded me that she hadn't been sure she wanted to live. I asked whether that had changed.

"It's all right, now," she said slowly. "My heart is open. It's all right now. I can still feel the light."

When I called this chapter "The Hardest Thing of All," I wasn't certain why I had, until I'd written it through. Maybe it's because it is the hardest thing to lose a cherished child. It's even harder to understand what Maggie understood. But there is nothing more healing.

When Jim was six, he wrote a little promise to his mother which she printed in the back of the book of his writings she had printed for his burial ceremony.

It seems so incredibly appropriate here, I'll let him say it for himself: "TO MAMA, IF I COULD...

I would give you a day in a land very, very beautiful. No worries or bothers. You could meet any man or woman, see all the worlds and ways that you, my mother would never believe. Mama, if I could, I would give you heaven."

That's why I think maybe he was there.

* * *

Post script:

What really happened, you may ask. It's hard to say. Days later my sister called to report that everyone at work told Maggie how much better she looked, rested, maybe or...well, she just seemed so...changed. "I am a different person,"" Maggie told them. And everyone could see it.

Did she see heaven? Did Jim help? What happened, whatever it was, whatever you choose to believe, it worked. That's the bottom line.

Chapter Nine

The Traveling Medicine Show

Healing on the Road

"Man cannot live without a permanent trust in something indestructible in himself, though both the indestructible element and the trust may remain permanently hidden from him."

—Kafka

Having lived with me and my "instincts" for so long, Harry doesn't balk when I change signals in our designated game plan and we find ourselves running wide outside or against the flow. Or throwing the long ball when everyone else would punt. Or whatever the metaphor is for "forget everything you know, this is something else again." This time, it happened in Prescott, Arizona in September of '91, before we had bought our house there and were just visiting as tourists.

We had been casing the bookstores of the town, of which there are an inordinate number for a place of that size. Every few doors, it seemed, there were new bookstores and used bookstores, spiritual bookstores, bookstores that smelled of incense and cappuccino and bookstores that smelled of moldy pages and leather bindings.

We had studied them one by one until we finally found a bookstore that featured the esoteric titles I coveted. Books on healing, on ancient rituals, on philosophy, psychology, Sufi books and Hindu books, Chinese herbal medicine books and, for good measure, William Blake and Joseph Conrad. That same store also sold knitting supplies. You could search the world over and not outdo the unique collection of bookstores piled up a mile high in Prescott.

Having chosen this one as best meeting our needs, Harry had just settled in, opening up Blake to re-read the most obscure passages he could find, and I was a babe in Toyland about to play in subjects I'd only dreamed of, when a feeling came over me.

"We have to go to the used bookstore across the street," I whispered, so as not to disturb the cashier, a mild-looking woman sitting among the wools and needles like a vision from Lewis Carroll.

"We will."

"No, I mean now."

"But we just got here. And this place has all the books you want. We were there yesterday and that place didn't have nearly the select—"

"—We have to go there, now," I said, closing a book on Wellness and beginning to walk out.

Harry closed the Blake, replaced it, and followed after me, less petulant than curious.

Every shop seems to take on the tenor of its owners or managers and, if you are paying attention, you can feel it the moment you enter. To me, the used-book store we now entered was an unfriendly place, the aisles narrow, the sales help suspicious. I quickly found the aisle on health, thinking that I must be there to find a particular book, that some odd volume must have summoned me there. But I walked up and down studying the titles in vain. Nothing caught my eye. I didn't even reach out to open anything.

Discouraged, I was about to apologize to Harry and drag him back across the street where the good books were, when a woman with a deep, whispery voice who had come in unnoticed by me asked the clerk, "Where are the books on the new treatment for cancer?"

"What new treatment for cancer?" I asked, before I could catch myself.

"I don't know," the woman said. She had very dark circles around her eyes, her hair was caught up in a neat, gray ponytail, and she wore sadness like a cloak. "I just need to read up on new ways to treat cancer."

I let the clerk lead her to the right section, and watched as she stood there without the slightest notion of what to do as the clerk left her to fend for herself.

"Maybe I can help," I said. "Do you know an author's name, or a title?"

"I don't know," she said, sounding exasperated, although that was clearly just a cover for pain. "My daughter has lung cancer." She looked at me as if, saying it out loud, she'd just heard about it for the first time. "She's going in for radiation treatment at one o'clock today. I'm just trying to find a book that might..."

"I don't know if there's anyone around here who does it," I said, "but hypnotherapy could be really therapeutic."

"What do you mean?"

"Well, visualization for healing, among other things. I'm a hypnotherapist and I've worked with cancer patients, so I know it works."

"Will you work with my daughter?"

"Oh, no. We don't live here. We're on the way out of town, we have to get back to LA. tonight. No, but if you could find someone who lives here and does it, that might really help."

"Couldn't you just—"

"Well, I couldn't work with her, you see? Because I'm not here. I'm just passing through. If you could find someone here, who could work with her, you know, regularly?"

Her eyes filled with tears. She didn't say another thing. She didn't have to.

"Well, okay, I'll work with her today."

"Now?"

"Yes, where do you live?"

"Well," she said, hesitating all of a sudden, "my daughter's at the shop next door. Let me ask her if she's interested."

She left and I wondered what I was doing. And what I must seem like. Some traveling medicine woman with snake oil and a promise.

When she came back, she had a sheepish look on her face. "My daughter says 'how much?'"

"How much what?" I asked, thinking she meant time or how many sessions, but she meant money. And I told her I would do it for nothing. No, not for nothing, for love. That's what it felt like, and you aren't really given choices in this matter.

"Follow me," she said.

So I found poor Harry back in the English poets section and said to him, "Harry, we're following this woman home. I have to hypnotize her daughter."

If you don't already think Harry is exceptional, get a clue. He put down the Poe and walked out without a question.

As I look back on it, they must have been very desperate. Imagine inviting to your home two such strangers from the bookstore (one of them a man 6'4 1/2" tall) for a treatment you know nothing about. I don't know what else we could have said or done to have reassured them and made it seem a safe and reasonable thing to do. Fortunately for all of us, it wasn't necessary. It was already 11:30 and the radiation treatment was to begin in an hour and a half.

We followed Betty and her family to her home and parked in the driveway behind her. In her modest, neat little house, shelves filled with memorabilia, we were introduced to Betty's sister and to her daughter, Leanna, the patient.

Leanna was a woman in her early thirties who had a soft and frightened face and the most beautiful, darkly lashed gray eyes I had ever seen. I had no time to waste, so I just took her into the part of the main room that served as a living room, asking everyone else including Harry to stay in the dining area. I said to her, "Are you ready to have me put you into a trance?" and she nodded, yes. And, just about in front of them all, I hypnotized Leanna with textbook ease. As we worked, everyone else seemed to disappear; neither of us was aware of them, as I took her down deeper into herself where we could ask the help of her unconscious.

Without having thought in advance about what I could do for her, and realizing that this might be the only time I could treat her, I decided that the best course was to "program" her unconscious, which means making suggestions in that altered state to the effect that she would have no adverse reaction to the radiation treatment, that it would go smoothly and the healing process would be beginning. I think that programming is the weakest part of work in hypnosis, but, especially in times of fear and trauma, the autonomous nervous system is especially open to suggestion. (See Chapter Twenty-Two on Emergency Medical Services work.) So this seemed my best avenue.

When I was as certain as I could be that her unconscious had absorbed and agreed to the ideas, I brought her back to full awareness and we joined the others in the dining area. Leanna seemed refreshed, but still frightened, of course. I took her phone number and told her I'd call her during the week to see how she was doing. Then we drove out of town, Harry all puffed up thinking what a nice way that was to spend the morning in his favorite town, me thinking life is kind of exciting when you're open to it. I had recently read a saying that you're only free if you're willing to take risks, and I imagine I was feeling kind of free on the way home that day.

When I called Leanna later in the week, she was more upbeat, and she told me she'd had no adverse reactions to the treatment and that it had gone very well. You know, when you do this work, it becomes painfully clear to you that its success isn't up to you. It is in the hands of the patient and her relation to herself and the universe. I was relieved and grateful it had gone well.

What I didn't know then, but subsequently learned, was that Betty and her family, including Leanna, had gone to New Mexico to watch the exciting mushroom cloud of the nuclear tests in the days before the public knew about the hazards of exposure.

While cigarettes can do great harm to the lungs, apparently Leanna's lungs indicated greater destruction than was caused by cigarettes alone.

* * *

Harry and I visited Prescott often that fall and bought little cabin right before Christmas. Every visit, we'd see Leanna. We met her 11 year old daughter, Sarah, during these visits.

Sarah's father, who does not live in this country, is Arabian and as a result, she has his golden skin and her mother's gray eyes with a greenish tint. It is a lovely combination.

To be 11 and have your only live-in parent critically ill is to be forbidden the natural adolescent nonsense and temperament. Sarah couldn't be annoyed with her mother or rebellious, lest she hurt her, or lest she lose her without being reconciled or kind. Her only recourse as a child who needed attention and who was rightly angry at the situation was to become somewhat sullen and unresponsive.

That put her at odds with her mother and grandmother, both of whom were already at odds with each other. When I walked into that situation, I realized that the illness was not the cause of the tension, but a manifestation of the dynamic already there.

Two dachshunds and two cats roamed the house. When Leanna and I worked, some animal or other had to be expelled from her room. Sarah would monosyllabically acknowledge us and go to her room or watch television without comment. There was a sullenness and a sense of disarray about the place that was not so much physical as in the air.

As I worked with Leanna it became clear that the angers she felt at both her mother and her daughter were keeping her from ease. We worked on clearing emotional issues, at visualizing, at healing journeys.

Her radiation treatments ended and there was nothing more they could do for her, it was said. She tried a shark cartilage treatment from a homeopathic doctor, and we continued to work together, but it seemed that the cancer had metastasized and gone to her brain.

Increasingly, I felt helpless and at a loss. My earlier successes had made me feel that if we truly wanted it to happen, anything could be healed. I had read enough legitimate cases of "spontaneous remissions" to know that those words are meant to be translated: we have no explanation of why this person just got well for no medically apparent reason. I firmly believed we could make her get well with our willing it. But, here she was, letting go.

I wish I could tell you that the "magic" in this one was that she turned the disease around and lived. It didn't work exactly that way. As she became weaker, however, her heart seemed to open. She and her mother reconciled. She grew closer to Sarah, who had begun, even before the inevitable happened, to forgive her mother for leaving her.

The last time I saw Leanna, she only intermittently opened her eyes. She was bathed and powdered and almost content, drifting in and out of delusions. When she saw me she said, "I'm glad you're here. You always make me feel calm." There was an irony to me in that, because all my life my high energy level and restlessness had made people insist that I made them nervous. When I met Harry, the static disappeared and when I studied healing, I helped others to find their own quiet centers.

"I had a dream that you and Harry and Abdul and I were diving for oysters," she said. I wondered if we found pearls. I felt she had. She closed her eyes and then opened them somewhat later as I sat there. "I see a lot of people around you," she said and closed her eyes again.

Later, she said. "I'm so glad we met. It was a blessing that I met you at just the right time." We both cried a while and I stroked her arm.

Betty called us a few weeks later to tell us that Leanna had passed over.

* * *

That was in 1991. After that, we saw Betty and Sarah often, whenever we were in Arizona. Sarah grew into a beautiful young woman, fell in love with a good man, graduated fifth in her high school class and entered college in the fall of 1999.

Sadly, the atomic cloud settled again, this time on Betty, and Sarah called me at Christmas to tell me Grandma was dying of lung cancer and would I come and make her want to live. When I arrived at the hospital, I learned that Betty had requested of the surgeon that if the cancer had spread, to simply close her up and let her live the rest of her life in dignity. Her wishes were ignored, and, while the cancer had indeed spread, the surgeon decided to remove a lung, so that Betty was now a helpless invalid. Being the fiercely independent woman I had always admired, she silently stared me down when I tried to work my magic on her, and said with her eyes that she was not planning on dragging this dying-business out. She had been through it with Leanna and wasn't about to put the few remaining loved ones around her, most notably Sarah, through it again.

She passed over with the new millennium and Sarah became our unofficial "goddaughter," becoming our little pearl in this sorry sea of sadness.

The rule in this work is "don't attach to outcome," and that means that when we help someone with an open heart, we have to believe that we can't really see the effect of our caring, but that the effects could, on some level, be profound.

Or, to put it another way, my father used to say that the world can always use more goodness in it, so you just put it in, no questions asked, and that way there's more of it to go around.

Interchapter 2:

Past Life Regression Therapy

*"If we could see ourselves and other objects as they really are,
we should see ourselves in a world of spiritual natures,
our community with which neither began at our birth
nor will end with the death of the body".*

—*Immanuel Kant, Critique of Pure Reason*

Whatever "past lives" may be, as you have seen in some of these cases, past life therapy can have a profoundly transforming effect on this life. That being said, they also can seem very "woo-hoo" to those who do not know the theory behind them. That makes working in this way leaving oneself open to ridicule and charges of "new age" nonsense. Why do I do it?

Working with people challenged by cancer, I constantly confront the issue of death. Partly because of our materialist culture, which turns from death in horror, people with potentially fatal diseases are frightened so profoundly, they may be unable to relax and get well.

I was desperate to find ways to calm their minds and I came up with two which have proven to work wonders.

I help them regress to "former lives," whatever that may mean to them. When in trance we experience our being in another form—living another life which we can feel as "us"—we feel we do live beyond our bodies. And we begin to see meaning in each story which a life's lessons presents.

Secondly, because of the advances of our technology, so many people who "die" are being revived on operating table. They bring back with them fascinating tales of these "near death experiences," which teach us much about what to expect on the other side.

What are past lives?

I imagine that "past lives" are one of three things, although with mysteries being by definition mysterious, they could be one of a million things. My three guesses are that that they may be:

1. really past lives or maybe even consecutive lives, if time is simultaneous, of which we are not aware with our conscious minds

2. a story we pull out of the "collective unconscious"—that pool of mythology and archetypes described by the great psychologist Carl Jung, which we all share

3. or simply stories made up by a part of our mind which uses stories or metaphors to clarify issues for us.

As I said, I'm quite certain it doesn't matter. As long as it effectively solves problems.

* * *

The Experts and the Theory

Transpersonal therapy is a formal branch of practice that assumes that we are more than the physical and biographically historical person who walked into the office with a presenting issue. I believe it assumes soul. And a good deal more.

I studied past life regression with Dr. Ronald Wong Jue, Winifred Lucas, Ph.D., and Hazel Demming, Ph.D. The two women are well over 80 years old, Winifred being, I believe, in her 90s. Hazel "went inside" when she was in her 70s to see how long she would live, and when she realized she had lots of time, she went back to school to get her doctorate!

At their Institute of Regression Therapy, psychologists and healers studied with great discipline, care, and scholarship, the methodology and practice of using regressions to "past lives" to help people heal into this moment.

What do others think past lives might be?

Dr. Brian Weiss wrote an instant best seller (*Many Lives, Many Masters)* and yet he was, at first, extremely reticent to publish his account of his experience with a patient whose phobias and panic attacks he had resolved through her regressions. Having graduated Phi Beta Kappa, magna cum laude from Columbia University and received his M.D. from Yale and holding the position of Chairman of Psychiatry at the Mount Sinai Medical Center in Miami, he was a man of science and medicine and as thrown by what emerged from his patient's unconscious as any traditional doctor would have been. Yet he felt compelled to write about it, defending himself by declaring that these parapsychological phenomena deserve more scientific study, that throughout time new ideas were always assailed, and that this therapy seems to work.

This is a field requiring courage and reminding us of another brilliant Einstein quotation: *Great spirits have always encountered violent opposition from mediocre minds.*

There are many good books in this field, and among those which make the case elegantly and persuasively I recommend: *Lifecycles; Reincarnation and the Web of Life* by Christopher M. Bache, Ph.D. and *Other Lives, Other Selves* by Roger J. Woolger, Ph.D. as well as anything by Brian Weiss.

Reincarnation helps explain all of life to some. Bache suggests that if we don't have reincarnation we have only two explanations for the hand we are dealt and for all of the suffering we see. The first is that suffering is random. The second is that God is responsible, but that still does not explain why children are born crippled or Serbs are allow to ethnically cleanse Moslems.

If we accept reincarnation, Bache says, then we inject meaning and "exquisite complexity and beauty" into life. "Themes started in one century are developed in another and closed in yet a third." Actions have consequences across time and lives and they play out a form of justice. "All is conserved; nothing is wasted."

Dr. Irving Oyle, in *Time Space and the Mind,* looks at it another way. He compares reincarnationists with alchemists who believe in "reincarnating anthropos," substituting DNA for the element which returns to life. He says DNA, too, "is immortal but creates for itself a vehicle of flesh so that it can become you in a physical body." And the part of you that is immortal is what he calls "empty awareness," the part which, when you wake up suddenly, remembers nothing of this month or hour, this house or city, but just IS. That you, he says, may go on and on. In any wardrobe of name and flesh, time and place.

But past lives could be just one's own personal myth. And if so, so what if they explained your present problems and gave your life meaning, and you were healed. There's a corny old joke about Uncle Charlie thinking he's a chicken and no one taking him to the psychiatrist because "we need the eggs." Whatever the reason, if past life regression solves problems, it make sense to keep getting the benefits, even if it doesn't seem to make sense at all.

From the Mind/Body studies (See Interchapter 1) we know that what we envision or imagine has an effect on our body, because by imagining we are talking to every cell in pictures. I have seen people lose afflictions, aches, pains, phobias by "recalling a past life" which involved an injury and then resolving it and letting it go.

Winifred Lucas, Ph.D. wrote in her book *Regression Therapy: A Handbook For Professionals* that she sees this therapy as remitting symptoms "more speedily and effectively than other therapeutic modalities were able to do." Because it also moves "in the direction of clarifying the spiritual nature of our existence," she says, "my cognitive side has been embarrassed to discover this, but the trend cannot be denied."

Whatever may or may not be factual about past life regression, it works for a lot of reasons, including because it gives meaning to suffering. And including because "re-living" a trauma and seeing it finished, completed, and having escaped from it into a future you know about, is healthy and freeing.

Someone with a phobic fear of drowning who is able to experience his/her own death, in another time and place by drowning, understands it and the "meaning" of it to that life and then awakens here and now—just might be able to let go of that fear.

We live with a constant fear of death because it is inevitable and awaits us personified by "the grim reaper." This metaphor is the other side of using metaphors to heal. It is a tragic mistake which spoils our joy and reeks havoc on our bodies. If we can assuage our trepidation and welcome every stage of experience, we can change trials into challenges and anxiety into ease.

We may not be able to fully know what it is we access when we go in trance to "past lives." Some like to take it literally and for those looking for "proof," there are a number of books about cases in which people in an altered state have remembered lives before their own in such intimate and accurate detail that explanations elude even the cynical, e.g., Dr. Ian Stevenson's *Twenty Cases Suggestive of Reincarnation* and Dr. Thomas Verney's *The Secret Life of the Unborn Child*, which details extraordinary information as evidence for in utero memory.

I personally do not think it matters whether we are talking about actual past lives or only memories which we draw from the collective unconscious.

Lucas uses the Mind Mirror, a biofeedback machine which monitors the mind of a person recovering past-life material, to further study this phenomenon. There are four wave states which the Mirror reflects:

Beta 13-30 Hertz (everyday consciousness)

Alpha 8-13 Hertz, (the meditating, creating state)

Theta 4-7 Hertz (one's personal unconscious)

Delta 1/2-4 Hertz, which used to be thought of as the sleeping state but is now considered the radar state, the state in which we reach for knowledge.

It seems that people in altered states recovering past life material are often in Delta. What is interesting about that is that if they were creating these stories, making them up, their brain waves would be of the Alpha frequency. So where are the stories coming from?

Lucas discusses the concept of a "mind field" and suggests that it is there that memories are stored. The Delta state, she suggests, may then be the radar state. The information seems to come in through Delta, go through the Theta state then into the Alpha, where it becomes images, and then up into high Alpha and Beta, she says "where it is remembered and recognized and evaluated and transformed."

I sometimes think of the brain as the hardware and the universal information as the software we all can access when we're tuned into it.

When the Mind Mirror also monitors the therapist, it can be seen that the therapists may go into altered states and Delta first and pull the patient there with them. As Delta tunes into mind field, perhaps where past life is stored, the brain slows down enough to pick up information in radar state.

Apparently, the more the subject is in Alpha, the more suggestible; the more in Delta, the more he or she is in his/her truth.

It is only lately, Lucas says, that people move with ease into Delta. In earlier times, it took years of Mystery School or yogic meditation to retrieve past lifetimes. We also seem to be able to be in Delta and Beta or Alpha and in Beta (our everyday consciousness) at the same time, which means we can experience the past life and comment on it, a completely new model. There you are seeing yourself as a little Dutch girl with wooden shoes growing tulips and at the same time, with another part of your mind, you are saying "this is weird."

What can we learn from looking at former lives?

We're not always Cleopatra in these lives, not always the hero. Partly, by experiencing a series of lives in which we are kind and evil, male and female, victim and persecutor, wise and foolish, we begin to understand that we are everything, capable of everything, and, having experienced the feelings of a host of divergent personalities, we can empathize with others rather than judging them.

That leads to love, and love is the most healing force in the universe. Chet Snow, Ph.D. calls love the "universal lubricant," and relates it to what Pythagoras called "the music of the spheres."

Ernest Pecci, M.D., put it this way, "There is a primordial Essence characterized by unconditional love, joy, serenity and wisdom from which we have become separated and to which we can return by moving out into the vaster realities of awareness."

There is no healthier state than that. The opposite of love is fear, and it is fear—of not having our needs met, of hunger, destitution, criticism, pain, abandonment—which causes our dastardly behavior and our illnesses.

So, of course, whatever we can do to alleviate the fear and live in love would provide us with health and tranquility. And, one on one, experiencing past life regression with a qualified therapist can provide a means to that end. It helps us to see and understand quirks, repulsions, longings, phobias in our present lives as patterns of lifetimes, helps us to develop our human consciousness so that it can begin to reflect love instead of fear, and so that it can release the self judgment which is the most negating thing that exists.

What about Karma.

Some people call it the law of cause and effect.

Some people see it as punishment for transgressions.

I see it somewhat differently. I imagine the Universe as a giant drum head and believe that everything we send out comes back to us. Not in judgment. Just back as we put it out, so we can feel its effects for ourselves and learn from it.

The value of experience, especially bad experience, is so that we can sympathize, identify, care from a position of understanding.

* * *

"There is no death. Only a change of worlds"—Chief Seattle

These days there are eye-witnesses to the other side. Sophisticated modern high-tech medicine enables us to bring technically "dead" people back to life and reports of "near death experiences" (NDE's) abound. Mostly they are similar to each other in nature, and people having crossed the line come back changed. Interestingly, they come back wanting to do good with what remains of the life they've been given back.

Generally, they go "out of body," looking down on themselves as hospital personnel try to save them. One blind woman "saw" during her out of body experience, reporting to the startled physician when she came back to life that he was wearing two different colored socks.

Once in the out of body state, they tend to move then toward the "light," often seeing people awaiting them who have died before. One of the clinchers that this is not fantasy is that when children have a near-death experience they might be expected to find a parent or someone they trust waiting for them in the light. But unless a parent has died first, that is not whom they see there, reports Elizabeth Kubler-Ross, M.D. who writes extensively on life and death.

On television recently, a little girl who had been in a car crash and recovered from a coma was reported to have said that she saw her mother and brother in the light. She did not yet know that they, and only they, had died in the accident.

During this process, some of the NDE-ers review their lives, bathed in unconditional love. See *Embraced by the Light*, by Betty Eadie and Dr.

Kenneth Ring's *Life at Death: A Scientific Investigation of the Near-Death Experience* and *Heading Toward Omega: In Search of the Meaning of the Near-Death Experience.*

"Proof" these trips are not simply the fantasies, for example, of someone under anesthesia during an operation is that many of those people are thoroughly monitored. They are hooked up to machines which read their functions. When they "die," their hearts may have stopped, but so have their brain waves, which show no movement. Whereas, if the patients were imagining the visions, the brain activity would register on the machines to which they are attached.

Imagine being convinced that life does not end with death—that our bodies are just cars for our souls to get around in and that, in fact, death is just a door. If we knew that, we could release our fears and let our bodies heal!

Some spiritual people suggest that if we can die in love and consciousness, we die in a unified way; if we die in fear, pain and suffering, those emotions re-form, the attraction is too strong, and they follow us from life to life. If that is true, then Harry is right and my work with Leanna was a success.

Here's how Dr. Ernie Pecci advises patients about survival anxiety: "You have a right to be here as long as you need to be to do what you have to do. And then you graduate; you've earned it. You can't possibly be responsible for your survival and your kids' survival; let go of it."

He concludes that pain and problems tell you that you are going in the wrong direction. Thank them, turn over the rock and see the gem. The three-dimensional world is not supposed to work in comfort—it's supposed to help you grow.

Dr. Jue uses transforming journeys (See Chapter Twenty-Nine) as well as past life regression to help his patients see their lives in a larger perspective. To see "the rightness of being," he says, the rightness of everything that has happened to you. To see that if you felt awkward or wrong, you were an ugly duckling who can now perceive him/herself as a swan. He sees his role as helping people find their integrity, versus fragmentation. Helping the person to come home.

Your whole nature is spiritual, he says, and this life and each of our many lives are part of the journey of the soul to make your whole life whole.

Chapter Ten

A Peek Through the Crack

Tiptoeing to the Edge of Trance

"There ain't no rules around here. We're trying to accomplish something."

—*Thomas Alva Edison*

Before beginning a healing, the great Native American medicine man of the last generation, Rolling Thunder, used to ask, "Why do you want to be relieved of this condition?" Such a question sets the mind in the right direction, imagining life beyond the present misery. In hypnotherapy, we often ask, "What will your life be like without this issue in it?"

Not everyone wants to change. John Kenneth Galbraith put it this way: *Faced with the choice of changing one's mind and proving there is no need to do so, almost everyone gets busy on the proof.*

Some people think it is more risky to step into the minefield of the unknown than to live with the pain that has grown familiar. And, if you want to help them, you have to know that, and respect that.

So, while this unauthorized session worked out well, I admit that it could be seen as an intrusion and today I would be much more circumspect about helping someone who was so clear about trying to avoid my aid.

Lena was a friend who knew me through my writing and teaching, but she was not among those fans of hypnotherapy and the occult.

Although she was suffering severely from two catastrophic losses, and although she trusted me as a friend, she adamantly stated that she did not want to be hypnotized.

Lena's losses crossed the generations. Her runaway, schizophrenic daughter died suddenly of a brain tumor, so disoriented and confused at the end, that she passed away estranged from her family that loved her. Within months of that tragedy, Lena's elderly friend Evelyn, whose journals she had promised to edit, died as well. Along with that loss, Evelyn's daughter-in-law destroyed or "mislaid" the journals so that Lena could not keep her promise. All of this happened within a year of the time of the day I am about to describe.

Lena had explained that she did not want hypnotherapy because she believed it had been misapplied in her daughter's case and had unleashed the multiple personalities that had made her final months so destructive and chaotic.

Lena also confessed that she was quite comfortable in her grief and pain, which had grown so familiar that she wasn't at all certain what she could replace it with or whether she would choose to let it go.

Healing can have rhythms in time and a mind of its own, however, and it does no good to insist that it conform to our agenda or presuppositions. So Lena and I were meeting for other reasons, to discuss some of our writings, although we often digressed to talk about life.

This day, she had remembered being beside a river in Japan years before and feeling a sense of expansion, of comprehension, of clarity as she studied the movement of the currents. It seemed almost as though, through the informal meditation of watching the waves, she understood how to solve her problems.

A resource! I thought. We all have resources if we can identify and acknowledge them. And if we can go back to them in our minds, we can bring the past into the present and leverage a neglected, overlooked but potent power that is ours.

"Can you remember that feeling?" I said.

"No." She didn't want to play.

"Can you try to feel it in your body, how it felt?"

"No."

"Maybe if you close your eyes…"

She didn't.

I closed mine and continued talking. "If you could see it in your mind's eye and remember again how it felt to have clarity, then you could just be leaf on the river, drifting lazily…" I spoke softly, escalating the pace just enough to cause a river-like momentum.

Finally, when I opened my eyes, hers were closed.

"Can you see it?"

"No. I see a big stone wall."

"How high is it?"

"High."

"Is there a ladder on the ground anywhere nearby?" I didn't want to risk another "no," so I kept on talking. "Could you pick it up and lean it against the wall? Then you could climb up and just look over; you wouldn't actually have to go over…"

"It's too short," she said.

Good, I thought. A short ladder is better than a "no."

But I was at the usual God-help-me-please state where I need an inspiration from a mind larger than mine. "Well," I said, stalling, "why don't you just walk along the wall dragging your finger along the mortar and see if any of it is dry and crumbly and if you might be able to loosen a rock and take it out."

"You're tricking me," she said.

"You know how mortar gets, and I'm only talking a little rock, just so you could peek through. Is there one that's loose, that you could just pry—"

"Yes."

Thank you. "Can you see Japan through the hole?"

"Yes. I can see the river."

"Good." Next, please God. And then right out of my mouth came, "Can you put a camera up against the hole and take a picture of it?"

She laughed. "You're tricking me."

"Can you?"

"Yes."

"Can you put a movie camera against it and make a movie and watch it tonight when you're lying in bed?"

She sighed. "Yes."

"And you could just…be a leaf on the river, floating down. And then you could have that feeling of clarity again, and maybe understand what you need to understand as the river ripples by just as it did before when you saw things clearly."

We both sat in the stillness for a while. Then she opened her eyes. It was time for me to leave. Walking me to my car she whispered, almost to herself, "And to think of all the time I've spent building a wall between…myself and my happiness."

* * *

That might be called waking hypnosis and it's as good as the other, more stagey kind, when it works. After all, we're in trance a large part of our lives. When you're driving home and you realize that you don't remember the trip at all, or whether you even stopped at the stoplights or signs, you've been in a trance. The next step, as you saw here, is to take the creative leap. Know that you have all the possibilities of the universe to call on; that you're only as limited as you allow yourself to be.

Of course, our minds are quirky, unpredictable, rebellious things. I later got an e-mail from Lena telling me that when she went to bed that night, she tried to play the movie from the camera, but she couldn't figure out how to work it!

I thought to myself, "You invented the blankety-blank camera, you could just have invented a red button to push to start it!"

But then, she wrote, after trying to work the camera and giving up, she simply remembered the river and then some answers floated along, too.

It doesn't matter how it works. Red button or no camera at all. It only matters that we have the answers and, when the moment is right, we can sometimes get to them. We **always** have our creativity.

Knowing **that** is the crack in the wall.

Chapter Eleven

Not Just in the Movies

The Newly Deceased Line Producer of Ghost Returns

"Belief is not the beginning of knowledge; it is the end."

—*Goethe*

Nothing about the request that I received to work with the man who had been the production manager of "Ghost" turned out as I expected.

It was during an exceptionally busy time for me in the spring of 1993, that I received a call from the wife of man who had managed the production not only of "Ghost" but of "The Terminator." He had developed lymphoma and they had heard I was a healer. Would I work with him.

Of course I would. The only problem was fitting it into my crazy schedule, which I am ashamed to admit was primarily taken up with work at the marketing agency, plus trips to our Arizona home on the weekends where we were committed to entertaining guests for the next two weeks. "I'll come to **you**," I said. "Would it be all right if we arranged it for two weeks from now?"

She hesitated, so I recommended that I send her some tapes that might help in the interim. In my travels in this field I have come across a number of healing tapes, some which I duplicate, not for sale, from choice programs I have encountered. I have made tapes of my own, as well, and so I made the cassette for her, put it in my car with a slip of paper on which I'd written the address, and drove to work.

When I arrived at my office, I grabbed what I thought was the tape and the address, and handed them over to an assistant. "It's urgent," I said, "life and death. Please FedEx this out right way for me."

Feeling mildly alleviated that I had done something good for these strangers in need, I worked through the day and got into my car to drive home in the evening. There on the seat next to me was the tape I had made for Dirk and Sabra.

What had I sent them? My mind raced through a review of what I had lately been listening to. In a moment of sheer panic I could only imagine I must have picked up the tape of zydeco music by my daughter's current boyfriend, George, which was raucous and wild and fine for tuning out freeway traffic. I was mortified. I had to stop Sabra from putting it on and being blasted away in a solemn and dire moment with the free-wheeling enthusiasm of the Louisiana band whose style is best suggested by the group's name—Loup Garou: French for werewolf.

As I walked into the house and right over to the phone, hardly acknowledging Harry, I must have looked like a person pursued by a demon.

Harry never misses a signal. "What's wrong?"

I had looked up Sabra's number and begun to dial.

"I can't even tell you," I said, knowing he would find out soon enough as he overheard my explanation, whatever that would be. I had not yet found words in my mind adequate to telling this stranger with a mortal wound what I had done. Whatever words I would choose, I knew I was so upset I could not bear to have had to say it twice.

"Sabra," I said, "it's Judith Prager. I'm so embarrassed. I FedExed you a tape today, but it's the wrong tape. You'll get it tomorrow, but please don't listen to it. I don't even know what I sent you, but I have the one that's meant for you right here in my hands."

"Dirk is in a coma," she said quietly. "He's in the hospital now."

Now my bearings were completely gone. Here I was babbling on about a tape to a stranger in such acute and tangible misery. "Oh, I'm so sorry."

She paused. "I don't know if I'm doing it right. I tell him how much I love him, and that I'll be all right, and thank him for providing for me, and sometimes a tear forms in his eyes and I don't know if I'm making him sad."

"That may be the only way he has of responding," I said. "I'm certain he hears you and needs you there. I'll send you the right tape right away and maybe if he listens to it, that will help ease his spirit, too."

"I'll take it to her," Harry said to me, "I'm going to L.A. tomorrow." I told her of his offer and she thanked him profusely for his generosity, which I happen to know Harry wouldn't consider it. He always says, if you're walking past someone who's on fire and you put out the fire is that a generous gesture? No, it's the least you can do.

"I don't know why," she continued, "but I've been singing 'Amazing Grace' to him."

"That's a wonderful idea," I said.

"I don't know the second verse. Do you?"

We didn't.

"I'm so glad you called," she said, breaking down, now. "I really needed to talk to you."

So, now I knew why I had made the stupid mistake with the tape. People in my field say there are no mistakes. As we talked, we both began to feel a little better.

Dirk passed over immediately thereafter and I never got to meet him. The friend who had given them my name called to tell me he was gone. And she requested that I work with the wife.

There I was, with my mixture of sorrow, remorse that I had not really been able to help, guilt, and confusion. Work with her? Doing what? I was a hypnotherapist who helped people with cancer heal either physically or spiritually, whatever was meant to be. I had never worked with their survivors.

We made an appointment and I spent the next week filled with prayer and dismay. I know that I am blessed with the ability to help console people about death, primarily because I believe that death is just a door; and this life we think of as all, is but a piece of something so extraordinary, we have not yet imagined it.

I can help people understand that we are so much more than we have allowed ourselves to seem. That we are not our names, nor the roles we play, nor the labels people give us. They can call us lazy and we can be lazy; call us stupid and we can be stupid; call us careless, brilliant, stubborn, negative, and we live up or down to the job description. But who we are, our souls, are much larger and just watching all the time.

Driving to her house, trying to weave myself into the fabric of this relationship, breathing its texture, feeling its patterns, I put into my now deeply-involved tape deck a tape of Hubert Laws' instrumental rendition of "Amazing Grace." Heading for this appointment with no clear plan, with no predetermined idea of how I would proceed, I asked my guides to be with me in this work, to somehow show me that they were there and I could call upon them.

I was driving a highway I'd never driven before, up the Hollywood Freeway up into the hills, feeling lost and frightened. Suddenly, as I rounded a curve in the road, the only lighted sign in this whole unfamiliar area blazoned brightly at me: "Braille Institute." At that very moment, "Amazing Grace" reached the part of the song at which these words flooded into my mind: "I was blind, but now I see."

I always say "thank you" to my guides. It seems like they like to be acknowledged, and, what's more, it seems that they come back more often when they think you're paying attention.

When Sabra opened the door, I knew immediately that I would like her, moreover that I could work with her, whatever that would mean. Pale and neat, she had a lovely, kind face and a natural manner that invited closeness and suggested familiarity from a forgotten time. She was clearly suffering, as this relationship had been the centerpiece of her life. And yet she was elegantly serene.

We embraced and I entered, noticing two cats, and I made an effort to say hello to them.

"They aren't themselves," Sabra said, wanting to defend their distant behavior. "They are in mourning. I'm afraid they're not going to be very social. Not only did they just lose their master, but there had been three and one of them just died of cancer, too." She paused. "I can only imagine that wherever Dirk is, he wanted a cat."

I don't know how guides communicate with other people, I just seem to know something I didn't know before and act on it believing that I've been guided. In this case, after having a conversation with Sabra about her beautiful relationship with Dirk and about his finally having had a chance to be line producer on a movie, I understood how tragic was her loss.

His new movie was to be released in August and it was called "Heart and Souls." It was directed by Ron Underwood who had directed "City Slickers" and it starred Robert Downey Jr. and an ensemble cast including Charles Grodin. The movie was about a baby who is born at exactly the moment that four people with unfinished business die in a bus crash. Rather than move on, they attach themselves to the child, who grows up to be something of a Yuppie. It is then that they learn that they may do one act to rectify their lives and then they must give up this plane. It is, in short, about entities.

I happen to work with groups of professional psychologists, Ph.Ds and counselors who do entity work, so I was intrigued. Remember, Dirk had also worked on "Ghost."

In order to help Sabra know that her spirit and Dirk's were eternal, had known each other before and would meet again on other planes, I suggested past life work: to learn where and how they had gone around together before.

First, my guides suggested, or I seemed to think it made sense that I do some energy work. I used the "Healing Hands" and "Therapeutic

Touch" I had learned at the Yavapai Medical Center in Prescott, Arizona. I sensed that it would be easier to put her into an altered state if I cleared her aura.

Clearing an aura is a deceptively simply process, but it requires about 15 minutes with the patient lying down on a couch as I move my hands along the invisible bodies above the one on the couch. She was proceeding nicely into what I could resonate with as a light trance when suddenly a loud, almost rumbling sound surrounded us. I work with my eyes closed, so I opened them to check on what was disturbing us.

It was the cats, each one perched on either side of her as I worked, purring furiously, radiating intensely like little generators. At that moment, I looked up in a doorway, and I got the distinct impression, although I never met him, that I saw Dirk leaning against the frame, in a relaxed, curious pose, his arms folded.

When I was done with that procedure, Sabra sat up and studied the cats. They were sleek and almost mesmerized as she carried them downstairs, surprised at their sudden interest, their odd vibrancy. They did not complain, just continued to hum as she left them to their own stupor.

When she returned I put her into a trance. Relatively easily, she returned to two "past life" scenarios. In the first she seemed to be in Spain centuries ago. She wore an elaborate gown, the crinolined skirt of which kept everyone at a distance. Everything there was formal and stilted, and although she found an energy that seemed like Dirk, and they danced, the gown an impediment between them, the distance seemed as emotional as it was physical.

In another life which took place in the West in the last century, she again found an energy which she identified as Dirk, but again there was coldness, distance. We didn't linger in either, since they were so antithetical to our goal of showing her how their souls had shared lives before and would again.

I took her to the Interlife, the "place" where decisions about the meanings of life are made, and we asked for an explanation. We saw that she and Dirk had decided to devote this life to learning how to establish and participate in the close bond; that, in fact, they had decided in this life not to have children because they had chosen to work on this relationship.

It was an unsatisfactory session for one as in need as Sabra and I was saddened. But if I have learned anything in my magical journey, it is that we control nothing, we are foolish to try to determine it, and if we accept with love and good spirit whatever comes, it will explain itself in its own good time.

So, as I was about to bring her up, I asked her whether there was anything else she wanted to do or say. She said she really missed Dirk. And then she said, sadly, "I'm not satisfied." Neither was I.

What could I do? This is out of our hands. But I thought, perhaps, if she "took a walk along the beach," she might find Dirk in her mind. Believe me, I had no idea of the consequences of such a proposal, but I seemed to have no choice.

There is a beach she loves, which she shared with Dirk and she easily saw herself there. Dirk was there, too, but there was a veil between them. She clearly felt he didn't want her to be with him. Now my despair grew doubled.

"Of course he wants you there," I said. "He loves you."

"But I just don't want to bother him. I feel like I'm bothering him."

"Well, tell him that everything is all right. Talk to him, to put his mind at rest," I said, grappling. I felt deserted by my otherwise dependable guides. Nothing seemed to be working.

There is a rule in hypnosis that a person in deep trance is never to be touched without announcing first that you will do so. That is because, when in an altered state, the person is "out of body," in a sense. In deep trance, one cannot even move without suggestion to do so, because the body is left behind as the work takes place somewhere else. So the effect to a person in trance of being touched by surprise is akin to, but worse than, those awful moments when you are awakened out of a deep sleep too quickly and can't get your bearings, don't know where you are, and feel drugged and disoriented.

Of course, I knew that, so you can imagine my surprise when my hand seemed to move by itself and place itself on Sabra's. I felt like Whoopie Goldberg being used by Patrick Swayze! If it wasn't Dirk's idea, I can tell you it wasn't mine.

And the instant I—we—put my hand on hers, her other hand flew to her eyes, which were still closed, and she said, "He's taken my hand and we're flying!" And she was off on an adventure with him which cut through the air in the room like a gust and left me well behind as they soared beyond walls and clouds and stratospheres and realms.

He told her then that he was joyful where he was and that he was just learning how to be there. They swirled and danced, floated and experimented. There was no stand-offishness now, not from former lives and not like on the beach just moments ago.

He explained that he had been not so much pushing her away as wanting her not to be sad for him. He was joyous, he insisted, it was glorious and now he had found her across the veil.

She might miss him, he added, but he did not want her to grieve.

* * *

When I called her the next day, I asked how she was doing. "The cats are back to themselves, again," she said. "They're running around, meowing."

"And you? Are you meowing."

"I'm better," she said. In fact, she went on in a few weeks to have a memorial at her canyon home for Dirk, inviting all the crew members from "Heart and Souls" including the director. I attended and overheard someone telling Sabra that he had explained to his son where he was going and that it was a memorial where everyone could get together and remember the good times and how they felt about Dirk. And, he said, his son really liked the idea of it.

I told her she was a beautiful inspiration to everyone, had shown everyone how grieving was really meant to be, and, while it had been up to Dirk to give his life meaning, in her dignified and open way, she had given his death a greater significance.

She remained frustrated that several of her friends and acquaintances had "heard" from Dirk in one way or another, even had messages for her, but he didn't seem to be trying to communicate directly with her. A channel had spoken his words to her, going outside with a pair of scissors to cut a rose and handing it to her saying, "Dirk says, you are my rose."

Sometime later, however, I received a phone call from her in which I learned that he was coming to her in her dreams. "Not in what I call 'story dreams,'" she said, although sometimes he appeared in those, too. No, these dreams were different, what some people call "lucid dreams." Very much like reality.

And always, in those, they made love. Danced as they had in the sky. I was thrilled.

Sometimes in these lucid experiences she could think to ask him questions like how did he feel getting from wherever he was to her.

"It's not my favorite part of it," he'd answered.

So she assumed it wasn't easy to "appear" to us. But it was worth it to him to make the journey.

His visits were both sexual and romantic. "But I wish he would talk to me, not just in dreams." she said. "I wish he would actually say to **me** 'You are my rose.' I want to hear words."

I had to smile. I used to think that things had to be said in words to be known, too, but I put it for her another way and I think she heard these words: "When you expect something in a particular way, it's like having tunnel vision. The only acceptable way for him to come to you is through that door. He might already be in the room, but you're watching the doorway. You know, he seeks you out across the veil through the universe, whatever it takes to end up in your arms. I think that's an exquisite way to say 'you're my rose.' Excuse me if this sounds odd, but if I were in your shoes, that's what I'd choose."

"Maybe you're right," she said. "It is very nice," I could almost hear her blush. "The last time he came to me was when I was in England. It was a passionate visit and I have to admit, when I woke up I felt very…girlish."

Is she satisfied now? I don't know. But it does seem to me, these days, that woman is meowing.

Chapter Twelve

Double Trouble

Abandoned with 18-month Old Twins, A Father Finds the Grand Design

"Touch a hole in your life and there flowers will bloom".

—Zen saying

Mitch hadn't wanted children. In fact, he'd had a vasectomy during his first marriage to emphatically make the point. When he remarried a young, fantasy-driven woman who read romance novels and thought Pepsi commercials represented a desirable way of life, he saw the two of them drifting into a carefree future of good times and easy laughter.

Although she would always choose dancing or shopping over going to the museum with him (he was an artist by vocation), his eye for beauty had been lured by her charms and he was well under her spell when she discovered within herself a previously unknown desire to have a baby.

Between his having to reverse the vasectomy and her discovering she had problems conceiving, fulfilling her latest desire became quite a project. Several fertility drugs later, her doctors announced to her that she had five fetuses in her womb and that, being a size two with slighter hips than a drinking straw, three of the fetuses would have to be terminated early or none would survive.

So by the time Ellie and Garret were born, they had endured a grisly selection process which left its traces all around them in utero. Not a propitious start in life.

But matters got worse when the mother discovered that "having a baby," actually two, did not fit the MTV picture and cramped her style. So, when they were 18-months old, she told Mitch that motherhood wasn't what she had expected or wanted and she walked out on the three of them.

By the time Mitch came to me for help, his fury at his wife scorched a path before him. "I want you to hypnotize me," he said, "so I can find out what our karmic deal is. I want to know why she did this to me and who owes who what."

I knew what he was talking about. He wanted to trace a "past life" to discover what gruesome Greek tragedy this ongoing saga was a part of and where it was headed.

"Not now," I said. "You're too angry."

He was bitterly disappointed, a state he felt permanently assigned to, but instinct alerts us that the work must be done at the moment when it is right to unlock the secret which would have stayed hidden only a week before.

Sometime later, when Mitch seemed ready, I told him I would work with him.

He went quickly into trance, looking for his wife (let's call her Suzie), down through the eons. The details of this process have somewhat faded from memory, but I recall that the first life we came to found him to be a fisherman in Taiwan in the 1300's. His name was Dey and he was carrying his baskets on a stick across the back of his neck. "Are you married, Dey?" I asked, thinking we could cut right to Suzie.

"Yes."

"Do you love your wife?"

"No."

"Why did you marry her?" I asked automatically, and just as automatically he answered, "It was arranged."

At times like these, when you recognize that the Mitch you know could never have thought of that answer, that it just would not have occurred to this thoroughly modern man, your respect for this process grows. He spoke that answer so naturally as Dey.

In another life, I believe in England, he heard a woman who might or might not have been Suzie drowning in a river, but did not choose to attempt to rescue her.

In yet another scenario, he was a Dutch carpenter who neglected his family in pursuit of his career. At the end of his life, he did not die a happy man, a classic verification of that piece of popular wisdom that reads, "Enjoy the people you love. No one on his deathbed says 'I wish I had spent more time at the office.'"

All of this seemed to have led us nowhere. So I asked Mitch to go before his "committee," who could help him understand the meaning of this life. This is an "Interlife" concept involving the notion that our lives are meaningful and purposeful and that we have agreed to incarnate in order to experience certain aspects of life and that for that reason, we encounter a particular combination of events. The committee knows all. It might be our own inner wisdom. It might be guidance. We don't have to know who's helping, as long as we get the help we need.

He asked his committee what this life was about and then he was silent for a while. I waited in wonder, myself. Then he said, "They're showing me shapes and textures. A lotus. Patterns." Another pause, then, "Oh, I get it."

I was not quite with him, but interested in how this was going to explain itself.

"They're saying they made me an artist and a Pisces because I never felt my true feelings in my other lives, I never committed myself to anyone, I never experienced my emotions. They said this life was meant to experience the connection, to really feel it, every drop of it."

When he came up from his trance, he was beatific, glowing. "I get it," he said.

Then he explained, "They put those two little kids right in my face, so sweet, so completely dependent on me, so that I'd have to learn the priority of loving, committing and caring."

He also added in surprise and perhaps relief, "It wasn't about Suzie at all!"

It was a truly wondrous explanation that put things into perspective. Mitch became an awesome daddy once he was given notice of his challenge for his life and its purpose. In a sense, this was all about creativity: the children and his work, the children of his imagination.

Awareness is the first step to getting it right. The next steps are up to us.

Stories About
Emotional Issues

Wholeness is wholeness and dividing this book into a section about emotional issues certainly makes no sense in that context. But often before illness manifests in the body, it tries to communicate with us through the dis-ease of uncomfortable emotions.

These stories are of people who found ways to change the trajectory of their lives through their imaginations.

Chapter Thirteen

Not Enough

How the Universe Lets You Know You Are in Your Right Place

*"The divine speaks in us, and it is exhausting to ignore it.
That is what makes us tired".*

—JSP

As you may have noticed, there are often times when, as a hypnothera-pist, I could have gone for the jugular. I could have taken on the "forces of evil," made Virginia confront her father, made Evie confront the per-son who betrayed her.

But my philosophy is that fighting something empowers it. You just think about it and dwell on it and pretty soon, it fills your life, even if you're "working on it" and "cleaning it up."

That is not to say that a good, clear understanding of what hap-pened and how you really felt about it are unnecessary to healing. They are invaluable.

However, there are times when my work ventures forth into realms beyond the literal, beyond the concrete. I play on the imagination to reach answers which transform problems, lift them up and out of the mundane, in hopes of providing a new and stunning perspective.

One client in particular surprised us both with the magic of our unlimited potential. A lovely, gentle woman, on her first and only appointment with me, Marsha quickly covered the old territory of pain by telling me about her troubled childhood, about her father's having kidnapped her at three and taken her and her sister to an orphanage.

Marsha had spent a significant amount of time working on her issues and clearing her understanding of herself and her relationships, but still she felt something was missing, felt, in her words, "like I'm not enough." Not enough as a partner to the man in her life, just not enough. Not enough of a woman. Not enough of a mother. Not enough.

Such a presenting problem seemed quite complex to me. Issues of self-esteem, of ego, stories and grievances to delve into. However, it occurred to me that there might be a way to get to the other side that did not involve trudging through it all again.

My first thought was that in trance she might find her inner wisdom, find a "guide" who would allow her to experience "what it would feel like to be enough." I felt that if she could picture herself as enough, she could move into that vision in her life. It seemed like a plan, but then, this work always has a way of proving that it has a life of its own.

I put Marsha into trance and asked her to imagine taking a walk on a beach. I described in detail the breeze on her face, the sun through the breeze, the sound of the waves and the gulls, the feeling of the sand beneath her toes. I used all of my imaginative powers to evoke hers.

Then I asked her to imagine someone coming toward her, a guide, and when she saw him or her, she should move the finger I indicated. She simply lay there.

"Take your time," I said, talking a little more about the scene, about the guide. Finally I said, "you may talk to me and remain in trance. What to you see?"

"I'm floating in space," she said.

No beach. No guide. All right. "Do you see anything else, any stars?"

"No."

"Are you in a vehicle or just floating?"

"Just floating. I feel heavy."

"What do you see?"

"It's purple," she said. "It's just all purple."

We seemed to be at an impasse. What could I make of this? Suddenly, I had an inspiration. "Could you be in a womb?" I asked, reaching for some way to quantify this experience.

"No," she said. We paused, as I wondered what could happen next. And then she started to cry, becoming very light on the couch, almost floating, with a smile on her face, crying softly, in what seemed like joy.

"What are you feeling?"

"Love. This incredible, beautiful, unconditional love."

I held my breath and watched her experience the sheer pleasure of it. Then these words came out of my mouth, sooner than I could think them. For surely, I had never had such a thought.

"Could you be in **God's** womb?" I asked softly.

To my eternal surprise and wonder she said, "Yes."

God's womb.

"Can you feel it in every cell of your body, in every ounce of your being, this love?"

"Yes."

"Can you hold it so that you can always feel it, just this way, flooding over you, filling your every pore with love?"

"Yes."

"And," I was a little afraid to utter it, afraid to break the spell and yet I had to take the chance. It was for this that she had come..."are you....enough?"

She hardly paused. "Yes," she said.

I asked if she could beam it out so that others could see it and feel it, God's love going through her, and she said she could.

We anchored it, so that she could go back to this feeling whenever she wanted to, and be enough.

After she left, I just sat in stunned silence, my little plans so tossed aside as something larger took over, said "excuse me, I'll show you how it's done," and left me in awe and appreciation.

In the wink of an eye, Marsha had found the perfect metaphor for the proof that all of us are created complete. Completely lovable. Completely adequate. Completely enough. We ARE all in God's womb all of the time, and it is only for us to realize it that it is "realized," becomes our reality.

So, I thanked her in my mind for the image of being in "God's womb" and ask you to hold it lightly in yours and see if you don't feel a difference. Just by acknowledging it.

Chapter Fourteen

Dialogues with a Fruit Bowl

A Phobia Explains Itself and Goes Away

"It is harder to live frightened than brave"

—*JSP*

This is one of my favorite stories because it unfolds like a mystery to a perfectly elegant conclusion. We find out who done it and why, in three brief sessions.

Melissa's mother was worried about her daughter's panic attacks. Although Melissa had been in conventional therapy, it had made no headway against the phobia which gave her sweats, palpitations and worse when facing her regular allergy shots. Her reactions had been so severe, they were having a negative impact on her ability to manage her busy work and home life.

Melissa's mother, another former student of ours, explained her daughter's situation on the telephone and said, "I just sat bolt upright this morning at six a.m. and saw your face and thought you could help her. You're lucky I didn't call you then."

We had known that she had an intellectually challenged daughter about whose difficult life she'd written stories in our class. We inquired and learned that Melissa was her younger sister.

So Melissa and I set up a meeting. She had a very responsible job at a major corporation, had just gotten married to a wonderful man with whom she had bought a beautiful house of their own and had every reason to rid herself of this phobia and live happily ever after.

We talked for a while and I learned that she had experienced anaphylactic shock at one time from the allergy injections and that had contributed to the fear. After all, they were injecting minute amounts of the very things she was allergic to into her system. But this seemed a case beyond the simple logic of those fears.

On the first session, because her belief system wasn't spiritual, we did not begin with guides and I knew that "past lives" were out of the question. We began by working to help her access the part of her that was "protecting" her by giving her these attacks.

While she was in trance, I asked questions and we used the "ideomotor" technique, which asks the unconscious to move a finger for "yes" and a different one for "no." Melissa was completely surprised when her finger moved itself. We did the work, encountered that part of her responsible for the attacks, thanked it for protecting her but advised it that it was frightening her and asked if we could find another way to alert her to the dangers. For example, could we have just a little feeling in her heart to which she would immediately respond? It said okay and we left it at that. But Melissa became fascinated that her finger moved itself and wanted to meet that part of her in "conference room." (See Chapter Twenty-Two for a full explanation of this amazing technique.)

However, at the second session, Melissa began by telling me that she sometimes felt as if someone was sitting on her chest when she had these attacks. I took her into conference room and asked who was sitting on her chest and she became exceedingly cold and frightened and nearly came out of trance. Rather than pursue that line, I thought to "take her" somewhere she liked to be and see if we could access her inner wisdom. So we imagined her being at Lake Arrowhead. There we met a guide. Waiting for her was Glinda, the good witch of the north. Glinda told

Melissa that she would be there for her and would reach down and save Melissa from the "vortex" she felt when she falls into a panic.

I still was not convinced we had solved the problem, but she did make me laugh when she asked "Doesn't everyone come up with Glinda as a guide?" In addition to Beth's angel and the "we" who helped Virginia, I've encountered Tinkerbell and a variety of others but never before, or after, the good witch from Oz.

We agreed to one more session. At our third meeting, she began by telling me that sometimes she felt that her life was perfect and maybe she felt a little guilty about that. I took her into trance and we tried to guide her to the origin of the attacks, in this life or past lives. She was unreceptive, finding herself in her own tennis shoes today.

Then I decided to try another technique that I'd learned but rarely used. I told her that when I counted to three and tapped her on the forehead, she would see a symbol that would represent her unconscious mind. She saw an orange.

I asked what the panic attacks did for her. The orange said that they protected her. I asked Glinda, who was also there, if Melissa really needed them to protect her and Glinda said, "No."

About this time I felt stumped. I became quiet and asked my guides for help. Suddenly, I found myself asking, "What would happen if Melissa **didn't** have these attacks?"

She frowned. "I don't like the answer." she said.

"What's the answer?".

"I wouldn't get the attention."

I asked if the part of her that wants these attacks would please step forward. Ideomotor. The finger moved. It would. It was an apple.

"What do you do for Melissa?" I asked the apple.

"Nothing. I just drag her down."

"Why do you do it?"

Melissa laughed. "Because I'm a rotten apple."

I felt a little at a loss here, but then I said, "Maybe Melissa doesn't pay enough attention to you. Maybe you're trying to tell her to be more a brat, more impish, to have more fun."

"I used to be like that," Melissa said.

"If instead of having the panic attacks, Melissa became a brat some times for attention, would that be all right? Glinda?"

"Yes."

"Orange?"

"Yes."

"Is there any part of Melissa that objects to this plan?"

"No."

"So from now on, instead of dragging her down, she could act up."

When she came up from trance, we put it all together. She felt guilty for being so lucky, having everything, a good marriage, a new house, a good job, while her sister's life was so unfortunate. And so she felt she had to be a saint and not let her bratty side out. The only way she could get attention and misbehave was to have panic attacks.

But now, whenever she felt the panic coming on, she could laugh at the rotten apple and act up just a bit and see if that didn't take care of the problem!

I met Melissa in the street several months later and asked how things were going. "Fine," she said. "Great. In fact, I'm traveling a lot on business and when I have to miss one of my shots, I'm disappointed. I just get them and it's fine."

I didn't ask what bratty things she up to, these days, or whether the conversations with the fruit bowl had continued. I just appreciated the twinkle in her eye.

Chapter Fifteen

Annie Oakley

A Therapist Reclaims Her Courage

"It's never too late to have a happy childhood."

—Milton Erickson, M.D.

Sometimes human beings get stuck, not because they are not equipped to move on, but only because they forget their strengths and get mired in memories of their weaknesses. In such cases, it's good to help people find their misplaced resources and remember who they are and that they are fully capable of bringing their talents, wisdom and good judgment into the present.

Christine was a brilliant therapist and a transpersonal psychologist with a knack for championing others in such a way that they felt empowered and connected to their own largeness of spirit.

It was not surprising, although ironic, that when she was faced with a frightening situation, all of her training deserted her and she was awash in fear. There are very few among us who can heal ourselves, and maybe the fact that we cannot is indicative of the larger truth that we need each other.

Christine and I had begun a friendship after we met in a group of transpersonal therapists who assembled monthly to study and share experiences. With her deep, perceptive intuition and her gentle ways, Christine shone as a unique and caring woman.

When she called to tell me that she might have to undergo hospital-ization for her frighteningly high blood pressure, and asked for my help, we both recognized that her physical symptoms were clearly expres-sions of an emotional situation. She told me that she was facing a very difficult personal and professional problem.

As a psychologist, she never doubted the role that turmoil could play in making her sick. But, in her fear and confusion about a pending law suit, she could not find her own way out of her emotional straight jacket.

If you've ever been in such a situation in which you know better but are still at the mercy of your emotions—and who hasn't?—you may have recognized that when that occurs we have several time periods churning around in us at once:

—we have the present and our view of present circumstances

—we have the past which superimposes itself over it

—and we have the future, on which we project from the other two.

So, if Christine wanted my help, we had to go to work on all three. Simultaneously.

"What's happening right now?" I asked over the phone, before we met for a session.

"I have been treating a child who was brought to me by her father. Her parents are having a custody battle over her. And her mother, who is an abusive woman who hides her destructive ways very well in pub-lic, is suing me!" She took a breath. "The child told the judge she prefers to live with her father, and the mother is claiming that it's my fault, that I poisoned her daughter's mind against her!" Christine's voice was ris-ing, her breathing accelerating. "She's dragging me to court so her lawyers can tear me apart and she's threatening to go after my license."

I said something consoling, feeling a great sympathy for Christine.

"And you know what else? I can't even protect the child!" she said, a clue to what was really going on. "The father got panicked and said he'd have to stop the therapy, and I had to say goodbye to the little girl. Right at this terrible moment in her life. Right when her mother might get her and punish her for telling the judge she prefers to live with her father." She paused, then began again, "As she was leaving for the last time," Christine's voice becoming very small, "the little girl asked for my card. I gave it to her although I said I thought she already had one. She did but she said she 'wore it out,' because she strokes it in bed before she goes to sleep!"

That is, in and of itself, a story that could make anyone's blood pressure rise. But the fact that Christine might have to be hospitalized made it evident that she was reacting not only in the present, but through the past, as well. We made an appointment to see each other the next day.

At the beginning of the session, we understood the present cause of her anxiety—the legal threats to her practice and to her person. Now, we had to see how the past superimposed itself on this situation, causing her particular physical and emotional reaction.

It didn't take long to learn about her own childhood, complete with an abusive, wild mother who had come at her with a knife, who had thrown cold water on her in her high chair, from whom she often had hidden under the bed. Christine was only six when her mother was taken away and committed to a mental institution. No one had been there to protect Christine. Clearly, it was this nerve that was resonating so loudly in sympathy with her client's daughter.

Some of these events we revisited in trance, where she was able to stop the scene and explain to her mother (in her imagination) how she felt about her unacceptable behavior. She explained to her mother how a mother is supposed to behave. She held a dialog with her mother, her mother insisting she'd done the best she could. Christine cried, she and her mother hammered it out, and before the session was over, there was some level of forgiveness and understanding.

That was only phase one of this process, but an important part. It is relatively standard therapy and it is useful *as far as it goes*. First, it was somewhat cathartic, relieving her of some of those pained feelings and helping her to appreciate the scene from her mother's point of view as well as her own as a child, which is different from how she would see it now.

After all, the mother you carry around with you is not the real person whom you call "mother." That person is or was out there, and, as we all are, she was different with every person she met. She was different with your father, with her own mother, with her teachers. She was even different with your siblings. And the mother you carry around inside you is someone you froze in your mind when you were a child. As you've grown, the real person may have grown and changed, as well.

So realizing that the internal mother is a figment of our own memory, seeing her now through childish eyes may allow us to be willing to concede that what we remember could have been distorted by our own impotence and innocence. We just clearly couldn't have understood fully what was going on, what she was going through.

Secondly, revisiting the scene tells us what tapes we are replaying in the present, what scenarios we superimpose on today. Christine could come to see that she is hiding under the bed again, feeling powerless as she did when she was an infant in a high chair, choking on the water thrown at her with no one there to rescue her. No wonder her blood pressure hit the ceiling.

Rather than spending more time revisiting the troubled past, going to other such awful scenes and cleaning up each one, I chose to have her rummage around in the past for a more useful piece of history to which to fasten her sense of self.

So, at the next session, although I realized that Christine's childhood was by and large grim, I asked her to remember a time when she felt very brave. I do believe that somewhere, no matter how small or vague, each of us has a resource we can draw on to remind us of our strengths. I think the universe has made certain that, no matter how dire the circumstances, there might be jewels in the mud if we can only see them as such.

In Viktor Frankl's *Man's Search For Meaning*, he proves the case of the power of a resource even in the bowels of a Nazi concentration camp. In the depth of his pain and degradation he remembered the love of his wife and, not even certain whether she still lived, he brought her alive for a fully empowering moment which he carried with him through his imprisonment. The theory that he developed from that experience explained that "the sort of person the prisoner became was the result of an inner decision, and not the result of camp influences alone." What that means it that we have at our base a spiritual freedom no one can take from us that makes our lives meaningful. It is ironic that it is often we, ourselves, who forget or subvert it.

Christine went into trance and pictured herself in a field of grass. I asked her to look around for someone to talk to, someone who could remind her of a time when she was brave. Suddenly, she noticed a lady-bug crawling up her arm. "It's whispering to me in my ear. It wants me to follow it," she said.

When she did, she suddenly saw herself on a bicycle. "Oh!," she said, "I'm Annie Oaklie!"

She was laughing and her face took on a lighter and more vibrant hue than it had since the lawsuit had filled her with fear.

"Annie Oakley?"

"Yes! I ride with the boys. We ride down the hill on our bikes. On the handlebars of our bikes!"

"Isn't that dangerous?"

"Yes, very." She was still smiling.

"What does it feel like?"

"It feels exciting!"

"Is it also scary?"

"Yes, of course," she said, obviously still riding.

"You mean…something can be scary and exciting at the same time?"

"Yes."

"And if you're brave, that's all right."

"Yes."

"So all it takes, in the face of something scary is to be brave?"

"I guess."

"Are you brave, riding down those hills on the handle bars of your bike with the boys?"

"Yes."

"And how does it feel to be brave in the face of something scary?"

"Exciting. Scary and exciting at the same time."

"Feel the feeling. Feel it in every cell in your body. In every muscle. Feel how it feels to be brave in the face of something scary. Know how brave you are. Remember how brave you are. You can bring that back with you. It IS you. You have it whenever you need it. It is YOU! Now and in the future. See and feel yourself as brave as you were on the bicycle, as brave as you are now, always."

* * *

Christine's blood pressure began to return to normal levels and she bravely went to court, where she discovered that the judge was savvy to the mother's scheme. Christine was excused from the case and the child was protected.

I especially like this story because it illustrates a predisposition of mine to go for the positive whenever possible and to use metaphors for emotions.

We did not ignore the past; we honored it. But we did not dwell any longer than necessary in the past that had harmed her; instead, we found a piece of the past that could heal her and we let her own it, turn it into her own mythology, her own definition of herself, as a warrior— Annie Oakley, a person brave in the face of something challenging, a person who found something that was challenging also exciting.

She had allowed herself to be dominated by the wrong "stuff" of the past; she had displaced the useful stuff. She remembered the fear, not the courage. And it was in remembering her courage that she became free to move ahead.

In fact, in remembering the courage, she got closer to who she was. That helped her to be free to pursue her life more completely because the person she was meant to be was now in charge.

Essentially, although it looks like we're simply being selective about history, the central power which is being called upon is the creative force. In this context, it is the power in each of us to shape pasts and experiences and values into an integrated personal mythology that recognizes our unique strengths.

Once the present has happened, it is done. Even as it happens it is not fixed in a solid medium. Any event is capable of as many "takes" and variations as there are observers. Once an experience has happened, it becomes part of the past. And as the past, it becomes less, not more, fixed than ever. All of the past is there to be shaped, however we decide to shape it, and carried into the future.

How we shape our pasts into our present and on-going mythologies that comfort us and help us to make the correct choices, is a function of the creative process, which is always available through guidance, example or self-transcendence.

We cannot deny our pasts as if they did not happen. They did happen. But what happened is perpetually up for grabs, affected by slippages in our recollections, by biases of perception, by selective focus.

Our flexible perceptions are not liabilities. They are assets. Each of us contains a creative force that when properly applied to the interpretation of the rich troves of our pasts and our value cores, yields perceptions that anchor us, that reinforce our unique strengths, and that propel us positively (sometimes even joyfully) forward. Each of us can be a hero in our own mythologies. Finding and charting that heroic path from the past to the present and beyond is a meaningful solution.

In short, we, each of us, have the power (some would say God-given, others would say innate) at every moment as we continue on, to re-create ourselves and go forward in new form. This is the core of the creative power. It is the basis of redemption that God or the universe or simply the miracle of life grants to us.

In the process, we re-learn the joy of play. As the great psychiatrist Milton Erickson declared: "It is never too late to have a happy childhood."

Chapter Sixteen

Changing the Past in this Moment

A Woman Sees Her Father's Love Differently

"A person's life is dyed with the color of his imagination."

—Marcus Aurelius

Dr. Larry Dossey reports on studies that show our ability to change the past, physically, before it has been fixed—that is, before we have turned our consciousness upon it.

At one of the Institute of Past Life Regression conferences, I saw a regression that I wanted to tell you about because it demonstrates how we can change the past emotionally in this moment. It's a different take on changing the past, one that has already been fixed in time. It involves changing our view of it from here, which can change everything from this point on.

Dr. Winifred Lucas provided the assembled group with a demonstration on a woman whose complaint was extreme. Her father had been so rejecting of her that she had been made to feel completely unworthy. Now a psychotherapist herself, she had "worked through" these feelings over many, many sessions with many, many counselors. But still, although her self-esteem was relatively whole, she could not shake the awful feeling that her father actually hated her, had no use for her, could not stand to be in the same room with her.

And to make matters worse, he had died some time ago. How could this be resolved?

Lucas took this woman, we'll call her Connie, into a series of "past lives" in which she recognized the men in the situation as bearing her father's energy. In the first, she was his daughter. After the mother died, the father had used her as both a servant and a lover, against her will. That life was very unpleasant and her feelings about her father seemed reinforced. He did not care for her, he only used her.

In the second "past life," she was his lover. The events seemed to take place in the farmlands of Europe in the last century. He was married to someone else, yet he was having an affair with her. In an effort to make him commit to her, she bore his baby, but still he remained loyal to his wife and rejected her outright. She refused to disappear from his life and at the end of this part of the session, she physically rose an inch or two off the couch as she "felt" him stab her in the back with a pitchfork and kill her.

I sat in the audience, wondering how this could possibly help her resolve her feelings of rejection by her father.

But we are dealing with forces larger than logic. There is a quote about logic/common sense from Vladimir Nabokov that I'll put in here, while you wonder how this story will end. He says:

"That human life is but a first installment of the serial soul and that one's individual secret is not lost in the process of earthly dissolution, becomes something more than an optimistic conjecture, and even more than a matter of religious faith, when we remember that only common-sense rules immortality out."

Lucas took the woman into the Interlife and had her ask her guides what the meaning of these lives were in relation to her present life. Much to my surprise, and as usually happens, the woman smiled. Of course. Now she saw it. Her father loved her so much, he was terrified that he would hurt her again, as he had in the past two lives. He was extremely attracted to her, but those feelings always seemed to end up hurting her. So this life he had frozen his feelings against her! But it was from love of her, not hatred, that he had rejected her. The coldness was necessary so as to resist the urges that drew him to her and not to cause her any further pain.

Whether or not this is true, her face changed, her demeanor changed, and maybe her life changed. If she could believe that her father loved her, really loved her, perhaps too much, she could feel differently about **herself** as well as him. She was not unworthy of his love. His coldness became a generous gesture. His love for her became real.

I submit this case to you because it shows two elements of this work which I so much admire. The ability to change the past in the present and the wisdom of our guides or higher powers which we can call upon to help us.

And when you think about it, there really is no past to change. It exists only as we carry it in our minds and bodies. Like the Japanese story, Rashoman, which, when told by each of the participants is a different story, so the past is again, in Einstein's phrase, relative to the observer, our particular view of it, not **the past**. So, if we can change it in our minds and bodies, that might be exactly where it needs to be changed.

As this woman begins to accept the idea of her worthiness, of her "lovability," of her father's "sacrifice," all could be changed about how she deals with the world and herself from this moment on. And it hasn't been just words. She's experienced it.

Chapter Seventeen

Lucy's Wild Motorcycle Ride

Learning to Go with the Flow

"You miss 100 percent of the shots you never take."

—*Wayne Gretzky*

As you read Lucy's story, see if you can find in your own life a metaphor that is *visceral*—that is, one that you can absolutely feel in your body, one that changes how you carry and hold yourself in situations where you don't flow.

Harry and I met Lucy when a friend invited us to join her and some of her friends for a series of luncheons. All of the people around the table were literary, intellectual and engaged in interesting work. Some were more outspoken than others. As is customary in such a group, there were those who dominate the conversation. Lucy's demeanor was reserved and somewhat formal. In earlier days, she might have been the librarian everybody liked but nobody really knew.

As we sat down, one of the group recounted an anecdote of a surprising adventure he'd had over the past weekend. In this competitive gathering, that quickly became the theme. Everybody elaborated on an unusual encounter or event since last they'd met.

People spoke up randomly, Lucy last. When she volunteered, it was shyly but with a sense of suppressed delight. "I rode a motorcycle last weekend," she said, an incongruous image. "Well, I rode behind the cyclist, I just was sitting there. In fact, it was very interesting. He said to me, 'Don't try to compensate for me. If the bike is leaning one way, don't try to lean the other. Just follow my lead and we'll do fine'. You can imagine," she said, "how hard that could be for me, to just, you know, let someone else take the reigns, so to speak. You know me, I have to control everything. But I did it. I just leaned whatever way the bike was going, and I hung on and followed his lead. And, oh, it was so thrilling," she said, her eyes widening.

Everyone was properly responsive and impressed with this unexpected report.

That seemed like a cue to me, so I whispered to her, as others talked amongst themselves, that she could use that experience as a metaphor in her life. "Whenever you come up against something that seems like you're going to fight it, think, 'What would happen if I didn't try to compensate, if I just followed and leaned into it?' You know how it feels to do it, now, you know it in your body and your mind, so you could just go with it and see."

She caught on right away and said what a wonderful idea.

I'd forgotten all about that exchange by the next time we had lunch. Lucy was very happy to see me again and put her hand on mine and said, "I used that method and it worked in two situations.' We were in a crowd at the time, so I simply said, "Great.' We all had lunch, talking about computers and spirituality and consciousness and experiments that helped explain the currently inexplicable and then it was time to leave.

On the way out, I took Lucy aside and told her I was working on a book and I wondered in what situations my suggestions had helped her. She paused, demure as ever, her Lucy demeanor proper and refined. "Sex!" she said, conspiratorially. "It was so thrilling! I just...you know, followed his lead."

"Wonderful," I said.

"You know, I'd been to a sex therapist and he'd said to me that I would never enjoy sex because I can't give up control! That's the problem, he said. What good did it do for him to tell me that? And I was **paying** him. But when I just leaned in and followed the lead, it was the most wonderful thing!" she said, adding, "I should pay **you** as my sex therapist!"

* * *

Exercise

What have you done in your life, like Christine's ride on the handlebars (Chapter Fifteen) or Lucy's motorcycle adventure, that could model a feeling for you that lets you step into other situations with a sense of your own power? Sometimes it is a small but glorious moment, like when you were the only one in the class to know the right answer or when you surprised someone and made them look at you anew. One client remembered how it felt to swing like Tarzan from a rope over a quarry, free and bold. Our strengths can be intellectual, physical, emotional or all of the above. Maybe you helped someone, even saved or changed a life. Maybe you comforted someone or something less strong than you. Like the movie, *It's a Wonderful Life*, our smallest acts might have had important repercussions and we, like George Bailey, might not have noticed. Take a moment to recall a memory of strength or accomplishment. Don't simply remember it, begin to be there again. Sit with it. Don't let it go until you feel it in every cell. Feel the courage and the exhilaration you felt then. That is you. That is who you are. Feel it, be it, and can carry it forward into the future. (Also see the last chapter about going with your strengths.)

Chapter Eighteen

Controlling Information Wisely

Testing Reflexes as She Comes out of the Closet

"Life is the art of drawing without an eraser."

—*Anon*

Although I believe that all of my work ties together in creativity, I rarely bring to the writing class Harry and I teach together at UCLA the therapy work that I am reporting here. One evening, however, Harry was not there and everyone who wanted to read his or her story already had. We still had another hour of class time and I decided to offer them an altered state experience to increase their imaginations. They readily agreed. So I put the class in trance and took them into a guided visualization.

I took them to four mountains, one in each of the directions, on which they either let go of something that they no longer needed or claimed something they did need. (More about this exercise in Chapter Twenty-Nine and at the end of this chapter.)

One particularly good writer came up after the class and told me that she saw but couldn't figure out what tool she "found" on the mountain on the north. I suggested that she might discover the answer in a dream.

The next week, driving to class, I "saw" what her tool was. When I got into the room, I drew it on the blackboard and stood in front of it when she came in. I asked her about her tool and she said all she could remember was that it was a stick with some sort of head on it, maybe like some kind of microphone. I stepped out of the way and showed her what I had drawn, poorly, I might add. It was a doctor's rubber headed hammer used for testing reflexes. She smiled.

What I knew about her from the stories she had written in class was that she was gay and had not yet revealed her secret lifestyle to many people. "This is your tool," I said, "which will allow you to test people's reflexes, their reactions, as you reveal whatever you want to reveal as you go along." She, of course, understood, without my having to add, "It's much easier on you and everyone to do it in your own way and at your own good time, measuring people's reactions rather than just blurting out 'I'm gay and I don't care what you think about it.'"

The exercise I did with the class follows. Try it for yourself and take your time interpreting your metaphors and symbols. They are there to help you and when you discover them, they not only guide you, they sometimes make you laugh.

Below is the exercise for your to experience for yourself. Chapter Twenty-Nine relates how it worked for me.

Exercise

Allow yourself to become relaxed in such a way that you feel your body becoming lighter and the space inside you becoming empty and quiet. Follow your breath for as long as it takes, knowing that your body knows how to do this and that it is not about "doing" it so much as "being" it.

When you are relaxed, allow yourself to imagine that you can float off on a cloud to the four directions, one at a time, landing on a mountain top in each direction and discovering there something that helps you on your life's journey.

Imagine your cloud. Is it big and fluffy, with a comfortable, couch-like cushion for you, or filmy and full of light, or even more like a magic carpet? It doesn't matter. Float on it now to the mountain of the West.

There, when you land, you find a blazing volcano full of fire and energy. Into the volcano you may toss something that used to serve you but no longer does, something you've outgrown, whether it be a job, a belief, a relationship, an attitude, whatever you choose and let it be transformed in such a way that it serves your adult needs. Take your time, as this is an important step. Or you may simply toss it and leave it behind, to be converted into more energy for the volcano.

Then fly to the mountain of the South, where you discover an animal waiting for you. Don't sensor your imagination, but let whatever shows up tell you what quality it is that he/she brings to you, a quality you need or may have forgotten you had. Feel that quality in your body, for example feline fierceness or eagle-eyed perception. Make that animal small and put it on a charm bracelet to take back with you.

Then fly to the mountain of the North, where you discover an altar on which there is an object that will help you on your journey. (This is where my student found her reflex tester). It is a symbol of your true essence, resources or vehicles you need to remind you of your destiny. Take some time to understand its meaning in your life, but whether or not you understand it now, save it, too, on your charm bracelet.

Then fly to the mountain of the East, where the sun rises and every day is new. See a sign for tomorrow and the days that follow. Let whatever is growing there become a symbol for your new beginning.

When you have all of your symbols, fly back on your cloud to the here and now and allow your mind to process what you've discovered over the days and weeks to come.

Chapter Nineteen

Tasting Victory
Success in Conquering a Life-Long Eating Disorder

"The proof of the pudding is in the eating."

—*Miguel de Cervantes*

When I first met Deanna, she was in her early thirties and for all of her life before that time, her diet had consisted of no more than ten items which she could eat without gagging. Namely, she ate only grilled cheese sandwiches, French fries, salmon, lettuce and sunflower seeds as a "salad," sugary candies, cheese and crackers, frozen yogurt, pizza without tomato sauce, peanut butter sandwiches and, strangely, burritos.

She explained that she had made herself learn to eat burritos by taking a few more bites each time and getting used to the bean part until she liked it. But the burrito could not have any varying texture in it, for example, no lettuce in with the beans, or she gagged.

She had never in her life tasted pasta, hamburgers, tuna fish sandwiches, fresh fruit or any of the regular meals we take for granted.

This eating disorder was a deep, dark secret that she told to no one, but one that caused her endless grief whenever she dined with company. When going out to restaurants, she had to hope that there was salmon on the menu, or she would likely just play with her food until her plate was taken away.

When she learned that I was a hypnotherapist, she confided to me about her situation. Socially it was a disaster for her. Going out with a date for dinner was anything from embarrassing to impossible. When her new boss took her out to lunch, she was mortified that she could safely swallow only the bread.

If she even tried to eat a banana or any fruit, she told me, or anything but that limited list, for that matter, she gagged.

To tell you the truth, I suspected molestation.

But I have found that it does no good to enter into these realms with an agenda or preconceived notions. So I waited until the moment when I felt that the time was right, and I put her into trance. Going back to early gagging only brought to mind a babysitter who had forced her to eat a banana.

I had her remember a rotten French fry she had recently eaten and had her imagine that all fried and sugary foods tasted like that.

Since her subconscious mind seemed not eager to get into the "why" of it, I took another tack. I invoked a "gatekeeper" in her throat, had her see someone there who was blocking the way of good food. I used the analogy of car, because she was attracted to cars, talking about good fuel making them run better and we asked the gatekeeper in her throat if he would be willing to allow a 30-day trial in which Deanna could eat good new foods without gagging and see if they both didn't feel better and like they were running more smoothly and with more energy.

He, or it, agreed to the trial period.

Then I had her imagine eating a bite of a new food one day, two bites of the food the next, and three the next and liking it then. Next I had her put that eating episode on film and speed it up so that within three bites she would have the "burrito" experience, accepting a new food and liking it.

When she came up from trance, she felt ready to try anything and everything. Thereafter, she tasted new foods every day. Like an infant, she would roll a bite of tuna fish or a taste of pasta in her mouth, frown, taste a second bite and then a third and say, "I liked the last bite the best."

Most foods didn't wow her, and she wanted to be wowed. Her first nectarine, which was perfectly ripe, made her eyes dance. And she fell in love with pasta pesto. But she can eat just about anything now, and that was the goal.

The most important response she had, after all, was the day she ate a vegeburger (I'm a vegetarian and she was joining me in a favorite) and she said, "You know, it's no big deal."

"Exactly," I said, smiling broadly. "It's no big deal."

So, sometimes it really doesn't matter "why." Sometimes, instead of tackling something head on and making a fuss, you can just jump over it like a puddle and get a fresh start on the other side.

More than a year later, I asked for an update on her progress. "It keeps getting better and better," she said. "Now when I go out to dinner on a date and we each order different meals, I'll look at his and say, 'That doesn't look too threatening. Can I have a taste?'"

"I'm not afraid anymore of gagging or trying new things. I just take a big gulp or bite. It took me a while to trust that I would keep the skill."

She knows that I appreciate it when people think in metaphors, so she was very proud of herself when she came up with this one: "So now instead of putting my little toe in, and then a bigger toe into the water, I jump right in!"

In fact, she's gotten so serious about nutrition, she often has wheat grass and a vitamin/power juice to start her day. And, she smiles, saying as she gulps down those odd elixirs "It's no big deal!"

* * *

Although eating disorders are not my specialty, on a recent occasion a physician who sends me patients he feels I might help sent a woman who was hypoglycemic and yet couldn't resist the chocolate brownie and ice cream desserts at her local all-you-can-eat salad place. "I take two, at least, even though I know I'll feel hung over in the morning," she said.

Debra was slim and attractive, but distressed at her lack of will power. What was the hold the brownies had over her? We talked for a while and discovered that such treats had been both rewards and punishments in her youth, not an unusual situation. Early on in her life, she had won a giant chocolate Easter egg in a spelling contest, and had eaten the whole thing in one sitting. At another time, she had lied in class and the teacher had made her stand in the corner while the rest of the children enjoyed cake and ice cream celebrating a classmate's birthday. Rewards and punishments.

Her hypnosis session was fairly straight-forward, untying the emotional connection and then discouraging the desire for the taste of the brownies and ice cream. Of course, when you remove something, it's good to fill the empty space with something else. She was just beginning a creative business as an artist and I had her visualize the "delicious" experience of creating great art and having people appreciate it.

She called me the following week to report on the effect. "Now," she said, "when I pass a chocolate cake, it just looks...**brown.** I'm not tempted at all!"

I thought that was wonderful and was delighted at how well our session had worked. As she was about to hang up, though, she hit me with the zinger. "So, it went great. Only one more thing.," she said pausing. I waited. "Uh," she said, shyly, "I'm just wondering, so, now, what should I do about the corn muffins?"

Metaphors, Magic, Myths, Legends and Guides

"I do not know how to distinguish between our waking life and a dream. Are we not always living the life that we imagine we are?"

—*Henry David Thoreau*

I had a dream one night that I was being carried in a rickshaw-type vehicle drawn by an animal. I realized that the animal was working very hard and when I looked closely, I discovered it was a squirrel that was pulling my weight. I was very upset and unhooked it from my cart, and as it ran away, its tail fell off, leaving a bloody trail. I felt awful and, later in a conversation with a friend, mentioned it. "Who was I so callously working so hard?" I wondered. "Don't you know that everything in your dream is you," she said. **You're** the one working too hard. Next time you're very relaxed, go back into the dream and ask the squirrel what it wanted to tell you."

I like to relax in the shower, so the next shower, I did call upon the squirrel, who obligingly reappeared. What was that dream about, I asked. Oh, it said, your friend was right. You need a good rest. You **are** working too hard. In fact, you're working your tail off.

Chapter Twenty

Dogs of a Feather

A Lost Dog and a Wild Response from the Universe

"Free from desire, you realize the mystery.
Caught in desire, you see only the manifestations".

—*Tao Te Ching*

To Kim and Steve, Tonka the golden and white puppy was their baby. He had his own toothbrush. He slept in their bed. Life revolved around walks and shared moments, his little tricks, their hidden treats. Kim carried his picture in her wallet and her conversation was filled with anecdotes in which he was the star. You have only to have had a cherished puppy of your own to understand how he filled her life with unconditional love and an innocence that melts the heart and turns grown people's vocabulary into monosyllabic slobbering of affection.

When Tonka was run down by a car right before Kim's eyes, the joy in her life began to evaporate. For half an hour she drove around, the mortally wounded puppy on her lap, seeking a pet hospital that was open and would see them. For half an hour, his muted whimpers stabbed at her heart as his blood soaked her skirt and his eyes silently pleaded with hers. They never made it to help in time. He sighed and was gone before she could bring his broken body to someone who might mend it.

For days, she could think of nothing else but the accident scene, which replayed in her mind, eyes open or shut, sleeping or waking until she wanted to tear the brain from her head. Feelings of guilt that she had let him run loose in a new neighborhood took turns with feelings of sorrow and loss, and she was left without a moment's peace.

When she asked for my help, it seemed that nothing short of bringing Tonka back to life would ease her pain. Ultimately, I wasn't able to help her the way she had hoped, so this is not a story about my vast and wonderful skills. But if we ask for help, when we pay attention we can hear the universe answer.

We had met Kim two weeks earlier at the wedding of Harry's daughter, Jennifer. Kim was soon to become part of our extended family, as Jennifer was marrying Kim's brother, George. Actually, the family really extended in that one stroke, as George was the youngest child of a brood including six older sisters, all of them pretty, competitive, and very protective of their baby brother. This all becomes convoluted when you learn that at one time, George had had two roommates, John Curry and Jennifer's brother Jonathan. John Curry had already married George's sister Holly, now George was marrying Jonathan's sister Jennifer, so the joke going around was that Jennifer's brother Jonathan should now marry another of the siblings and we could accomplish something close to a remake of seven grooms for seven sisters.

Holly was extremely pregnant–everyone thought dancing at the wedding would certainly bring the baby on–and I spent some time with her telling her my theories about altered states and childbirth, telling her tricks she might do for her own comfort and so that she could avoid anesthesia as much as possible. (Anesthesia is suspected in infant cerebral palsy). Kim listened intently. All she wanted to talk about was hypnosis and what else I could do with it. I had the feeling I would be seeing her again, soon.

It rained up to the half hour before Jennifer and George were to walk down the outdoor aisle, then the sun shone brilliantly, water drops glistening off deep green foliage making bowers all around them, and even though both sets of parents were divorced, everyone was civilized, courteous, and festive. Jennifer had a guitarist play a Vivaldi piece instead of "Here Comes the Bride," as she walked down the aisle. It was an unexpected touch, amplified by Jazz, Jennifer's dog, who had been tied to a tree and was watching the proceedings politely. When Jenny, escorted by Harry, her dad, came down the aisle to the classical music, Jazz, upon seeing her favorite two people strut their stuff, gave out a handsome war-hoop. It made everyone smile. Kim told us how she loved Jazz and that she often brought Tonka over to play with her and used her as a role model.

Holly danced all night without losing the baby, and after brunch the next day we headed home for L.A.

When we got the call from Kim several months later, she said that in her despair, after Tonka was killed, my face came to her. And she thought I could help her, so she was flying 3,000 miles, at great expense, to see me right away. At that time we lived in that shack I'd described and really had no place to put her and Steve up, so they went directly to a local hotel. Harry was on a train going to a friend's wedding in Michigan, and when I went to see Kim and Steve at the hotel, they were so clearly devastated that I put their suitcases in my car and took them to my humble home. There they could sleep on the simple, homemade couches Harry had fashioned when we'd first moved in.

I had some ideas about how to transform the loss into an opening of their hearts and Steve went quickly into trance. He proved to be a good subject and was able not only to see the big picture but to have a personal revelation.

But Kim was resistant. All I could offer her was my presence and sympathy and, while she seemed to be reviving, she would tend to lapse from time to time as the vision of the accident replayed in the back of her mind.

I was scheduled to go that weekend to an Institute of Noetic Sciences conference in San Francisco, to further study the nature of consciousness. Harry came back and we traded off: Kim and Steve became his charges. He decided to take them out to Arizona where we owned a cabin.

Going to Arizona is, for us, like traversing primeval territory; all the elements combine differently than they do anywhere else. It is as if we were touching the stars, sensing the scent of the desert on our skin, seeing coyote songs. When thunder and lightening light up the sky from horizon to horizon, it is like being inside one of those energy balls filled with electricity dancing vertically, horizontally, diagonally.

And when there is a rainbow, well…Well, that is another story. Once, when we were driving through a violent Arizona storm, it abruptly ended and the sky show, not finished dazzling us, produced a giant rainbow from the horizon on one end, across the celestial ceiling, ending, landing, straight ahead, down in the road a few miles before us.

"We're going to drive right through that rainbow," Harry said. He loves to make pronouncements. I usually humor him. Not this time.

"We can't," I said, forgetting it was Arizona, forgetting I was with Harry, forgetting that it only takes believing. "A rainbow is an optical illusion. You can't drive through it; it will disappear when we get there."

"We're going to drive right through the purple," Harry said, smugly.

"No way," I thought. But we were coming closer and closer. And still it remained before us, planted as if growing from the center yellow line. Then, like some special effect from Industrial Light & Magic, we drove directly, clearly, undeniably through the rainbow. Through the purple, to be precise. I could almost feel it coloring my face, my hands, my chest. And as I turned around to see it behind me, it was gone. An illusion, just as I had thought.

After the rainbow passage, the sky turned gorgeous, the setting sun lighting up the clouds violet and orange, everything so "round," Harry said. "Not flat, like a child's drawing of the sky and the clouds. There's such a…roundness." And so there was, as if the clouds were layers of veils, one in front of another, a depth you could reach behind and embrace, richer oranges and deeper violets than I had ever seen. We pulled over to the side of the road, got out of the car and held each other around the waist, watching the sunset.

So when Harry said he was taking Kim and Steve to Arizona I thought, good. It'll do them good. Maybe they'll see a rainbow. In the meantime, I was at the convention in San Francisco doing "serious" work, studying my new chosen field. I thought they'd just gone off to play.

But Harry always fools me. Although he looks like he's not paying attention, like he has no plan at all, things just seem to happen around him. He's the most natural magnet for meaning I've ever met.

They went to Arizona, had a lovely stay at the house and were driving back to L.A. when Harry began to get tired. He'd been thinking of coyotes, thinking that seeing a coyote in the road would somehow cheer Kim up, because they were so doglike and yet wild, because they were yellow and white like Tonka, just because. So he had been calling to them in his mind, asking them to put in an appearance, but it seemed it wasn't to be.

Harry had driven through Arizona and was back in the wilds of Eastern California when he became tired and asked Kim if she'd like to drive, which is very rare for him. She said, "Sure," and took over the wheel.

Harry was in the front passenger seat when he saw it happen as if in slow motion. In the dark, a coyote waited at the side of the road and fixed Harry's eyes with his own. "Don't worry, don't do anything. This is as it's supposed to be," the coyote's eyes told him, faster than he could react.

And the coyote stepped out in front of the car.

Kim screamed and veered away. Time stood still. She held on to the wheel, skidded, and missed the animal while seeing its familiar white and gold coat, just like Tonka's, as clearly as Harry had. It had stepped into the same side of the car that was the one that had hit Tonka.

And this time, the animal wasn't hit.

It was as if Kim had been given another chance. It was in her hands this time, and this time, no one died.

Harry caught his breath and grabbed on to the dashboard, after the fact. As I had turned to look at the rainbow, he turned to see the coyote, but it wasn't there. So, he thanked it in his mind and relieved the shaken Kim, driving the rest of the way home, himself, thinking about how it had communicated it all to him, thinking about how it was all of a piece.

When I called in from the conference, he told me what had happened. "Oh, I get it," I said, "I come all the way up here to be at a conference about the mysteries of life, and you go off and do them by yourself!"

But that wasn't all. The next morning at 5 o'clock the phone beside my bed in the hotel rang. I answered and heard Harry saying, "No matter what you hear on the radio, we're all right."

"What?"

"There was an earthquake in Los Angeles, a pretty big one. It rolled and seemed to go on forever. But we're all right. Although it scared the shit out of all of us. Kim's had a trip she'll never forget. I think she's looking at everything a whole new way."

It seemed I missed a lot that weekend. As Dorothy found out, you don't need wizards, it's all in your own backyard.

Grief over a lost animal is not trivial, even in the cosmic scheme. Dr. Brugh Joy quotes a Western mystic, who said that "there were two ways of dealing with problems. One was to transmute the problem and the second was to wear it out!" If I can, I try to help people transform it into understanding. In this case, Kim just went through it, the going "directly into the problem and allow[ing] it to manifest completely." She re-lived the accident and made it right. It still did not make sense as an act by itself, but she was done with it.

When we were little, my mother used to explain to us that a mother's heart is not a like pie which has to be cut into smaller and smaller pieces to allot love to each child. A mother's heart was like a rubber band, she used to say, stretching to encompass all whom she loved.

Kim went home, waited a while during which she healed, and got another puppy, in memory of Tonka, who was different from, but part of, the spirit-of-dog, which Tonka represented. She hasn't forgotten, but her heart as grown.

Interchapter 3:

On Time and Synchronicity

"For those of us who believe in physics,
the separation between past, present, and future is only an illusion."

—*Albert Einstein*

"By looking at a moment, we shine a light on a part of eternity
and think it is a 'when' instead of a 'what.'"

—*JSP*

When Harry and I took our past life journey and landed in the same place, we had crossed some sort of boundary in time. How was that possible? Why are there people–even some scientists—who contend that the passage of moment to moment strung out in a long line that connects birth to death, life to life, age to age–what we refer to as linear time–is an illusion? It seems so obvious that time goes from minute to minute. That there was a past, that we move into the future. What more is there to say? How could it not be linear?

And what difference does it make whether it is or not?

I figure there are two major reasons why it's important to know what time really may be.

1) It's not good for our health to think that time is linear and that we are on a collision course with decay and death. Dr. Larry Dossey says that we live in a period of "time sickness," proven by the dramatic increase in death by heart attacks between 8 and 9 in the morning on Mondays. Other species don't die because it's time to go to back to work. So, it becomes a matter of health to free ourselves from the tyranny of time and perceive its elasticity.

2) When we understand that time may be simultaneous and not linear, we may be able to explain how we can know something "before" it happens, how we can instantly connect with other minds, how everything that seems to be a "coincidence" is really part of a pattern, a dance all happening at once, and we can even change the past in the present.

I used to think I was crazy to be the only one who couldn't get a fix on the idea of "last Wednesday" or "an hour ago." But lately, there's support for other ways of looking at time, other ways of recognizing that we may be trapped in an idea, a construct, when we think that time "moves," that it is a thing.

How real is it, I asked myself.

First of all, what is time as we measure it? Arbitrary units. We say it takes twenty-four hours for the sun to next appear in the same place in the sky, but we could as easily say it takes 11 zondras or 700 skijolis, or 2 jahazafazis. We say there are 60 seconds in a minute and 60 minutes in an hour, but there could also be 10 whazzats in a bazurki and 10 bazurkis in a day.

We made that part up.

The part we didn't make up was that the sun does have a cycle, as does the moon, as do the seasons. And primitive man believed in cycles, not linear time. He believed that time was measured by the returns. If we were thinking along his lines, we'd think most days exist in a flow, but Christmas, for example, is real time. And the reason it is real is that this Christmas brings back every other Christmas. Rituals were thought to "coincide" with all other of the same rituals, all of them living in that alive moment.

That makes more sense to me than trying to pin things down by turning a calendar page from May to June. Every time we go back somewhere to a place we knew a long time ago, part of us goes back in time, too. And then, suddenly we have slipped out of "linearity." So be it. It feels good, to me.

You go back to a place that was meaningful to you and you are nearly swept away by a great gust of the past blowing into the present and embracing you. You are ageless. It's not about "now" at all. That's the difference with kyros time.

Chronos time is linear time. Yesterday, today, and tomorrow. But kyros time is all time packed into this moment. It is all you are and have ever been and will be, here with you now. Not just added up to present a total without the column of numbers, but every detail, as densely packed into this moment as the breath you are now inhaling.

We think the three-dimensions are limited, and we've packed our fourth dimension—time—into the same rigid carton. But as bounded as the three-dimensions may seem, we feel the squishy edges of time and have to wonder. Could time be boundless? With no boundaries in time, could it be that time provides the portals of exit and entry?

This might be the place to talk of String Theory, but even those who work with it admit it's a hard concept to wrap one's mind around. I'll just suggest that if the scientific exploration of the mysteries of life and matter are of interest to you, that you read more about both String Theory and Chaos Theory so that you may be disabused of our mistaken notions of reality.

Is it possible that in this moment you can change everything that is and was? By deepening the intensity? By changing how you feel about someone or some thing? By learning that the person you thought had betrayed you had really saved you, can you change how you feel about him or her, how you see everything that was and is? Can you change history in this moment? I think so. History is what we carry around with us, and I believe we can make it right in this moment. And that is what religious people call "grace." (See Chapters Ten, Fifteen and Sixteen)

David Bohm, the British physicist and one of the fathers of the "holographic universe" theory which is discussed in Interchapter 6, also has a theory to explain Kyros time. He calls it the "implicate order."

What we see on the surface, he explains, is the "explicate order," what is considered the Newtonian universe. But behind the scenes every thing and every being and every moment is densely packed with hidden underlying ground. Much is "enfolded."

The simple explanation I have encountered goes something like this: think of a television set. You look at it in your living room and see your favorite newscaster reading a story about a fire on the evening news. In your living room, it looks simply like a television set with a head on the screen. But behind that television set there are all the parts and wires that make it work. And behind that, there are television waves carrying it through the air. And behind that, there are people in a studio putting the newsman on the camera, and behind the newsman is a writer who wrote the news and behind the writer is the fireman who made the news and behind the fireman is the arsonist who set the fire and behind him is his father who beat him when he was a child. Well, we can go back further, but implicate orders may just be infinite, so we'll quit here. The point is, all of this exists even though all you see are the flat, dancing images on the video screen.

Chronos (linear) time is like the video screen. Part of the explicate order. What we need to do is to begin contemplating the implicate that lies beyond.

Among the classic ideas Einstein shattered was that time was uniform throughout the universe. Again he showed that time was relative to the observer. As far as I am aware, he never discussed stepping out of time, but everyone has had that experience in dreams. You enter a room you've never entered before and you simply "know" everything you need to understand. Without a background briefing. Instantaneously.

Sometimes, and it is quite a thrill, we can experience "knowing" when we are awake. Something comes clear to us so quickly that we know it instantly, although to try to explain it to someone else could take forever. "Enlightenment," the Buddha said, "takes only an instant, but one could be preparing for it for eternity." We think mundane thoughts in words (about the laundry, dinner, the bills, the weekend plans) but we perceive great concepts at a level of understanding beyond words and then try to place them in a verbal context.

The holographic Interchapter, 6, should help illustrate how we pull the information from the universal holograph into the holograph of our own minds when we get that "ah-ha!" phenomenon.

But "knowing" is clearly "out of time," and not a product of how much thinking we've put into it. It is also where inspiration comes from, where artists get their visions, where scientists dream of a snake eating its tail and understand the configuration of the benzene molecule. Einstein did say something to the effect that putting his brainstorms into words was the harder part, and secondary.

If time isn't moving, isn't linear, one-way then why does it *seem* so much like it is?

Try an analogy. Einstein used analogies, what-ifs, because they came to him as pictures before he had the explanations.

Imagine you are standing at a railway station waiting for the train to come in. It has to take a sharp curve before it comes into sight, so you've positioned yourself so you can see the first car the minute it hits the station. Here it comes, now. And you see the engine. Now the engine, which is moving away, and the second one, which is right in front of you. Oops, there it goes, moving away, and here's the third right in front of you, and so on. You have to wait to the end to discover that the caboose is striped red and white with a banner across it. You've seen each train car as it rounds the curve and presents itself one by one, replaced by another, frame by frame. Tick, tock, tick, tock.

Now imagine that you're in a helicopter flying over the scene. What do you see? The whole train, all at once. The engine. The caboose. Simultaneously.

The analogy's not perfect. The train is, after all, moving, which the modern theory goes, time is not. But the point of it is that what of if you can see, and in what order, depends upon where you're standing. Einstein even suggested that someone standing somewhere else might see something else happening *first*, a different order in time.

Or imagine that you have a telescope which you move horizontally from left to right and you see all of life only that way, in a line in one direction. That does not mean that the scenery exists only when you see it or in the order you see it. Time may be laid out like the vast mountain ranges and we may be stuck with three-dimensional eyes looking through a telescope we call "time." Or maybe we're not so stuck.

A Richard Bach analogy: simultaneous time can be imagined if we picture walking into an appliance store and seeing all the televisions turned to different stations. Whatever set we decide upon, focus on, is the "reality" we are involved in, but the rest goes on, if we have the other sets to pick it up, all at the same time.

* * *

The Magic Part: Synchronicity

I'll quote the Addams family; since I've quoted everybody else:

"Coincidence?" the members of the Addams family would ask each other, rhetorically throughout their movie. "I think not!" I happen to agree with their conclusion.

If time is not linear, but only appears to be, if it is, in fact, simultaneous, and we only see a small portion of it in a limited order, then what is it around the corner that we might get a peek at? And, are we getting peeks that we deny? And is everything related in ways we cannot see when we observe it from our limited viewpoint?

Everyone's had deja vu's and precognitions. The feeling that you've seen something before, been somewhere before, heard this conversation before, even though you're certain you don't know how that could be. The intuition that something's going to happen, for no good reason your logic can explain, and then it's happening, much to your dismay, or confusion, or even pride.

Carl Jung, (the famous psychologist and contemporary of Freud's), was the father of synchronicity and its first major student. He started back when it seemed almost ridiculous to make a fuss over coincidences. Jung defined synchronicity as "the coincidence in time of two or more causally unrelated events which have the same meaning."

In F. David Peat's book, *Synchronicity: The Bridge Between Matter and Mind*, he writes that synchronicity involves internal and external parallels that unfold "according to a hidden dynamic order." He writes of Austrian biologist, Paul Kammerer, who made a study at the turn of the century of coincidences and unexplained clusterings of events which seemed to him to be the visible signs of a pattern he called "the umbilical cord that connects thought, feelings, science and art with the womb of the universe which gave birth to them."

Although it was risky at that time to delve into such a field, even Einstein admired Kammerer's work, which he called "original and by no means absurd."

* * *

"Coincidence is God's way of remaining anonymous"—A. Einstein

My personal theory on synchronicity.

It is that all of the universe is a web of connected, simultaneous meaning. And that whatever we choose to focus on, that is what materializes from that pulsing web. To use an everyday situation which might help demonstrate this, imagine pulling out from your closet a skirt or shirt which has in its patterns all the colors known to our experience. Our eyes see them all as a swirling mass of colors, none particularly primary. Then let's say you pull out a turquoise belt or tie and put it against the fabric. Suddenly, all the turquoise becomes prominent, it calls attention to itself. Put a red belt or tie next to it, and the focus is on the red in the pattern.

In a similar way, when we focus our attention on one aspect from the soup of possibilities, we become more aware of all of its manifestations.

It figures in the chapter on Kim and the dog (Chapter Twenty). It's in the chapter on the widow of the producer of Ghost, when the Braille sign appeared to bring Amazing Grace to life.

Think about the *I Ching*, Tarot Cards, and other historical forms of non-causal connections. In as much as they work, they could also demonstrate this "integrative tendency of the universe."

Keep a synchronicity diary.

Begin to look for signs of all kinds, answers to your prayers and questions, and see where you may find them.

Next, acknowledge them. Thank them.

Prove to yourself and then enjoy the realization that the universe is whole and listening.

Surround yourself with wonder. "Wonder," Aristotle said, "implies the desire to learn; the wonderful is therefore the desirable."

Chapter Twenty-One

Connecting on the Astral Plane

"Anything you can do, or think you can, begin it.
Boldness has genius, power and magic in it"

—*von Goethe*

In the days when a Shaman was both healer and wise man, he worked on a level often called the Astral plane. That is a place in consciousness where we meet and go beyond our limited brains and bodies.

In hypnotherapy and trance states, we are able to contact that plane in ourselves. But once there, can we contact others? There is a lovely book by Jose Stevens, Ph.D., called *Secrets of Shamanism: Tapping the Spirit Power Within You*, which I read one night before going to sleep. It was full of the kinds of ideas which it is hard for us to accept, believing as we do in our limitations. Such as being able to visit other people in the astral plane.

One of his exercises called for going into a light trance, finding a power animal, going with the animal down a tunnel, and then well, after that I seem to have taken off by myself. First I was in a cave where all of me flew apart and there was nothing left but a pilot light. I had taken people with leukemia and cancer on similar journeys, knowing that they were angry at their bodies and that if they could experience a rebuilding, cell by cell, deeply at the cellular level, they might provide new instructions to their cells. But this time, I was looking for a new start for myself or at least the experience of reconstructing myself. So I flew apart and just enjoyed the sensation. It felt slightly odd, but I was not concerned. I enjoyed the out-of-body sense I had, and all went predictably until I decided it was time to begin to reassemble myself.

At that point, the guide whom I had taken with me on this journey, Grandpapa, interceded. He said, "Why don't you stay apart for a while and go around exploring? I'll keep your reflection whole for you, here in this mirror, so you can come back to it," and he held up my reflection in the mirror to show me that there would be, somewhere, a memory of how to reassemble the parts.

The plan seemed to make sense, and so I decided to go off into Harry's dream. Suddenly I was there, watching his dream. He was dreaming about some puppies, random puppies I did not recognize. He does have a favorite dog in the world, his daughter Jennifer's Golden Retriever, Jazz, but these dogs were something else again. I don't know how long I lingered in his dream before I found myself lonely for my body and ready to pull myself together. Maybe I feared it would be more difficult than promised and I just bolted in panic, it's hard to say.

Much to my delight, it went smoothly and I thanked Grandpapa and my power animal, moving back up through the tunnel to the entrance. Slowly I opened my eyes.

Harry was stirring in the bed beside me and I thought I'd catch him before he forgot his dream. "You were dreaming about puppies," I said.

"Yes," he said sleepily.

"Not Jazz. Puppies."

"Yes," he said, looking at me oddly, and turning over to go back to sleep and continue dreaming.

I soon realized that it is very impolite to go into someone's dream, or mind, uninvited, and I have not tried that again.

However, not too long ago, my daughter Daniele's boyfriend at the time, who was quite psychic, was, in my opinion, not treating her right. I had only met him once on a trip to New York where they both lived, and being on the opposite sides of the country, we were still relative strangers to each other. When Daniele told me that he had gone home to Louisiana to visit his family, I figured that would be a good time to have an astral conference with him, so I went into a altered state, focused on him, and said, simply, "Get with the program. Be nice to her or leave her alone, please."

I don't know what I thought would happen, but I felt so helpless to ensure her happiness that I guessed nothing would be lost. I did not mention to Daniele that I had "visited" him in this way and forgot all about it until the next time we spoke.

She told me that her boyfriend was back and he had said to her, "Your mother is very powerful."

"What did he mean by that?" she asked. I was embarrassed, caught. He was more psychic than I thought. I thought he'd just get a *feeling* and not know it was *me*. So I had to tell her. She laughed and said, "No trysting on the astral plane!" which I thought was a very clever response. And I promised to stay out of his mind from then on.

But we did have one more verification that he and I are cooking on the same burners. Daniele came out to Los Angeles to visit us during the summer of 1993 and one of the things I did for her at the time was called a 'Magnetic Cleansing,' part of the training I'd gotten at the Yavapai Medical Center. It was meant to clear her aura, and to me she was looking very light and bright when she left.

She called after she'd seen her boyfriend to report that he had said, "Your aura looks very clean." "My mother cleaned it," she said, and then she laughed and said to me, "It makes it sound like a T-shirt!"

* * *

The magic comes to me slowly. I have asked for it that way. When I pray for it, I ask to be given it to help myself and others and I ask for it "as fast as it is safe for me physically, mentally, emotionally, spiritually, psychologically and socially." I don't know where I got that little mantra from. Wherever it all comes from, I guess.

I test it and I try it and I see meaning in everything. One day I was looking at a cloud and thinking that if I concentrated on it, I could make it dissolve. I started staring it down and it began to change before my eyes. Instead of dissolving, it seemed to grow into something dreaded looking, something fierce, a gargoyle, a monster. At first my heart leaped and pounded and then I remembered the East Indian word I like so well, Namaste, which means the soul in me salutes the soul in you, whether or not I like your personality, appearance, whatever. So I said to the cloud, in my mind, I know your face looks frightening, but I see your soul and salute it. And the cloud dissolved.

When I told my friend Louis about this incident (he is a psychic who practices geomancy or feng shui, the Asian art of knowing the effect of the arrangement of the environment around us on our being), he told me that his wife, Beverly, who is a channel, had a similar experience only more frightening. She had been dreaming about a monster that meant to kill her and she made herself awaken from the dream. But when she opened her eyes, the monster was still there, and she knew she it was entirely serious and deadly. And she knew, also, that she could only dissolve it with love. So she did. But it was terrifying for her.

I said I guessed I was lucky that mine was just a cloud, and Louis said, "No, that's your deal with the universe. You've asked for it to be safe."

That's true. But what Beverly and I both remembered, in order to win the day, is important. If you've ever played with the woven straw, pipe-like "finger torture devise," you know that when you put your index fingers into it and try to free them, the harder you pull, the more stuck they become. The only way to free them is by pushing—the opposite direction from the way you want to go. That is the way of everything. When you want to fight something, try instead the approach of loving it into submission. At the very least, it puts more love into the universe.

These are not really tales of "power" but they all are meant to show the kind of power that we have with our mind when we believe in it. Check out the Interchapters for the science behind all of this. And then, if you choose, fix your mind on seeing the magical in everything and claiming it.

Interchapter 4:

Non-Local Effects and the Nature of Consciousness and the Paradigm Shift

The same heart beats in every human breast.

—Matthew Arnold

The indestructible is one: it is each individual human being and, at the same time, it is common to all, hence the incomparably indivisible union that exists between human beings.

—Franz Kafka

How could I get into Harry's dream or send a mental message to my daughter's boyfriend hundreds of miles away?

How is it someone can "feel it" when you are staring at them? Even from behind. Why is it when you think of someone, out of the blue, they call you?

Some people agree with the Nobel Prize winning scientist Erwin Schrodinger, who said "The overall number of minds is just one." Some people think that consciousness is fundamental in the universe, not locked in what we in three-dimensions perceive as time and space. And that it might, in fact, be proof of the soul.

Shortly before his death, Heisenberg published a paper which contained the proposal that certain fundamental, mechanistic common-sense concepts such as 'being composed of' and 'having distinct and nameable parts' may be meaningless for the ultimates with which physics seeks to deal. And physicist Bohm expressed the same sentiment. "One is led," he said," to a new notion of unbroken wholeness which denies the classical idea of analyzability of the world into separately and independently existent parts."

Can we mentally influence others at a distance? Is mental intentionality a causal action having distant effects?

I heard Dr. Larry Dossey speak at the Harvard University Conference on Spirituality and Healing on Distant Intentionality. He cited experiments in which individuals could inhibit the growth of fungus cultures by concentrating on them for fifteen minutes from a distance of 1.5 yards.

He told of experiments in which animals were influenced, specifically mice who were awakened more quickly from general anesthesia, if they received positive mental intent.

He told of a wild experiment in which 80 test cell groups of 15 baby chicks, who like to be in the light, "willed" a randomly moving robot carrying a candle in a dark room to move closer to them. The robot was in the vicinity of the chicks 71 percent of the time, whereas in the absence of the chicks, the robot moved in a random trajectory.

He reported on tests on blood platelets from human volunteers which were treated by healers to increase the activity of the enzyme monoamine oxidase.

Most impressive, of course, are the experiments with human beings in which those who were prayed for in double-blind experiments (no one knew who was being prayed for, not the doctors, not the patients), had significantly fewer side effects or problems after their operations than those who were not prayed for.

Dossey calls the healing effect of prayer, "eternity medicine." He insists that, "If you take away the willingness of love and deep, empathetic healing, these studies don't work. You have to care—use the heart in compassion, empathy and love."

Marilyn Schlitz, Ph.D., Director of Research at the Institute of Noetic Sciences, spoke after Dossey and told of other experiments on intentionality and non-local or transpersonal consciousness.

A person wired with equipment to measure his autonomic nervous system was being watched at intervals by someone in another room through a video camera. Could the "observer" who was nowhere in sight "get" the attention of the volunteer by staring at his television image? And would that awareness have a physiological effect?

The positive answers to this and other studies of intentionally influencing the healing process in Israel for hernia patients and another pilot study here in America for AIDS, make her consider that the intention of the physician or experimenter may be more important than we thought.

"If practitioners can influence patients at these transpersonal levels, this requires that practitioners be more thoughtful about the psychological, social, and spiritual ways in which they interact with people…In fact, these data support the idea that we are interconnected at a level that has yet to be fully recognized by Western science and that is very far from being integrated into our world view."

Of course, if our thoughts are shared, we must then be more thoughtful and responsible for not only our actions but how we think and interact with people, she concludes.

* * *

Harry says "Everything important happens off the page." You have a conversation with someone and you walk away feeling bad, although it seemed to go well. Or you walk away feeling great, and all you did was agree that it was a nice day. The communication went well beyond the words. Some of it happens on the astral plane and we can keep it going with our thoughts, thoughts which we are then required to use for healing, for good, for opening doors.

There are scientists and philosophers who have posited this inter-connectedness in various ways. The British biologist, Rupert Sheldrake, envisions a "morphogenetic field" which connects us all so that when some of a species learns something, all of them suddenly "get it," a sort of hundredth-monkey scenario. In this theory, awareness is shared by a critical mass, and through that intangible field, beings understand something all at once. In some of his experiments, Harvard psychologist William McDougall taught rats to swim water mazes and measured how many attempts it took them to learn. What he found was that each successive generation learned faster than the one before it. As reported by Kenneth Ring in 1983, in tests both in Scotland and Australia, "The first generation of rats learned to negotiate the maze almost as fast as McDougall's last generation. Training pigeons seems to make all subsequent pigeons smarter. Athletes break records every single year. The bar, the level, gets higher as we as a species master it. Children today are born knowing how to function in a world dominated by electronics, although their elders toss the VCR instruction manual over their shoulders in frustration. Pierre Teilhard de Chardin's idea of a Noosphere, an invisible planetary web of evolving consciousness also applies here.

* * *

A Sidebar on Uses and Abuses of the Non-Local Field

I have no desire to get into the middle of the abortion fray, but I have one story that suggests a possible solution. A friend became pregnant at a most inconvenient time, just as the man she was living with was throwing her out and her job was precarious. While she might have loved to have a child when she could offer it security, protection and love, she felt that this child would be born to chaos and sadness. So she decided to have an abortion.

I had heard of hypnotherapists whose experience included asking the soul of the child to leave and having the fetus self-abort. While I had never attempted this, and I do wonder how the soul of the child might feel, should it be asked to leave and decide not to, I mentioned this approach to my friend. She had already made the appointment and was determined to go through with the procedure, but was willing to give my approach a try.

I put her into trance and she made quick connection with the baby's spirit. She explained the situation and told it how she loved it and wished that she could provide for it and how she hoped, if it would leave now, that it would be willing to come back at time when she could give it all the care and opportunities it deserved.

She felt better the next day and the following day woke up and was headed for the abortion procedure when she decided to speak once again to the spirit of the fetus. To her surprise, she couldn't find it. It didn't seem to be there.

While she was certain it had gone, she did go through with the abortion, and the tissue was removed. However, there is a sense in her mind that the baby understood and that it was by mutual agreement that this pregnancy and birth did not occur.

In my experience (see the Green Light Meditation in the Exercises at the end) we can not only contact others on these other planes, but know when we have and what their response has been. Perhaps there are other ways to use these abilities wisely, not intrusively, as we have no right to interfere with others, even when they seem to be harming themselves.

Therefore this warning: If ever you decided to "contact" someone, do so as if you were encountering that person in the material world. Ask politely before you "give them light" whether they will accept it. All of the approaches I talk about in this book rely on a heart-centered approach to life and a realization that everything we do affects everything else.

* * *

Interconnectedness and the Paradigm Shift

"You are everything, and everything is you."—song lyrics

Back in the mid-'90s, I was writing my dissertation on the Paradigm Shift, busily proving that it was already on the way and that it will be shortly be an invisible fait accompli. I complied evidences of such a shift. There was the explosion of electronics from the computer to the internet modeling for us what kind of beings WE might become. I speculated that these devices ultimately will have existed only to help us understand that our brains are the hardware and the universe is the software.

There were events such as yard sales to illustrate how the apparent stranglehold of corporations was an illusion and we had choices we were exploring as a people (and this was before "the people" confronted the World Trade Organization in Seattle and stopped them, at least momentarily, in their tracks). There was talk radio and chat rooms and ways for people to "congregate" beyond time and space. And so much more.

But how, I wondered, would this change happen within us? What would it take for us to move up the evolutionary ladder from ape to angel?

My thesis included the concept of chakras and civilizations. Outside of Western medicine, it is believed that energy enters and leaves our bodies through vortexes called chakras, the Sanskrit word for wheel. The major chakras line up along our spine, from the base to the crown of our head. They are aligned within proximity to our major nerve plexus and our endocrine glands which regulate and control everything from our growth to our emotions.

They are counted up from the base of the spine, and each chakra has a set of behavioral components associated with it. My thesis suggested that the paradigm shift would happen when enough people "get it" (the hundredth monkey principle/ an idea whose time has come). And the "it" they get is that when we are heart-centered, everything changes. This is not a new message, but a new presentation of it. That, as with the individual, so with society (as above, so below, ontogeny recapitulates phylogeny, and more echoes you'll find in the other Interchapters.)

* * *

Society began at the level of the **First Chakra**, which is also called the Base Chakra, located at the base of the spine, and its focus is those essential, life-and-death needs that had to be met. You hunted, or were hunted. You built a shelter or you froze to death. You suckled at your mother's breast or you perished. Although we have grown beyond simply the basic kill-or-be-killed lifestyle, it is still true about humans that most of the cruel, evil things we do to this day stem from our fears that our needs will not be met. What if we will not have enough, will not be loved enough, will be abandoned, left to freeze, starve, be in perpetual want...

As humans evolved, they moved as a society to **Second Chakra** considerations—community, procreation, creativity, generation. This chakra is located in the area of our reproductive system. We joined with others in tribes. We developed lore and laws. We sang songs around campfires, made love, made families not just babies, made pottery, necklaces, weapons, garlands.

As societies became more sophisticated—likely the ancient civilizations, surely the Roman and Greek, and in modern times, during the Renaissance,—people at all levels eventually became preoccupied with the business of the **Third Chakra**—me! The ego. Located at the solar plexus. (You can see how this societal movement parallels the growth of an infant. Just as ontogeny recapitulates phylogeny—the fetus re-enacting all the stages of physical evolution of life on earth from finned and tailed animal to human embryo—so our growth from infancy re-enacts the path on which humans must travel to evolve. First crying for the breast, then awareness of those around him/her, then, suddenly, aware that he/she is not mommy—is, in fact him/herself.)

Self-awareness leads to contemplation and philosophy. But, of course, to focus on ourselves to the exclusion of others is not reaching our highest state. It cannot lead to anything beyond the most elementary morality. That is why religion may seem imposed on us arbitrarily. For us to live up to our full potential, we must be both self-aware and aware of others, acknowledging their self-ness AS our own.

As the paradigm shift comes upon us, we must move from the third/ego chakra to the **Fourth Chakra**, located at the heart, which relates to love in all its forms, from self-love, to romantic love, to unconditional love.

The paradigm shift relies on our leading with the heart chakra. It is by feeling what another feels that we can become psychic, that we can develop traits of understanding that go beyond sympathy into empathy; that go beyond the gesture to our experiencing how interconnected we really are.

Recently Harry picked up a bamboo flute he sometimes plays. It's an ancient Japanese wood instrument called a shakuhachi, and it has five holes and no reed or whistle aperture. It is very difficult to play and there is no written music for it. When you play it, it simply sings through you. Harry started to play and I stepped into the room, leaning against the doorsill. When he was finished I said, "You want to know something funny? I knew exactly the notes your were going to play before you played them."

"You want to know something funny?" he said. "I knew you did and that you were going to say that."

"Was it because I thought it that you played it, or did I just read your mind?"

"I don't think that's the question," he said. "I think the music just is. All music exists. Some people just mark it down." He even speculated that after someone has written great music and died, when we play it, they know.

Maybe so.

What is important about all that is that, if it is true that we share consciousness, then **everything counts.**

Nothing that you do stands in isolation. Everything that you think and feel and say and do affects the whole, all of us. And, of course, you are affected by all that happens around you. But you are responsible for your own emanations. And how you respond to those of others.

What would life be like if you knew that everything counts, that nothing can be dismissed or swept under the rug? If you knew that everything you think feel, say, do and don't do—all of it not only defines who you are in every minute, but affects everything and everyone else? There is immense power and responsibility in knowing that.

I don't know who Lauren Eiseley is, but I saw this quote of hers and knew it belonged here. "One could not pick a flower without troubling a star."

Chapter Twenty-Two

Into the Conference Room with Morning Light

*"The difference between being **a part** and **apart**
is a matter of the space we put between us."*

—*JSP*

Every time I do this work, I'm afraid. It seems to take a courage that is nothing like jumping out of airplanes or lion taming. My feeling is not like fear of public speaking (which studies have shown is the number one fear among most people, beating out even the fear of death), or fear of failure. It is something visceral, which seems to dissipate as I actually do the work and help people. Nevertheless, my hesitance has become a mystery to me.

Although I had studied a conventional kind of hypnosis and been certified by the man who had put on the conference I had attended, I realized that I needed another way into the work that would work for me. I didn't want to simply be a practitioner. I wanted something closer to, oh, you know, magic. That's where Alchemy and the Isis Oasis came in.

Now, magic is a wonderful tool, but it is only a tool. Unless it has a spiritual base, it will lead to frustration because it is ultimately not ours to control, only ours to share. And selfish motives do not include sharing. When we acknowledge the holy in everything and everyone, we are working in the area where the magic resides.

Someone recently said to me that people are like onions, just layers upon layers, but without a core when you get to the center. That's a very sad thought. And it's the opposite of what I believe. To me, the only reality is the core–the rest is layers and layers of ephemera. Roles played, costumes worn, opinions carried about like so many purses and hats.

I wanted to work with their core. I wanted to really help heal. It is said in the healing field that just the act of acknowledging another's soul begins the healing. I have found that to be true in my work. When I don't know what technique to use with someone, it has been my experience that angry or badly hurt people can be transformed by the simple act of our being present for them, simply because we are listening with all our heart.

                              * * *

Exercise: Here's some magic you can do right away, yourself. Stop judging, stop trying to change people, stop needing to prove yourself right. And just really listen. See if you can detect a change in the other person when he or she is honored by your complete, caring attention.

But, I was looking around for a spiritual way to do this work when I met Valerie, a flight attendant who had studied Alchemical Hypnotherapy at the Isis Oasis and convinced me of its wonders.

So I called David Quigley and said I wanted to study with him. He suggested that I take the full, three-week course, but I only wanted to learn a few of his techniques, most specifically his "clinical issues" methods, because I worked with cancer patients and needed all the approaches I could learn.

And I wanted to study a little technique Valerie had talked about called "Conference Room."

Because I was already a credentialed hypnotherapist, David acceded to my request, and I packed my things to join a class in its last week of the semester.

Harry drove me up to Santa Rosa to the hotel where classes were held. Beyond the wine fields, along small country roads, it suddenly appeared before us, the Isis Oasis, complete with a violet-colored, Egyptian temple and an assortment of exotic animals.

Suddenly, I got cold feet. It looked like summer camp for Hippies. I was about ready to turn around and leave when a rotund little woman in a long, multicolored skirt and a cheerful, moon-round face introduced herself as "Morning Light," and I was trapped. Harry had gone off to make friends with the llama—he'd read that you can calm them down by exchanging breath, so he breathed into its face and it fell in love with him, as everyone who knows him does. By the time he returned to rescue me from this obvious mistake, I was surrounded by Alchemists wanting to incorporate me into their merry little band. And then, before I knew it, Harry was gone and I was abandoned to the company of people who so thoroughly fit the "California-touchy-feely-love-and-bliss" stereotype, I was seriously considering hitch-hiking the 300 miles back to L.A.

Of course, once you begin to look at the world this new way I am suggesting, you realize that nothing ever is what it seems. This training turned out to be very rigorous and brilliant, the people were very earnest, and Morning Light? Well, she took me on a trip that topped them all.

Morning Light lived in a trailer with a big Chow Chow named Bear. Money was tight for her and, because I hadn't been there for the first two weeks to interact with people and be part of the mutual practice, I asked her to spend one night taking me into the "Conference Room," for which I would pay her.

The theory, which I have found works excellently and which I love to use when people have dilemmas, is that in conference room, the many parts of you, the many people that you are, can confer on the problem and what is more—here's the magic aspect—secrets you've kept from yourself can be told.

Often what happens is that there are reasons why we do things which are not the reasons our conscious mind makes up. The reasons at one time served a purpose, but now they may no longer be useful. However, that part of the mind that continues the behavior doesn't realize that that strategy is no longer working or doesn't want to give up the behavior, even though it may no longer be appropriate. In trance this can be discussed and negotiated.

Here's an example: a heavy woman swears she eats less than all her friends, diets constantly and can't lose weight. In trance, some voices, some parts of her, talk about dieting and how they keep her from overeating, some talk about how she's too busy to cook good food for herself, some feel sorry for her, some are angry at her, and then, like a lightening bolt from beyond the rest, a part of her admits: "I keep Lois fat because when she was little someone said what a cute little girl she was and hurt her, so I make sure she's not a cute little girl any more."

The therapist has to thank that part of Lois for protecting her, has to say something like, "Thank you. Lois has been safe since she's been fat. But she's 46 years old now. Maybe there's a better way you can protect her from being molested." And the negotiations begin. David's brilliant theory also insists that you give that part another "job," let's say making sure that Lois goes to the karate lessons that have been agreed-upon to protect her from harm. It's quite a nice methodology.

* * *

For conference room, you need an issue. I chose the question: Should I do this healing work as a profession? I had been earning a good salary in advertising, something which was very easy for me. Because I have a terrible memory, there aren't a lot of good jobs which suit me. But a bad memory and a good imagination were the perfect combination for someone expected to be creative every day. I always have to make everything up, anyway, as I'm always in the dark about how I did it yesterday. So I liked advertising, if not for its morals, at least for its suitability to my talents. But I knew there was another reason, other than earning power, that made me ask this question. Something about doing this hypnotherapy work frightened me, held me back. My real, unspoken question was why was I afraid to do this work?

Morning Light, her chandelier earrings dangling gleefully, sat beside my bed with the '60s Madras bedspread in the modest room, pencil and pad in hand. She had a long, body relaxing induction, the kind I often find boring, and as she took me into trance, I wondered whether I was really in an altered state or whether I would just have to pretend so, out of politeness.

As the induction wound down, Morning Light stated the question of whether I should do this healing work and counted me down a stairway and through a door. Then it was up to me to furnish my conference room with tables, chairs, and all my many parts.

I was surprised to find, sitting sprightly and first at my table was my cheerleader saying, "She can do it. She can do anything she wants to do. She does advertising, she does writing, she does art, she always succeeds at whatever she does. She could do this, easy."

At about five o'clock on my round table, my artist and writer parts shared a seat like Tweedle-Dum and Tweedle-Dee, saying, "No, she should write, she should be a sculptor."

When we got to about 9 o'clock at the round table, someone who named herself "Ms. Demurer" appeared, saying the equivalent of "after you." Suddenly, I got a cramp in my left leg. It stopped me for a moment, and I was afraid I'd lose any trance I had, but we continued and other parts spoke up.

We went around the table again, and when we arrived at Ms. Demurer's seat, I got another cramp.

Morning Light, experienced little dumpling that she was, said "I'd like to talk to the cramp in Judith's leg."

Imagine my surprise when it said, through me, "All right."

Morning Light said "What are you trying to say to us?"

And it said, again through me, "She shouldn't know why she's afraid to do this work. She's not ready to know, yet."

My heart sunk. That seemed not only ominous, but ultimate. Where do we go from here?

But Morning Light was not deterred. One of the wonders of hypnosis and the mind is that it is infinite. Everything is possible. There are no dead ends.

"Could she proceed with this work without finding out why she's afraid?" Morning Light said, so logically, I wondered why I hadn't thought of it. "Could she just do as much of this work as she wants, without knowing why she's afraid? And then find out one day when she's ready?"

"That would be all right," the cramp said.

* * *

That was years ago, and I still don't know, although I can guess— can't you?—what I might have done or been or known which makes me frightened today. I can tell you that I still enter every session with trepidation and hesitance, with prayer and concern. I once asked my guides if they would please speak up a bit and they said, no, they wanted me to listen harder.

Everything in the universe works by opposites–there would be no dark without light, no way to describe what dark is except by comparison; no big without small, a thing is only relatively big or small, compared to something else; no wise without stupid, no right without wrong. I guess in this work we're never supposed to be confident or cocky. Modesty and fear of failure are built in to ensure that we struggle to get it right every time.

And so we are blessed by having it not be easy. I know it. It's just hard to remember that it's a blessing, sometimes.

Chapter Twenty-Three

Hypnosis for Medical Emergencies

The following story is not so much about magic that happened to me as about magic we can pass along. A nurse whom I had met through Leanna, the woman I had worked with in Arizona, invited me to study with the nurses at the Yavapai Medical Center, the main hospital in Prescott. The nurses were studying Healing Hands and Therapeutic Touch.

One of the people I met there was LaRayne Ness, who works at the Emergency Rescue Division of the hospital. I told her about a video I had seen called "Hypnosis in Medical Emergencies," and explained that, when rescue workers knew about the effect of what they said on patients and accident victims, they would know how to say the words that would facilitate better, quicker healing. She was interested and so I gave her the full story. Then she invited me to address the EMT workers, the nurses, and the fire fighters on this subject.

It was a thrilling moment for me. I thought about all the people I could influence, all the health care workers and the patients, and I was amazed that I had such an opportunity. Since I've got your attention, I'd like to tell you some of the things I told them.

* * *

When a person is in an accident, he or she is in an altered state. Fear, rampant emotions or shock put them into a highly susceptible position where their own judgment is suspended. At such a time, what you say can influence their healing.

For example, if you see someone (even in a coma—they hear you!) who seems to be in bad shape, it can only harm that person to overhear you saying so. But, on the other side of it, positive suggestions can help them as readily. The reason (as you may already have read in Interchapter 1) is that every emotion that we have generates a physical response. When we are embarrassed, we blush, when we are excited we can get aroused, when we are frightened, even by a nightmare, our hearts pound, our hands sweat, we feel faint. Our thoughts give rise to physical manifestations.

It has been shown that autonomic nervous system functions (heart beat, respiratory rate and the like) can be influenced by words alone. Doctors in operating rooms are becoming aware that even people under anesthesia hear their words at some level and can remember them when put in trance years later. Wise doctors are now realizing how important it is to take care before they speak, as they are operating not simply on an inert body but on a whole human being who is a mind/body. I recently developed a series of tapes/CDs for Cedars-Sinai Medical Center which are being used before, after and during cardio-thoracic surgery, so that patients not only don't hear harmful words during the operation, but that their inner healing is initiated by positive visualization.

So, should you encounter someone in an accident, even non-medical personnel can help, not by moving or even touching the victim (never do that!), but simply by making positive suggestions.

The best positive suggestions of course come from trained personnel themselves, because they can establish what Don Jacobs, Ph.D. calls a "contract." For example, a firefighter says, not that it's going to be all right—even a person in shock might not believe that—but the follow-ing: "I am John Doe with the fire department. The worst is over. I'm here to help. Will you do as I say?" That's the contract. If the person says "yes," you can talk directly to their autonomic nervous system.

Even if you're not a medical or rescue person, should you find someone in an emergency situation, you could still simply say, "I'm here to help. The worst is over. Will you do as I say?" If they say, "Yes," you can suggest that they concentrate on slowing down their breathing to a comfortable, natural rate. You might suggest that, as soon as the wound is cleaned, they should stop bleeding and not waste their blood. Believe it or not, they can and will stop bleeding. You might distract their attention from their pain by asking them about non-injured parts (for example, if their leg is apparently broken, you might ask them to scan their body and see how the rest is). Pain is a matter of awareness. If their awareness is transferred away from the pain, you are giving them some relief until medical help comes.

There is also a portion of the program about burn victims. If you get to a burn victim before an hour has passed, you can suggest that they imagine the burned area in a cool stream, in a bucket of ice, packed in snow. If they can do it, there will be less inflammation and less scaring when they are treated.

My partner and fellow therapist, Judith Acosta, CSW, and I are currently writing a book called *Verbal First Aid*. It will provide the general public, as well as emergency rescue people, with this valuable information.

This is everyday magic. There are seven medical doctors on the video made by Dr. Jacobs, many of them from the Berkeley Hospital Emergency Room, who state that they wish workers in the field would apply these techniques before the patients are brought in.

I gave my lecture to a room full of skeptical-looking, cowboy-style firefighters, EMT workers and nurses. Their expressions were inscrutable. I did show them snippets of the video, of the Doctors testifying to the truth of this work, of a fire captain reporting its effects. I gave them the captain's name and phone number and said, "If you don't believe me, call him. He'll be glad to talk to you about it. And try it for yourselves." And I left.

Later on, prepared for the worst, I called LaRayne to find out how she thought it went. She said she had been watching the audience, not me, the whole time I spoke, and that they were transfixed; that they hadn't talked to each other during my address, as they usually did, but were silent, listening. What's more, she told me she had overheard the Rescue Workers remind each other, "be careful what you say." She said that they had heard me. That was all I'd hoped for.

Chapter Twenty-Four

Grandpapa and White Eagle

"The good walk in step. Without knowing anything of them,
the others dance around them, dancing the dances of the age."

—*Franz Kafka*

Before I found Grandpapa, my guide, I thought that when I went into trance and found a guide, I was just making it up. After all, when we do altered states work, whatever is made up is considered as valuable as that which seems to come deeply and automatically. We are often reminded that even that which the client invents on the spot is part of him or her and therefore a valuable contribution to understanding. After all, you might make up a butterfly and I might make up a teacup and that's just for starters.

Whatever **you** would make up, it would be something entirely different from what someone else would envision, so, its being unique to you, it tells a therapist about how you think.

I was introduced to guides by Valerie, a flight attendant. She had just completed three weeks of Alchemical Hypnotherapy and made it sound so rich and spiritual, I asked her to demonstrate it for me, on me, in her motel room at lunch.

As we walked to her room, she told me about her guides, among them a Native American who always presented her with a feather when she did a good deed. Since this was before I was aware of the holographic universe and synchronicity, I granted her her illusions but didn't believe them, myself.

She also told me of a woman guide who wore old-fashioned armor. She said with amusement that this guide had the strange name of Minerva. The fact that she did not know that Minerva was the Roman goddess of war gave a certain credence to the reality of these manifestations.

"You're kidding," she said to me when I pointed out that there "really" was a Minerva in Roman mythology who dressed a lot like her guide. "Well," she said easily, "that explains it."

I lay down on her bed and she put me into a trance, something all of us students thrived on doing for each other. Whenever an instructor said, "Get into a comfortable position," and began an induction, another friend from England used to say, "*Do* me. I'm a hypno slut." The truth is, the altered state is a natural one to us and a pleasure to bask in. Being in an altered states allows the whisper of intuition to be heard. In fact, studies have shown that when people are drunk, they can commit acts that, when they become sober, they forget. But make them drunk again and they can remember again. So it is with altered states. When we are only in our conscious mind, we cannot retain or grasp what we know, all that we know, all that we have always known, unless we allow ourselves to drift into that altered state from which we've come, before we thought our conscious mind was all and everything.

Hazel Demming, Ph.D., describes the mind as a sphere, with the conscious mind being only an equator-like slice through the middle. Below it is the fullness of our subconscious mind and above it is the fullness of the supra-conscious mind or the collective unconscious, or maybe the universe.

We make the mistake of thinking that the conscious mind is all, when it is just a tight and rather rigid fraction of all we are.

In fact, the conscious mind is sometimes said to be able to do only four things:

1. provide short term memory
2. provide rationalizations for our actions (usually wrong and after the fact, but necessary, lest we go mad)
3. provide will power (which is highly over-rated, or we'd all be slim, non-smoking paragons of ambition)
4. and be logical, analytical.

So, once you've known the feeling of meditation or trance and seen how it draws in the wisdom beyond the limited conscious mind, you are always ready to return.

Valerie began an induction I hadn't experienced before, very leisurely rather than the dramatic "sleep now!" type I'd learned, and led me down the path of my unconscious. I met a Native American named Pathfinder who wouldn't talk to me (and still hasn't, but was the one who suggested without words that I let Beth's guide come up with her visualization). I think Pathfinder was meant to make me disabuse myself of the love of putting everything into words and to begin to understand what "knowing" is. Knowing is non-verbal and instantaneous. The way we know in a dream all we must know about a scene the moment we encounter it. His very insistence on a kind of wordless telepathy taught me much.

Pathfinder took me to a man on horseback who only laughed and led me to Virginia, who looked very like the Empress on a pack of Tarot cards. She has been with me ever since, to guard my health and provide white light whenever it's needed for protection.

Although these were not the guides I necessarily would have chosen for myself, they did seem somehow figments of my own imagination. I mean, just because a character appears in your mind when you're doing this work, what makes it a guide, rather than simply a pretend wish? Well, maybe we are everything, all connected. I didn't have a theory but I thanked Valerie from my heart for the experience and as we walked back to the afternoon session, she stopped and knelt down to the sidewalk before her foot and said, "Oh, here it is. I must have done a good job," and picked up a perfect white feather lying across our path.

It wasn't until months later, when meditating in my unique way, part trance, part dream, that my understanding of guides changed. I was at our Arizona home. In my meditation I had meant to go in my mind into the little stone house on the property, but found myself instead in the rundown greenhouse out back. I was not alone. Waiting for me there was an older man who introduced himself as Grandpapa. It was a time of late afternoon sun in my vision, and, although I often directed these interviews, this one had a different tenor.

At a loss, I said, "Grandpapa, tell me how I can be more loving." I hardly remember formulating the question; it seemed to ask itself.

Then he began, getting comfortable in a seat next to me in a shack that has no such seats. "I'll tell you a story."

Great, I thought to myself, *now I have to make up a story. What am I going to–*

But he wasn't waiting for me to construct anything. "All of God's children got together," he began, "holding hands, and they formed a huge circle. In the center of the circle, an egg appeared. And it grew and it grew and it grew."

I couldn't imagine what would come next, where I would take this story, but I wasn't telling this story—

"And it grew. Until it cracked open. And inside?" he said, pausing for effect. "inside were…all of God's children."

I was stumped.

"If you want to be more loving," he said, patting my hand, "see yourself as more loving."

Maybe Grandpapa is merely my inner wisdom. If so, it hardly matters. He has been back, always helpful. And it seems to me I feel him touch my hand when I call him.

* * *

I have other guides, as well, including a Native American spirit named White Eagle. I learned later that there are writings of White Eagle, but I don't know if they are the same being. My guide, like his predecessor, Pathfinder, doesn't much care to talk to me. But he had an elegantly silent way of assuaging my doubts about my healing abilities.

While in my car on the way to visit a client, I began to wonder what I could do for her that would help her get through the ravages of indecision over a wrecked relationship. She was one of my writing students and someone to whom I personally felt very close, so when she asked for my help, I'd agreed. Now I drove along a Los Angeles Freeway trying to imagine which of the techniques I'd learned I could apply to elicit her own understanding.

I decided to ask my guides to tell me what to do. That's a mistake in the first place. What kind of a guide wants you to give away your responsibility? Not the kinds I like to work with. So, in answer to a stupid question, White Eagle stood up from the ground where he had been sitting in all his glory, and brought forth a dazzling headpiece. It had an eagle's head and shoulders on top, cascading down from which was a waterfall of white feathers in all directions. He walked toward me and wordlessly put it on my head, where its face was elevated high above mine, with the feathers wrapping around me like a cloak. Then he turned his back and walked away.

Part of the work with spirit guides is understanding their subtle messages. White Eagle was saying to me, "You do not need me to make you a shaman. But if you think you do, put this on. Now you're a shaman. But you were already. If you want the trappings, you can have them. But it doesn't make you wiser. You are already as wise as you need to be to do this work."

An end note on this chapter happened recently when Harry lay beside me, playing the shakuhachi flute. His tune, made up as he play, took me back to White Eagle's village.

White Eagle came up to me, studied me for a moment, and then placed a mirror in my heart.

I came up from the trance confused. Words, again, failed me. I had to live that heart-mirror to understand. The next time I had an emotional reaction to a conversation, I went inside and looked at myself in the mirror in my heart. It showed me the shallowness of my thoughts and transformed my mundane image into what I could be by simply changing my attitude—a reflection much more appealing.

To see how this can work in your life, see Finding Guides in the Exercises at the end of the book.

It is very nice to have this kind of support and serenity inside. In truth, the outer world is a reflection of the inner. Your life is about the grace with which you live.

Chapter Twenty-Five

Family Matters

The reason it is hard to believe in psychics is that sometimes they are wrong. Also, there are phonies who say they are psychic, give you a lot of generalizations about how "troubled" you are when you come to see them—an easy assumption—and "read" your responses to compound a picture which seems insightful to you in your already admittedly troubled state.

The psychic, Todd, who had seen Beth's cancer was not a phony (See Chapter Three, Beth and the Angel.). Here's how I know.

My father's name was Al and looked like Clark Gable, except that my father had a stiff leg. He had the biggish ears, the famous mustache, and the sad, telling lines around his deep-set eyes. Later, as Sean Connery began to lose his hair and get those wizened eyes that always move me, pictures of him always brought back my father in the later days of his life.

My father had been my hero, the ideal dad. He could fix anything, remove splinters like a surgeon, and play the old philosopher, my favorite of his roles. All my life, however, while my sisters saw him has invincible, I always saw his suffering, his fragility. I always regretted the accident that had happened long before I was born, which had caused him to walk with a limp. He had been 19 years old, a potential baseball player, subbing on the farm team of the Philadelphia Athletics (later to become the Oakland A's), full of the wild, untrammeled spirit that made one of his teachers turn his name from Alexander to Smart Alec.

When, running or catching or fielding or whatever, he hurt his right leg, and through a series of mismanaged medical moves, the cartilage in his knee became gangrenous. In the days before antibiotics, that meant the cartilage had to be removed, so the doctors took it out. They sewed his knee up, a big scar across where it used to bend, and sent the kid with the promise out into the world a "cripple."

From that time on, his leg stuck out straight whenever he sat down, it stuck out to the side when he showed us how to ride a bicycle, it made his walk down the block, step-limp-step-limp, so very characteristic for all of our lives. Including my mother's, who also never knew him any other way.

It must have contributed to his shyness. Smart Alec became just Al, wise, witty, retiring. People often asked him if his stiff leg was the result of a war wound, and he'd wished it were, but in fact it had kept him out of the war. It never kept him from anything else we could notice. He was a businessman, an avocational artist, even an excellent golfer in his later years. And he was ever the philosopher to me.

My father died in 1986 in California. I was at his deathbed, in fact the last person to see him alive. In fact, I was the one who had to tell the nurses not to cut open his throat for a tracheotomy which would allow him to breathe for another day or two in pain before the disease that had wrapped its gnarled fingers around his lungs and squeezed them dry could claim him. I was the one who saw him stand up, rip from his arms and face and body the apparatus which wired him to life, and give it up rather than live as an invalid. He had already lived gracefully as a "cripple." That was enough. It was so like him, that even as I cried for help, and even as they told me they could only prolong the suffering, I knew it was time to let him go.

In his book, *Reinventing Medicine*, Dr. Larry Dossey writes about deathbed scenes where the dying are talking to someone or something other than those gathered at the bedside. One report even had the mother and daughter both actually seeing the angel to whom their husband/father spoke. When my father was dying, his last words seemed not addressed to us and they were full of possibilities. He said, simply, "I won the game. I won the game."

Since he died neither rich nor famous, to me that observation confirmed that goodness is its own reward.

At the funeral, I gave the eulogy, calmly, addressing him, rather than talking to the crowd that turned out. Lines of people who formed at the door, each one with a story of something he'd done for them which he hadn't mentioned to anyone else. "I know you loved your father, but I loved him, too," they said it almost word for word. And then they'd relate how he'd fixed something for them, or driven them somewhere when he was really on his way somewhere else, always with a smile, always generous.

People would ask him about how he did something, his sculpture, his repairs, and he'd always say, "Oh, anybody could do it, it's easy." But to be like him, well, truly, anybody could do it, it was certainly easy, but no one else seemed to think of it. He had read a book called *The Magnificent Obsession,* about the secret of life being helping others and not taking the credit for it, and he had lived it. He'd help and run, leaving them to wonder "who was that masked (limping?) man?" His was, in a small way, a magnificent life. And that surely seemed how to win the game.

We still lived in New York, at that time, and because I was able to pretend upon my return home from his funeral in California that he was still just a telephone call away, I decided not to mourn his passing. That was before I worked in this field and had learned two important concepts: one, that it would be better for me, and him, if I mourned his death, and two, that he was in some ways better than "just a phone call away."

* * *

Years went by, we moved from New York to the infamous boat, from the boat to the shack on the beach, and I began studying hypnotherapy, as you already know. By the time I worked with Beth, I was ready to check out Todd.

I had known people before who claimed to be psychic, who generally told you what you wanted to know and promised you success, even those who offered to pray for you for a price (you can do that yourself—you've got a direct line). But Todd had been so vital to Beth that I had to meet him to hear what he had to say to me.

As I told you, Todd lives in a little shack behind his mother's house in Culver City. You may wonder why "real" psychics aren't rich, and that is a good question. I think it has to do with two things: The way the universe works and the nature of people who go with the gift,

Todd begins with prayers and has you bring 10 questions in a sealed envelope. If he hasn't answered them all by the end of the session, you open them up and ask away. But he does seem to hit all or most.

There was nothing that transpired that was worth reporting in detail that day, except for this one incident, which may register with you as it did with me. Todd had me stand up against a white wall so he could see my aura and also the spirits who were with me.

Remembering Beth's angel, I was particularly anticipating this event. I stood up, he read my aura and then he said, "There are three spirits around you. One is Rose, do you know a Rose?" I did, it was my mother's mother, but in the confusion of the moment, I said I didn't. There was also a baby spirit around me, which hadn't revealed itself yet, and would be impossible for me to bring into the world. So far, I was disappointed.

Then Todd said gently, "Where is your father?"

"He's dead," I said.

"He's right there with you. Beside you." He hesitated, puzzled. "Can I ask you a question?" he said.

"Yes." I guessed there would be no angels for me. Maybe Todd wasn't so perceptive after all. It was easy to say my dead father was nearby.

What was his question, how long ago did he pass away? Was my mother still alive?

Todd leaned forward in his seat, looking, it appeared, at the wall to my right, puzzled. I waited for his question about my father, not altogether interested.

"I just wanted to ask you," he said, speaking slowly, "what's the matter with his leg?"

* * *

I have this on tape. I brought it home to play to Harry. I played it for my sisters. They just shook their heads. "Don't tell Mom," one of my sisters said. "She likes to think that in Heaven, Dad's leg is perfectly all right!"

After that, I believed in Todd. He said, "You didn't say a prayer for your father when he died, did you?"

"No."

"He wants you to," he said. I was surprised. My father had never seemed religious. It was only later that I read that it really makes a difference to spirits to be prayed for. So I went home and said a prayer for him. And I started crying and crying and hardly could stop.

Oh, I thought, Daddy, being the generous creature that he was, he had me say a prayer for him, for *me*.

But, because there's always more, if you look for it, it turned out he might have wanted it, needed it too. Because, after I said my prayer, he started appearing to the family in very helpful ways.

* * *

The summer of '93, my daughter was going through a life crisis and came to visit us in Los Angeles in the hopes of seeing her life in a new way. I took her up to David Quigley of the Alchemical Hypnotherapy school and she had two sessions with him to try to understand and unlock old patterns.

One of the most important aspects of his work involves finding people's "resources." What do you have to call on inside yourself that helps you know who you are and what you think? (See final chapter for an enhancement on this thought of going with your strengths.)

My daughter's father had loved her but his way of showing it had been judgmental and damaging. As she began to understand in these session, because he had courted her and then rejected her, courted her again and then judged her badly, her relationships with men were suffering. Although she loves and admires Harry, he had come on the scene too late to be a good role model, and when David had her go inside to find a resource, a "guide," she found one. It was my father.

"Grandpa's face was in front of me, so large," she said later. "It wasn't like a dream. I saw every feature. You know how, in a dream or a memory you just get a sense of a person. Well, he was *there,* his face as clear as life." I believe she went home transformed, even if, as often happens, going home means living in the conditions which made you crazy in the first place, which in her case was partly life in New York City. When I later asked her what it meant that she saw Grandpa, she said, "You know how you have no place to rest, like if you hate your job and you're fighting with your boyfriend, and there are mice in your apartment, and nothing is going right and there's no place to put your mind? It gave me a place to put my mind, to rest my head. With Grandpa."

That fall, my sister Stephanie came to visit us in Prescott. Her career as a romance writer was just budding, she already had an agent for her first book, and was working on a time-travel, romance novel which was to takes place in Sedona and other areas near our Arizona cabin. She is also a confirmed skeptic, a non-believer. She is certain there is nothing but this life, that when it's over, it's over. And that it is all meaningless, so you should just hold on to what you've got. I don't argue, it only makes her upset.

However, she had a telephone phobia, because of which she couldn't seem to call anyone, herself, and had to rely on her husband and son to contact the outside world. Therefore, she thought maybe hypnosis could cure it. Sure, I said, knowing full well she wanted, at least subconsciously, to prove there was nothing to anything I was doing, knowing getting her into trance would be like pulling a donkey who'd decided to sit.

Her husband and son went off to shoot pool in the wild and woolly pool halls of Whiskey Row, and I had her relax on the couch. I started with breathing, went into all the tricks I knew, and, because lately I've been able to feel in my body how deeply in trance someone I'm working with is, and to see it in their "aura," I could tell that she wasn't quite there. However, I had her try this and then that, all of the "mechanical," clinical methods I had learned. Visualize the phone. Repeat phrases. Go into her body and say what it was feeling. When it feels afraid, what does it want to say? "I'm afraid." Of what? "Just afraid." Go inside the knot in your stomach. What's there? To every "what are you seeing?" there was a predictable "nothing." Even the old hypnosis trick of "If you *could* visualize something, what would it be?" didn't seem to work. She just shrugged.

Finally I decided that nothing would be lost to try a more spiritual approach. I had her take a walk on the beach in her imagination to find a "guide." "Someone who knows the answer for you will be waiting behind the next sand dune." I didn't even hope, I just did it.

And then she smiled. "Daddy's there."

"Daddy."

"He's young. It's before his leg is hurt. He's in a bathing suit." She starts to cry.

"Go over and talk to him."

"I don't want to."

"Why not?"

"I don't want him to know I'm having a problem. He always liked it that I took care of my own problems. He liked me to be independent. I don't want to burden him with my problem."

"Maybe he wants to help."

"No."

I didn't want to miss this chance. Something important was coming up for her and she was turning her back on it. Desperately, I suggested, "Then tell him about all the good things he's missed. Tell him about Arika's going to college and how well Alan's doing and how well—"

She smiles. "He knows."

I may have gasped. She didn't seem to notice. My sister, who believes in nothing but this life, seeing her dead father and telling me *he knows* what's been going on since he died!

"Why don't you just go sit down yourself somewhere on the beach and see if he comes over to you."

"All right."

She is quiet for a while. Then, "He's coming over."

"Good."

"He's sitting down next to me, but he's not looking at me."

"That's fine."

All of a sudden she starts to laugh. "You should hear what he just said about Mom!"

"What did he say?"

"He said, 'You think I thought Mom was perfect? I knew she wasn't perfect. You don't have to be perfect, either.'"

Whatever was happening, she was fully aware she was having a real experience.

When I brought her up from trance, I never mentioned to her about the obvious contradiction in her beliefs. She was shaken up, and wanted to do more work the next day. I was amazed.

But once we started, the next evening, she was even more loath to go into trance and nothing seemed to be happening. Even asking her "higher self" what benefit this phobia provided her didn't help. Generally, when we have a behavior pattern that appears to hurt us, it provides us with a secondary benefit. A bad back may be a pain, but if you can't work and somebody else has to support you because of it, it provides a secondary benefit. A cold that comes when you've been working too hard makes you go to bed and slow down. And there is a part of us, accessible in an altered state, which knows what the benefit is. Since she could not acknowledge that this phobia did anything beneficial for her, and since she was getting restive, I brought her back up from trance. Days like this make me remember that I am not the one who makes this happen, I am just the one who is there to help it happen, and it will unfold in its own sweet way, which it did moments later, when her husband and son returned to ask how it had gone, was she changed?

"It didn't work at all," she said.

"That's good," they said, almost in unison, "because we like you the way you are."

She had been walking from one room to the next and she literally came to a dead stop and turned to me. The benefit wasn't hers! It was theirs. They liked her helpless. She was just going along.

Later, I talked to her a little about it, about finding other ways to assure them that they wouldn't lose her if her novels took off and she became famous and independent. To assure them that she still needed them, not as an invalid but because she loved them.

A few weeks later, she called to report that she had spoken to the car repair man on the phone about her son's fan belt and had called the plumber about some pipes. It didn't happen in hypnosis, but all it has to do is happen. Once we get it, we're free. I'll also report that she also called her agent about her new novel and is now a published author of many successful romance novels.

* * *

I have one more family story to report that doesn't relate to my father, but ties in with all the rest. I have another sister named Shelle; she's the middle one (I'm the eldest). Her husband, Jeff, calls her a Zen master, because she seems to take pleasure in simple tasks and finds enlightenment through them. One day in October of 1991 she was washing the kitchen floor when she thought she heard our deceased Grandmother, our mother's mother, Rose, say something to her. Shelle couldn't make it out, so she actually said, out loud, "Speak up!" but there was no more. As it was our Grandmother's birthday, Shelle related it to that and let it go.

Three weeks later, our mother went into the hospital where she was to die. The doctors examined her and declared that, three weeks earlier, she'd had a silent heart attack. At exactly the time when <u>her</u> mother was trying to talk to Shelle. Maybe she was trying to talk to me through Todd, when I forgot who she was in my moment at the wall. Maybe if I could have heard, I could have done something for my mother. I don't know. It must be very hard to pierce the veil.

An odd note, however, about how thin the veil might be: After my father, an avocational sculptor, died, I found myself, a woman who couldn't draw water from a well, taking up sculpture myself and spent nearly four years in passionate work. As suddenly as I started, I stopped, imagining that both my father and I seemed to be done. After my mother a romance-reader and would-be writer, passed away, my sister, Stephanie, began writing romances and has become very successful in the field. I guess our mother had more to say.

By the way, I went back to Todd once more, for a check-up. Since he'd diagnosed Beth, I though he was a reliable resource in the esoteric medical department. He started pulling things from the air as he usually does and he said to me, "What does the name Paula or Pauline mean to you?""

Odd name, don't you think? It was my mother's. "It was my mother's name."

"Where is she?"

"She's dead."

"She wants you to know that she's happy and with someone named Joseph. Is that a brother or her father, a husband, perhaps?"

There was only one man my mother ever loved, the man to whom she was married at nineteen years old, with whom she shared forty-four happy years, all but the last six years of her life. He looked like Clark Gable and was called Al by everyone who knew him. Only his immediate family knew that he had another name. His older brother, named Alexander, had died as an infant, and their mother had liked that name so well, she wanted to give it to the next child. Since it belonged to the son who had passed away, she named the next child Joseph Alexander. Joseph was my father's real name.

Interchapter 5:

Grids and Gestalts

"…when we were in training to be night fliers in the Navy, I learned, very strangely, that the rods of the eye perceive things at night in the corner of the eye that we can't see straight ahead. It's not a bad metaphor for the vision of art. You don't stare at the mystery, but you can see things out of the corner of your eye that you weren't supposed to see."

—William Meredith

"Everything important happens off the page"

—Harry Youtt

Before science discovered the quantum universe, only those material things that we could see and measure with our five senses were deigned worth studying. These days, science can prove esoteric concepts such as that prayer works (they call it a "non-local effect," which makes it sound more credibly technical) and the concept that our bodies are in actuality 99.999 percent void. Non-material.

That's because we're made up of atoms and each atom, if you could enlarge it to see its structure, is mostly space. Each atom has a tiny nucleus the size of a dust speck in the center, a football-field sized void of nothingness beyond, with electrons orbiting around it also the size of dust spots and as far away from the nucleus as the bleachers are from the fifty yard line. That's what we're made of.

Unless string theory is correct, in which case we're made of something incredibly smaller. And vibrating.

It's also believed that we can see only 6 percent of the known electromagnetic spectrum. We can see light waves. We don't see the gamma waves in the room with us right now, nor the beta waves, the X-rays. If you turned on a radio or a television, they would go on because, right now, there are radio waves and television waves in this room as well as microwaves. We don't see them, or even the ultra-violet or infra-red light some of our fellow beings on the planet (bees, snakes) can see.

So, if we don't see 94 percent of what we **know** exists (not counting what we don't know about) and we're made up of only .00001 percent actual matter, how can we possibly deny the goings-on in the realms that remain invisible to us?

Houston Smith, Ph.D., in a guest lecture given at UCLA in 1995 talked about the limitations of science, and the movement from modern to postmodern sensibilities. He said there are at least six things that the scientific method cannot wrap itself around. (He used the analogy of a fish net that catches lots but lets lots slip through.) These six things beyond science's measure are:

1) *Values.* While science can measure things like good or bad consequences of smoking, it can't measure what is normative (by that he means what people want and like) and intrinsic (perhaps choosing to smoke and enjoy it, even if that choice also means taking the risk of dying young).

2) *Meaning:* He says that science can deal with equations, but not with existential meaning, meaningfulness to someone, what is the meaning of the whole, the all?

3) *Purpose.* Science can deal, he says, with teleonomy, the biology of science. It cannot deal with teleology, the final causes. What is the point of something's being the way it is? It has been said of the

scientific method that it systematically rejects the concepts of a purpose and of final causes.

4) *Quality*: Science has no problem with measuring quantities. It could measure an increased heartbeat as you watch a scary movie, but it cannot measure how your being experiences it. It cannot measure the quality of how you experience your life. Or even whether we experience a color in the same way.

5) *Invisibles.* There are those things that either have no physical, material, or visible components, and those things science could never disclose. He says the current scientific view of the big picture is that the universe consists of 70 percent cold dark matter, 30 percent hot dark matter and a pinch of everything else. But what they really mean is that if it's not material, it's literally not on their radar. Does that mean it doesn't exist? Of the known electromagnetic spectrum, only 6 percent is visible. But we have Geiger counters and sonar detectors, so we know about some non-visibles. Without a machine to measure it, science discounts it or pretends it couldn't be there.

6) *That which is superior to us.* This is my favorite aspect out of the reach of science. Whether we're talking about extra terrestrials, angels, God, if their intelligence is greater than ours, we can't measure them.

There is no proof that these things exist, but if they do, science is not going to tell us about them. Stephen Jay Gould says "Absence of evidence is not evidence of absence." But as far as science is concerned, there's no "point" talking about all these six categories which comprise and inform such a vast portion of our lives.

Smith uses the analogy that our feeble attempts to scientifically study those with superior qualities would be like a dog trying to analyze whether mathematics exists by subjecting it to the sniff test. This thought brought me to my theory about theories and grids.

There are many windows into and out of healing. Perhaps as many as their are healers, who each tend to have an approach, a system which "explains it all." They write a book about their theory and go on the circuit.

I have been in what might loosely be called "the healing profession," for the last decade, much of which, while my clients got well, I berated myself for not having a theory. Deepak Chopra likes the Auyervedic system. Caroline Myss created a chakra-Tree of Life-Sacraments system. John Bradshaw gave us a whole system based on the Inner Child. The brilliant Dr. Larry Dossey focuses on non-local healing.

My friend, Julie Motz, who wrote *Hands of Life*, is theory personified. Her theory, very sophisticated, has to do with four primary fluids of the body: cerebrospinal fluid, blood, lymph and synovial fluid that lubricates the joints. These four relate to THE four feelings: fear, anger, pain and love. These relate to the four forms of energy: electromagnetism, gravity, the nuclear force and the weak force.

It seems every healer has an angle, owns a corner.

And here I was, healer without a system, a method, even a grid.

In my mind, being without a grid means being at a loss for the ability to fit concepts like time and matter into squares like calendar pages and rooms. For example, I have always teetered precariously on the outer edges of linear time without the grid that everybody else seemed able to put on top of "now" or last Wednesday and plot out like a graph. There was yesterday, and last week, and tomorrow and 1979. Those were hard concepts for me. I always felt that, while I couldn't remember exactly what I did last Wednesday, Wednesday was not so actually identifiable as the day I went to school and then to piano lessons and then home. It was a seamless part of all the days in which I went to school, all the piano lessons, all the time at home. But not the times I went to Grandma's.

"We do not remember days, we remember moments." Cesare Pavese

But there are native peoples who grasp and relate it better. They believe that time is circular, a concept we've now labeled kyros (as opposed to linear chronos) time. In kyros time, all Christmases are stacked. Every Christmas you experience relates not to December 24th of that year, but to all other Christmases. All your birthdays are in the same time zone, and the times you spend at your favorite getaway—those are separate and apart from any day/date/year designation—they are somehow all one. That is how it, all of life, has always seemed to me. (For more on Time and Synchronicity, see Interchapter 3.)

And while I worked hard to pretend I could also function with the grid system (what day is it, again, and what month?), I knew I saw things differently. (Of course, when we all understand string theory, and space and time are officially declared illusions, I will be vindicated.)

Naturally, having been inept at explaining my "take" on time (and matter, for that matter), I hesitated to offer an explanation of my methods of helping people heal themselves. In fact, I had not even articulated it to myself when the issue was brought to a raging boil.

I was asked to speak at a conference with the above-mentioned Julie Motz, who declined sharing a podium with me although we were friends. She believed her methodical way of proceeding was scientifically serious, and had nothing in common with my methods, which to her were not. In so many words, she expressed her dismissal of my approach to healing as, "You just **love** people well."

At first, I was taken aback. It had the intonation of an insult, while I unexpectedly had the inclination to say "thanks."

When I considered my approach in a cooler light, it seemed to me that what I do somehow involves moving my vibration "up" or getting into an altered state myself, then taking my client with me. Lately, I don't even have to formally "put anyone" into trance, just be with them and they can experience it. One client described it this way: "When you talk like that, the room around you gets dark, and I see you as if you

were at the end of a tunnel and I have to blink to keep you in focus."
What happens when we are both there tends to be unpredictable.
Sometimes, I believe, even providing opportunities for spontaneous
remissions from cancer.

Exactly what theory can I make of that? Well, I have one and I'll get
to it, but it isn't a grid, it's more of a Gestalt, an ah-ha!

I started thinking about Smith's dog's grid, doing a sniff test on the
world as it sees it. "Okay," Rex would say, "the world is divided into
four categories.

Those things that smell good and taste good;
those things that smell good and taste bad;
those things that smell bad and taste good;
and those things that smell bad and taste bad."

Now that's not a bad way to explain that particular material, sensual
level of experience. That might cover all the possibilities, but it is all the
possibilities for a very limited sphere of influence. It does not allow for
a view of anything above its limits.

In the same way, it seems to me, when we put a grid on a limited level
of awareness, we get a limited grid. If, for example, like Julie, you are
interested only in what happened from the moment of conception to
the moment of death, you can create an entire system which touches a
lot of bases. However, its natural boundaries creates its limits.

What if Einstein had limited himself to the known? He solved cosmic
riddles through imagination, through visualizing himself traveling on a
beam of light. Very unscientific.

Some time ago I went to a medical conference on "Spirituality and
Medicine." Papers were presented which concluded that those who
attended church a certain number of times suffered less stress than their
non-church-going counterparts. When I questioned the absolute connection between church attendance and spirituality, I was told,
"Church-going is measurable and we are a science. The medical model
requires that something be measured." Researchers couldn't tell the

quality of the experience, as Smith would have it, only the quantity. And the fact that it was reproducible.

The near-phobic denigration in a modern (but perhaps not postmodern) scientific world of anything "beyond measure" is one reason that so little attention is paid to the massive documentation that has been collected in Japan and now in America on spontaneous remissions. No measuring there. In fact the most famous medically documented case was of an Italian man whose entire hip was eaten away with cancer. He made a single trip to Lourdes, bathed in the water, opened up his belief system, his spirituality, and grew a new hip. Doctors in France and Italy both had before and after X-rays and yet it is still considered dismissibly "anecdotal." Beyond measure.

* * *

As for my grid: I believe we are not only all interconnected, but connected, too, with the universals, the ultimate in ways that will astound us. We can use altered states to be in touch with that higher level of awareness and it is increasingly easy to attain these states as our whole population moves up the "morphogenetic field" or the "noosphere" (see Interchapter 4 on Non-local Effects). That means you won't need *me* to take you there; you'll find your way yourself.

Creative imagining is one avenue into that state and for purposes of this book, I'm using the metaphor of metaphor to explode the prison of limits that has characterized three-dimensional life. I'm using the illusion of allusion to melt hard forms and make them malleable. I'm offering you Alternity—the domain of endless possibilities and inviting you to move in.

Exploring
Interconnectedness

This is an exercise I'm sure you've tried, but you may never have thought of it in this context. Stare at someone who is not looking at you and see how long it takes for that person to "feel it." It doesn't matter how far away they are. It doesn't matter if you know them or not. They'll become aware of your eyes on them and look up. Why? Because we can be aware of things we "know" beyond the use of our five limited senses. You are almost tapping them on their shoulders with your glance. Amazing, unless you recognize that there is more to our awareness than we are aware of.

Chapter Twenty-Six

The Diamond and the Ghost on the Queen Mary

"To die, to sleep;
To sleep: perchance to dream. Ay, there's the rub;
For in that sleep of death what dreams may come..."

—Shakespeare: Hamlet, V

The Queen Mary is a luxury liner with a daunting history. The elegant, gracious ship of kings, presidents and Hollywood royalty, it was the means by which the rich and famous made the journey across "the pond," the Atlantic Ocean between the United States and England. Before conventional airplane travel, anyone who was anyone took the voyage, whether in the grandeur of first class or not.

If you had been a fly on the porthole, you might have seen Sir Winston Churchill, General Dwight D. Eisenhower, Queen Elizabeth the Queen Mother, the Duke and Duchess of Windsor, Henry Ford, Jr., Aristotle Onassis, Michael Todd, Fred Astaire, Lionel Barrymore, Charlie Chaplin, Gary Cooper, Marlene Deitrich, Douglas Fairbanks Sr. and Jr., Clark Gable, Greta Garbo, Elizabeth Taylor, Mary Pickford, and Liberace walking her decks.

After a splendid career as luxury liner in the thirties, she became known as the *Grey Ghost* during the Second World War, ephemerally eluding the Nazis as she transported troops and then transporting British war brides when the war was over.

These days she is docked, a regal hotel and tourist destination gracing the shoreline of Long Beach, California.

When I worked in advertising for Ogilvy & Mather in New York, I had the opportunity to create a promotion to attract tourists to the Queen Mary.

The story we created for our event was that, shortly before the war, the Queen of England had given the Crown Jewels to the ship's Admiral to keep them safe from the "Nazi hordes" and that the Admiral had hidden a diamond aboard the Queen Mary. He had kept an elaborate journal with clues as to where it could be found, and now, after his death, the public could pick up a copy of the journal at Crandall's Jewelers or on shipboard and test wits with the enigmatic diary. The person who found the jewel could keep it.

(There's an amusing inside story, here. We had originally planned on awarding a prize diamond worth $100,000, but the winner would have an enormous tax obligation on such a gift, and might have had to sell it to pay the taxes, so we offered a diamond of lower value instead, a mere $30,000, thereby making it more affordably win-able.)

I scoured the decks for a perfect hiding place, worked diligently to create labyrinthine clues (someone else had "found the journal" and marked it up with further clues before it got into the publics' hands, so that there were two layers to puzzle through) and created a handsome, "leather bound" journal in which hints were buried within tales of the sea.

One hundred and eleven people found the diamond (it was hidden inside the metal bar of the clothing closet of the captain's quarters) whereupon, according to the rules, whoever wrote the best essay about why the Queen Mary was a "gem of an experience," would be the winner. I wanted to send each and every one of those who had solved the mystery a certificate of congratulations on being so brilliant, but I was told there was no money in the budget to do so.

Years later, there were rumors that the Queen Mary might be sold to the Japanese and taken away, and Harry, who had a weakness for boats (you may recall our little around-the-world episode), especially luxury liners with a brilliant history and which are notoriously known to be haunted, decided we should spend the summer living shipboard.

Every day I left for work from Long Beach and returned "home" to the liner for dinner and a walk around the deck. It was extremely romantic, especially because we often had nooks of the ship to ourselves during the week at odd hours.

One early evening we were sitting alone in the richly Art Deco Observation Bar having a cocktail as the sun traced long, late afternoon fingers of light across the room from the forward end of the ship.

We had been talking, debating about the nature of time, my asserting my belief in its being non-linear, Harry asking for a "before" and "after" to hold his place. (There was a funny odd quote which agrees with us both: *Time is God's way of keeping everything from happening at once.* To me, that can be explained that everything does happen at once, but, being human and therefore locked in time and space, we perceive everything through that window of time. See Interchapter 3 on Time and Synchronicity if this discussion or thought intrigues you.)

In a brief pause in this quantum conversation, my eyes softened and drifted over to a table nearby, where a man with a pencil-thin mustache and a boutonniere lifted a martini glass and toasted me.

It just took a second.

Harry is very subtle. He was looking at me and asked quietly, "What just happened?"

And when I heard his voice, the man disappeared and the table was again empty.

"I just saw one of your Queen Mary ghosts," I said.

Harry had seen him, not to his face but in *my* face, and there was nothing more to say.

We had dinner at the Promenade Grille and retired to our room. As I lay in bed that night, just before I fell asleep, I had another other-worldly sensation. I felt the same ghost from the Observation Bar slip into bed beside me, discretely, considerately, respectfully, just for a moment, and then he was gone.

When I told Harry what had happened, he wrote a story, which became a one-act play, about the events of the evening. It was told from the point of view of the ghost, who doesn't realize he has crossed the veil of time. He has written a letter to his friend, describing the events of the evening. He had become fascinated with a "wildly unusual woman who talked of waves and particles and seemed to have landed aboard the ship from some inexplicable place as it sailed for Cherbourg."

We hope one day to see Harry's play performed in the Observation Bar, just as it happened that night.

Chapter Twenty-Seven

A Near-Accident Experience

The discipline of spirituality took me over without so much as an "if you don't mind." My longings changed from a desire for success and fame to the urge to "be of use."

My meditations also have a mind of their own. One day while driving the customary hour to work in Orange County, I had my car's lights on because the morning was foggy and I thought to myself, "How can I remember to turn them off?" Then I thought, "I don't want to just remember when I get there that they're on. I want to be AWARE that they're on, the whole trip."

Now, strange as that seems, that's a metaphysical challenge. Awareness is the hardest state in which to live. I imagine that "the enlightened ones," by whom I mean Buddha and Jesus and Mohammed and beings of that magnitude, are great in part because they can hold awareness. As for us, try as we may, we drift into idle thought within seconds of the determination not to let it happen.

So I drove, fighting drifting thoughts, trying to stay in awareness and being aware that my plan about the car's lights was really a test of being aware of God. Which of course I failed. (See Mantra Exercise at the end of the book.)

Shortly thereafter, on January 22, 1997 (I mention the date because on the next day there was an astrological phenomenon in which all the planets made a configuration in the sky of a six-pointed star which was considered a turning point in the New Age), I was driving again to work and this time it was raining.

"I am very aware of God," I said to myself as I drove. Forget the lights. I went straight **for** it, this time. "I am very aware of God."

May I say here that I don't know what or who God is, and my awareness is of grandeur and majesty and unconditional love, clear but not specific.

As I was thinking that thought, I was driving on "the 405," the San Diego Freeway, at 60 miles an hour. The pavement was slippery as the new rain mixed with significant deposits of oil on the road. And in a moment I began to skid.

I went from the far left (fast) lane, into the next lane, then back, then back to the next lane and then finally back into the fast lane where I swerved, head on, into the dividing wall and then whirled around to face the oncoming traffic.

On the freeways in Los Angeles it is not unusual to see a car spun around (you always wonder how that happens), usually quite smashed up with a number of cars behind it equally destroyed. As I began the spin, in my mind was the terrible fear for those behind me.

And then as suddenly I was enveloped in total silence. It felt as though the hand of God had reached down and quieted everything. And when I looked up, I was facing three lanes of oncoming traffic—all of them stock still, waiting for me to turn around and proceed.

Not a screech of tires. No one moved. Three lanes of traffic that had been going at 60 miles an hour were frozen in silence, watching me.

I was instantly mortified, put my car into reverse, turned my car back on its course and started driving in the dead silence, when I felt my car filling with angels and I started smiling and crying and saying "Thank you, God, thank you, God, thank you God," all the way to work.

When I got to the office, I called Harry and all I could say was, I just had a near death experience, and it was very gentle.

* * *

This is not the first book on this subject I have written. I have written a book on the paradigm shift. I have written on book on the science and medicine of the paradigm shift. I was shy about writing about me, thinking it seemed somehow like bragging.

In the same way, I had resisted telling anyone of this incident. I thought it sounded too much like I thought I was special. When I finally mentioned it to my friend, Tahdi, she said, "No, we have to inspire each other, tell each other those stories." Then she paused. "You know, I was looking at the sunrise this morning from my place in the canyon and at first there were just colors spread out across the sky and then slowly, gradually, it all gathered, all the power and the colors and the rays, into a ball and the sun rose. And I thought to myself, the sun doesn't say 'don't look at me, I'm not that important.' It says, 'Look at me. Isn't God's grandeur amazing.'"

So, I told you this story.

Chapter Twenty-Eight

Levels of Awareness

I may be misquoting the Buddha, but I believe it was his thought that your life is not about what happens to you but about how you take it, what you make of what happens to you.

You have probably heard the old Asian story meant to illustrate that we can't even know when we are lucky and when we are not. It is about a man whose most valuable "possessions" are his son and a beautiful Arabian horse. He treasures these two above all else and considers himself a lucky man for having them in his life. Then one day, the horse runs away and the man is devastated. He has lost half of his treasure. The horse returns the next day, bringing with it a beautiful mate. How lucky the man feels! Now he has three treasures. His son leaps on the new horse and rides around the property until the horse stumbles and throws him, and the son breaks his leg. How unlucky the man is; his son is hurt, what a tragedy. Then the king's soldiers come to the man and tell him that the country is at war and all the eligible young men must enlist in the army and go off to battle. But his son cannot go; he has a broken leg! How lucky that he broke his leg—

As you can see, "luck" is not only fickle, it is not always what it appears. A wise person makes every effort to see the good, the meaning in all that happens to him or her. When you trip over a rock, pick it up and turn it over; you may discover a jewel of understanding when you examine the other side. If you understand that life is not about what happens to you, but about what you make of what happens to you, you can go beyond expectation or desire, the belief that only what you think you want to happen to you is worth experiencing.

Thinking that x or y is the only thing that will make you happy gives you tunnel vision and precludes the possibility that you don't know what really will make you happy. And what is worse, you won't be open to seeing it when it appears.

Expectation is the containment of pleasure. Meaning is the answer. Through meaning you can welcome everything that comes as a messenger and know you invited it and can learn from it.

What is Your Level of Awareness?

How you go through life, how you view what happens to you, depends upon your level of awareness. It is not just a simple matter of "positive thinking," not a question of "putting the best face" on something and pretending it's all right. In some ways that could lead to more pain, as the repressed thoughts, angers, feelings emerge in eye twitches, stutters, or even inappropriate rages for having been denied, unexpressed.

No, I'm not talking about pretending everything is just fine, even when it's not. "Levels of awareness" are actual ways of seeing things differently.

Imagine you are a traveler, a visitor to a sacred temple, let's say in India, in Egypt, a place of history and majesty. You are with a heterogeneous group of people and you are just an observer, watching how they view this imposing sight.

Some, on the most basic level of awareness, are bored and wondering when lunch is. They may feel tired, cold, and, if you asked them they'd probably tell you that the temple is very nice, but they saw one like it yesterday and all they can think about right now, thank you, is that their feet hurt.

Others in the group may be at a mid-level of awareness. You see them noticing the great craft that went into building the temple, studying the art, the sculptures, the architecture, the curve of the ceiling, the way voices vibrate off walls. If you address them, they may remark on how impressive a structure it is, wondering when it was built and reading inscriptions and plaques to learn more.

There may be others, however, at a higher level of awareness. They stand in awe of all that has gone on before, seem to be stunned, to be able to feel what it means to be there. If you talked to them, and they could catch their breath, they might tell you that they were experiencing a "knowing," a sense of wonder, an understanding beyond words. And if you are perceptive about it, you will notice that they don't seem to be tired, or cold, or bored, or uncomfortable. And it is likely their feet don't hurt.

That is how and why to get to higher levels of awareness. That is why, as we evolve, the ugliness around us won't matter so much, the fray, the noise, the base angers and petty, ego-driven needs. When we are evolved, we will be heart-centered, we will recognize and understand each other's souls, we will see the meanings and grow and learn. And our feet won't hurt.

* * *

When Dr. Victor Frankl came out of the concentration camp at Auschwitz, he not only wrote *Man's Search For Meaning,* but devised a theory of psychotherapy called logotherapy. While Frankl's theory begins with the search for meaning, he writes that, "Ultimately, man should not ask what the meaning of his life is, but rather must recognize that it is *he* who is asked. In a word, each man is questioned by life; and he can only answer to life by *answering for* his own life; to life he can only respond by being responsible."

How can you take that step? How can you take responsibility for your own life? Frankl asks you to take a look at your life as if it has already happened and yet you may change what has happened in the future. In an extraordinary "categorical imperative," he words it this way: *So live as if you were living already for the second time and as if you had acted the first time as wrongly as you are about to act now!*

Look at your actions as if you would have a second chance and could get it right before you get it wrong.

That would require quite a high level of awareness, don't you think? To do it, you'll have to step out of your life, imagine yourself having already lived it, not being altogether pleased by your choices and being offered those choices again. How can you do it better? As soon as you know, first of all that you **can** do it better, and secondly that **you** can do it better, you are on the road to higher awareness.

Of course, Carlos Casteneda would then insist that, since you now know that you have choices, you must always make the choice that comes from *impeccable integrity*. You see, it gets harder as it goes along, but it is well worth the climb. When you live with impeccable integrity, you never have to apologize to others or to yourself for having fallen short, whatever outcome seems to happen in the objective world.

"Oh what a tangled web we weave, when first we practice to deceive," Sir Walter Scott said. But if we don't deceive, we don't even have to remember the lies we told so we won't get caught in them. Doing the honorable thing also turns out to be doing the most freeing thing.

When you step outside yourself in this way, too, it helps you to see what one of my mentors, Dr. Ronald Wong Jue calls "the rightness of being." That it is all being staged for your benefit. And sometimes it has to be pretty loud and awful to get your attention. That's why it's best if we can all get to a high level of awareness in a hurry. It may spare us a lot of grief and move us quickly along to understanding and the evolutionary leap.

Chapter Twenty-Nine

Taking a
Transforming Journey

On the second Friday of the month we would meet at the house of Ronald Wong Jue, Ph.D., a group of five to six therapists, to practice new transpersonal techniques on ourselves and bring them to our patients and clients. Ron is the leader and he supervises our altered states and guides our journeys.

First we talk about what has transpired in our lives since last we've met. I tend to keep to myself unless something amazing has transpired, in which case I volunteer. This day was meant to be a quiet one until Dr. Jue surprised me by turning and saying to me, "Are you in advertising? Somebody said you were. I only know you as a healer and a writer."

"Yes, "I said, mortified. "I'm in advertising and it becomes increasingly intolerable every day."

"Why is that?"

"Because it goes against everything I believe." I could have explained that it is inimical to my spirit; that being part of a system that encourages people to work themselves silly in meaningless jobs to have enough money to spend on meaningless possessions which it is my job to entice them to want, makes me feel like a thief of their wholeness. Instead, because it was too large a subject to get started on that morning, I simply said, "I'm a vegetarian and one of my clients manufactures beef jerky—"

For some reason, that struck the room as the funniest thing they'd heard all day.

I laughed, too. It was all so incongruous. To redeem myself, I told them about writing this book. And that felt right. Fortunately, the focus faded from me and we began our work of the morning. (You can try this journey for yourself at the end of Chapter Eighteen.)

Dr. Jue said, "get comfortable," then he spoke softly about being aware of our breathing and took us into an easy trance.

He had us "go to our healing place," from which we could look out to the six directions: North, South, East, West, the sky above, the earth below. On the four corners there were mountains to which we were to journey. First to the mountain on the West, where the sun sets. There, we were told to release anything which no longer served us, whether it be a job, a belief, a relationship, an attitude, whatever we chose. Then we returned to our healing space. We flew off then to the South, where our power animal awaited us, a source of strength, and we were to feel where in our bodies (in our chakras) we held these powers, where they manifested.

Again we returned home. On our next journey, we went North, where we were to discover on the mountain an altar which held a symbol of balance, our true essence, resources or vehicles we needed to remind us of our destiny. After we returned home again we made our last trip out, to the East, in which we would find a garden, whatever growing there being a symbol for our new beginnings.

Our journeys completed, Ron brought us up and asked us to describe what we'd encountered. Everyone around the room spoke in turn, some experiences being more profound than others, all being a reiteration of each person's personal theme. It was fascinating how consistent each was to the person's own life's path as we knew it.

The session was to end at one o'clock and at ten minutes to one, the floor was supposed to be mine. But I had neither liked nor understood my journey, odd for me, since I had helped interpret everyone else's to grateful acknowledgements, proving my skills as a therapist.

"Judith?"

"Oh, I mustn't have been concentrating, this time. It wasn't very fruitful. Time's up, anyway, I'm glad to pass. There's nothing much to tell."

Ron has always been quite passive with me, but this time he spoke up. "You know you do this quite a lot," he said. "You dismiss yourself," he went on, gently shaming me into sharing.

So I began telling it rather quickly in what I thought was a lighthearted way. "At the Western mountain I decided to let go of my persona that I use when I am afraid to show my intellect or wisdom. I become ditzy and everyone laughs at me and then no one is threatened. I saw it as a clown costume and I tore it off and threw it into the fire of the volcano.

"At the Southern mountain I met my power animals, including a new one, a dolphin."

"You're still doing it," Ron said. "Rushing through this as if it wouldn't be of much interest to anyone. As if it is supposed to be dismissed."

I slowed down. "On the North mountain I saw the altar, which looked like it might be in Tibet, in the Himalayas, like ancient, corroded metal, and on the altar, the thing which was meant to be my symbol of balance, my true essence, the resource I would need to remind me of my destiny, was a single tear. It turned into a crystal, then back into a tear again.

"And when I got to the mountain in the East and was looking to see what was growing in my garden, I saw nothing growing, nothing, and I said, *something grow!* And then suddenly, babies were growing in my garden, hundreds of babies, a whole giant field of them."

I fell silent, almost embarrassed about these odd visions. But Ron smiled. Reminding me, but not in so many obvious words, that we teach what we have to learn, he pointed out that because I dismiss myself, I help others not to dismiss themselves. It is a theme of my life and it is what I do as a healer. I let people see what is not to be dismissed in themselves, what they deny, and help them be reborn whole.

About the babies, Ron said, "You are a spiritual midwife," and I realized he had said that to me in other contexts, that he'd had that vision for me before. Now I had seen it for myself, in so many symbols.

And the tear? Everyone seemed to come to the conclusion that it is the tear of emotion, which I later figured out was the tear of empathy. It does seem that that is how I help people, by feeling what they are feeling and then turning it with magic (the crystal) into a way they can see themselves so that they can be reborn, whole.

I tell you this story not so much because it is about me, but because it is about the way the magic I am here to tell you about works. Here's a little theory behind transformational journeys.

First of all, if you allow everything you encounter that stops you to become a metaphor, pick it up, acknowledge it, examine it, and thank it, it will tell you why it is there and in what way it serves you. I promise you, you will see everything in a new light.

It is transforming to see something troubling as a sign from the universe that it is listening, instead. In transformational psychology there are three stages of changing dross to gold.

First, you must realize that most of our experiences in life are actually **projections**; they come from within us, as **our interpretation of the event.** Ron puts it this way.

There is the *event*.

Then there is our *interpretation*.

Then our *judgment*.

Then our *reaction*.

But the last three of those come from inside us. The only thing that may be outside is the event.

A simple example might be when a person is mugged in a strange city. That is the *event*. It stands alone. Then what happens? The event is interpreted by the person. The *interpretation* might be that it was a personal attack. The *judgment* might then be "I wasn't careful enough." Or,

"The world is a terrible place." Then comes the *reaction*, which might be that the person becomes paranoid or never visits strange cities again. But everything about this story except for the event, the mugging, has been a product of the person to whom it happened.

The second stage of a transformational journey occurs when the person "owns" these projections. When the person knows that he/she gets to see it any way he/she chooses.

Let's be really idealistic for a minute and pretend our mugging victim is able to find out who the mugger was, goes to his home, and discovers that the person was in desperate straights, needing money for medicine for a loved one.

Admittedly, this is stacking the deck, but how would it change the interpretation, judgment, and reaction?

Or what if the victim decides to invent something that prevents muggings, or helps other victims. Is that too idealistic for you? What about the mother of a child who was killed by a drunken driver and, instead of interpreting it that life is meaningless, formed MADD (Mothers Against Drunken Drivers), which has altered the way we all see drinking and driving and has probably saved hundreds, if not thousands, of lives.

By then, you're at stage three, which is realizing that what is experienced externally is really experienced internally. It's all about you and how you take it.

W. Brugh Joy, MD, in his book *Joy's Way*, writes about the Tibetan Buddhist approach to transforming problems. "The highest and most difficult is to transmute the problem," which is what the MADD mother did when she turned an event into something positive and meaningful.

The second pathway "is to ennoble the problem, to treat it is a necessary and important steppingstone of experience in one's unfolding."

And the third pathway is "to go directly into the problem and allow it to manifest completely...[while making] a portion of one's awareness into a witness that observes the problem. In this way, understanding may come."

Often that means going through it, increasing its intensity. The great psychiatrist Milton Erickson invented a whole method of treating people through altered states which utilized this kind of reverse psychology. If someone came to him weighing 200 pounds and complaining about his/her fat, Erickson would say something like, "Come back to me when you weigh 300 pounds," effectively prescribing the symptom until the person has had enough and can give it up.

"I believe," Dr. Joy writes, "that some of the negative qualities of emotion, such as anger, fear, hostility and depression, are functioning properly only when they lead to insight or when they act as a signal to the outer mind that a flaw in perception or in understanding is occurring."

That's why transforming it is so important. And why it is so important to realize that "the negative response is a signal from inside and not a fact of reality from outside. Your fear does not mean that there is necessarily a real danger, and your depression does not really mean that you are at the bottom."

Of course we all have problems, and many of them are "real." To my way of thinking there are two ways to deal with them. The most obvious, and least useful way is to resist and resent them, in which case they seem to hurt all the more, because of the focus we put on them. The healthier way is to transform them using metaphors, pictures in your mind or stories that help see the situation in a new light and your own powers in brilliant strength. (See final chapter.)

In our hypnosis training we learned about the surprising way the brain works. Try this exercise and see for yourself:

EXERCISE: We were instructed to "close your eyes and picture or imagine any animal you like, any animal in God's kingdom. Except the elephant. Don't picture an African elephant with those big ears charging at you, or an Indian elephant with the little house-seat and someone riding in it. Or a *circus elephant with big, sparkley decorations on it, don't picture a circus elephant...' And pretty soon we were all laughing, not able to thinking about anything else! Your mind doesn't hear the "don't", the "not," it only sees the pictures.*

If you think "I won't be unhappy. I hate my body. I'm not going to eat brownies," or any other admonition that focuses on something you want out of your life, you are simply inviting it in, like it or not. And that is what happens with resistance. You spend all your energy giving the thing that is making you miserable more power. Turning it into an elephant charging at you.

In this way we set up what Dr. Jue calls a Resonance Pattern. We program ourselves, "I'm a loser," "I'm a victim," and our reality complies to make it so.

The alternative, as we've been discussing, is to transform your problems. Seeing them metaphorically can change the picture in your mind. As Dr. Jue says, you can't be a knight without a dragon. You can't be Tarzan without a crocodile pit. Any kind of hero you want to be requires the challengers to test you. You need your parents playing whatever role they play in your life so you can be you and grow your way out of the situation.

All of the healing that we do, including the physical repairs when our burned skin grows back or our broken bones knit, is a movement towards stasis, towards balance and wholeness. Opposites provide the energies which propel our eternal balancing act, our highwire tilting first one way and then the other in our journey toward wholeness.

If you can think of all there is, all of life, as a metaphor, a play to illustrate something we need to experience, and the universe as meaningful, then understanding becomes the way to transform all sadness. And transformation becomes a matter of our simply being our own magic decoder rings.

Interchapter 6:

Matter, Quantum Physics and The Holographic Universe

"If the doors of perception were cleansed,
everything would be seen as it is, infinite"

—*William Blake*

"'Mastering Reality' Means Limiting the Possibilities"

—*JSP*

Here's the Interchapter that puts it all together: the marriage of science and mysticism.

Part I: Three-dimensional reality

People talk about "reality" as if there were such a thing and we could all agree upon it. "Get real!" they say if they think your head is in the clouds. Often, it's "harsh reality," we have to deal with, which means if you'd like to see it another way, you're a dreamer.

And this reality of theirs, it's not very flexible. There's reality and then there's the way you might like it to be, might wish it to be, but reality doesn't bend, no sir.

Well, then how about all of those people, going way back, who aren't so sure this reality stuff is all that hard and fast. Plato saying what we perceive as reality is but a shadow of it against a cave wall. Buddha saying that this world is only an illusion.

In Emanuel Kant's *Critique of Pure Reason*, he said it another way. What he figured was that all we can know about what's "out there," is only what we can see through our limited senses. We interpret everything through our personal filters. There is no real, objective reality out there.

An example, an analogy? How we see color.

If a baby were told that "red" was called "blue," how would we ever know, when he saw an apple and called it "blue," whether he saw a "blue" or a red apple? How, in fact, do you know that you and I see the same "red" apple? (Some might argue that we can tell when people are color-blind, but that means we know what they don't or can't see, not exactly what they do see.) What I see as red can in no objective way be compared with what you see, except by the length of its wave. But then it is a wave, not a color. Color is perceived inside us, subjectively.

All of reality, Kant said, whatever is thinkable and nameable, conforms to the inherent structure of our minds. That includes material objects, time, space, causality, etc.

Sir John Eccles, the eminent English neurologist and Nobel Prize winner puts it this way: "I want you to realize that there is no color in the natural world and no sounds—nothing of this kind; no textures, no patterns, no beauty, no scent." They reside in us; without our participation in the universe, all that does not exist.

Einstein contended that the real external world "rests exclusively on sense-impressions," and that "all knowledge about reality begins with experience and terminates in it."

Why has it taken us so long to discover that three-dimensional reality is not "out there" at all, but is a function of our perceptions? I believe there are three major reasons why we have been trapped in this illusion.

1) We trust our senses. That has tended to mislead us, but it is an honest and understandable mistake. Even when we know better, we'd rather believe our senses. That's why this information that goes against our senses isn't easy to impart. For example, when trying to communicate it, I sometimes imagine myself on some prehistoric or perhaps Early Roman talk show in the Coliseum. The host is jovial, close-minded, and confrontational. I say to him, "Our senses tell us that the sun, moon and stars go around the earth and that the earth stands still. But I'm here to tell you that the earth rotates around the sun and through the stars. And that the moon rotates around the earth. Oh, yes, and the earth isn't flat, but round and it rotates on its own axis every twenty-four hours."

Could you imagine his response? "Ladies and Senators, this woman would have us believe that the earth is spinning but we can't feel it, and that people are living on the underside of what she imagines is a globe. How are they standing there? On their heads? Anyone with one wit of sense can see that the Earth is the center of the universe and the universe spins around the Earth. Thanks a lot for all that useful information. Guards, feed her to the lions."

Point being, though what I've said is true, it is still almost impossible to think of the sun and moon's activities as anything but rising and setting.

Conclusion? Even if we wind up believing that reality isn't reality at all, we will, of course, act as if it were. Even though we've just shown that seeing is not necessarily believing.

Anyway, what we see is not so much a product of what's "out there," but of the structure of our eyes. If I were a frog, I would see mostly shadow and movement. If something were small and moved nearby, I'd try to eat it. If it were large and moved, I'd jump away to avoid being eaten. If it didn't move at all, big or small, I wouldn't see it.

If I were a cat, I'd see in black and white; a bumble bee, I'd see infra-red, which now I cannot see.

As it is, we can see only our limited color spectrum and only in three-dimensions. That's all right, but we should know it's limited. The visible spectrum is, after all, less than 10 percent of what we have learned about, so far, as the electromagnetic spectrum. That means we *can't* see more than 90 percent of the *known* electromagnetic spectrum.

There are two more thoughts about seeing that make what we see even more ambiguous:

The first is that there is a part of the brain that simply interprets what we see. In his book, *The Man Who Mistook His Wife for a Hat,* Dr. Oliver Sachs told us of people whose interpretive facility has been damaged. They are able to "see" things (that is, their eyes register objects as they've always done) but they are not able to recognize or know what they are. It is as if they had just landed on a planet of new shapes and configurations and everything before them presents itself as a mystery, a puzzle. Is this a cup to drink from or a shoe to wear? Is this person I see clearly before me and who claims to be my wife of 30 years actually my wife? Yes, I recognize her voice. This means that "seeing" is in part seeing and in part interpretation of what is seen from a different part of the brain.

What's even more dramatic is that apparently "less than 50 percent of what we 'see' is actually based, at all, on information entering our eyes. The remaining 50 percent plus is pieced together out of our expectations of what the world should look like," says Michael Talbot in *The Holographic Universe,* on studies begun by Karl Pribram of Stanford University and followed by others. Our eyes may be the lenses, but the brain makes it up, fills it in, filters it out. *Half of our seeing is not seeing at all, but assumptions.*

* * *

So, why should we care about what else might be "out there" that we can't measure? Because that is our source of infiniteness.

Then there's Robert A Monroe. In trying to figure out "where" he goes when he journeys out of body (or where we go, perhaps, when we dream), he writes about Locale II. As we now know through quantum physics (details to come), all of what we think of as matter is really waves and particles or maybe even vibrating strings. Therefore, there may be an "infinity of worlds all operating at different frequencies," one of which is this physical world. "Those world can share the same space as do the various wave frequencies in the electro-magnetic spectrum." Monroe's speculation: where we go when we dream or go out of body might just be here, in the space we share with things from other frequencies we can't see.

Or, putting it another way, imagine having only a Geiger counter to measure what is in the room around you in which you now sit reading this book. Imagine yourself blind-folded, relying on the machine to tell you what is beside you. You set the counter out to click off what's there. It wouldn't measure the furniture, the depth or breadth of the room, how hot or cold it is, whether music is playing. It wouldn't register life itself, the people, the cat sleeping on the sofa, the bird singing in the cage. It might even say that nothing is in the room, because it, a Geiger counter meant to measure radioactivity, doesn't see anything else. What if we, relying on our five senses only, are like that Geiger counter?

Good analogy, but then someone will say, what about stuff we bump into? It makes no literal sense to say that there's no "out there" out there if you can't then walk through that wall. Here are some of my thoughts on that subject. First of all, we bump into stuff in dreams, and none of that is "solid" as we experience it in three-dimensions; secondly, it is through a sense—touch—that we know things are solid, and that, again, is subjective. (If you told that same poor, misguided baby that soft is called "hard," would we know what he feels when he pets a rabbit and says "hard?" Would we think the problem was in his fingers rather than his vocabulary? Would we think, how sad, the rabbit feels hard to him, he cannot enjoy the feeling of soft?)

And thirdly, if everything is waves and particles moving in profusion, as quantum physics suggests, then maybe "solid" is an illusion. Here's my speculation: all of reality is like a wheel with spokes which is spinning so quickly it appears solid and through which you cannot poke you hand, even though, if it came to a stop, we would be able to see that it is made up mostly of space!

The philosopher A. Eddington put it this way: "I very much doubt if anyone of us has the faintest idea of what is meant by the reality of existence of anything besides our own egos."

Well, how come, then, we've all agreed that reality is as it appears and it is outside of us and everything is separate and apart if that's not really the case?

I said there were three basic reasons why we're stuck believing that three-dimensions are "reality" and the first was that we trusted our senses exclusively.

2) We have succeeded so well in three dimensions that we have decided that the proof of something's existence is that we can use three-dimensional means to measure it! We have mastered three-dimensions so thoroughly, made such great progress in it, that we now believe that only that which can be measured by our three-dimensional tools is "real." What a trap. Now we're locked in that rhetorical tautological system. We have to be able to "prove" something is real three-dimensionally, or we discount it. That was, of course, until the advent of quantum physics.

Which leads us to our third reason we've been victims of the three-dimensional belief system.

3) Cartesian philosophy and Newtonian physics. On November 10, 1619, Descartes had a dream in which he saw the universe laid out in logical, mathematical order, a giant scheme that was formulated, regular, predictable. The symbol, the analogy he used was a clock: the universe and all there is, is a ticking mechanical clock, ticking away with regularity, made of disparate pieces. Descartes' ruminations also resulted in man's being divided into two parts, mind and body, with

the body affecting the mind, but no influence going the other way. In his scheme, the mind did not affect the body. (This was important, because the mind is not logical, not controllable. It is unpredictable, not orderly, and therefore it would be a sorry universe that responded to thoughts rather than material substance and laws.) The body, too, was a machine and with the acceptance of that model, we lost the religious, social, metaphysical context of larger meaning, lost it to self-centered individuality.

A century later, Isaac Newton picked up the illusion of a mechanistic universe and explained the "laws" which predict natural events— mathematical, mechanical laws of the universe. No longer was the universe a web of interrelated occurrences; it was a lifeless structure of lifeless design. In *The Quantum Self*, Danah Zohar says that, according to Newton, "Things moved because they were fixed and determined; cold silence pervaded the once-teaming heavens. Humans beings and their struggles, the whole consciousness, and life itself were irrelevant to the workings of the vast universal machine."

When we bought into Newton's universe, we agreed to see everything as solid and discrete, and so we have. We made a pact with the three-dimensional world, a pact that has "worked" so well, we've been stuck in it until Einstein had a dream of his own and Relativity Theory and then Quantum Physics were born.

Judith's simplified version of Quantum Physics with apologies to everyone who knows better. No, I won't even try. There is nothing simple, or easily comprehensible about it. Even the people working in the field and speaking its language find it so mysterious, many prefer to talk in equations.

All right, then, here are the experts' words. (For readers who's rather just find out what it all really means to you, jump ahead to the third part of these Interchapter notes: The Holographic Universe.)

* * *

Part II. Einstein's Revolution

Because both Relativity and Quantum Physics deal with matters so enormous (the universe) and/or so very fast moving, or so minuscule they are invisible to the eye, the applications to daily life are not readily obvious. One important effect of these discoveries, however, was the realization by many thinkers that it was possible and even wise to learn to live with paradoxes. Brilliant metaphysicians had known this all along, but somehow it was too painful to hold conflicting thoughts in one brain without a fast and final resolution.

Ancient wisdom had often referred to opposites making the whole, the yin and yang. They had told us that there is no such thing as the idea of big without the idea of small. Big is relative. A cat is big to a bug, a cow is big to a cat, a car is big to a cow, a hill is big to a car, a mountain is big to a hill, the planet is big to a mountain, and this planet is small compared to a lot of other things filling our skies. There is no right without wrong, no good without bad, no faith without doubt. There is no foolish without wise. There is even no life without death, and if we ever find ourselves enjoying eternal life, it'll have to be thought of as something else, like beingness, as opposed to nothingness.

The greatest contrast of all occurred with the head-on collision of ideas when Einstein's special theory of relativity assaulted all that was smugly established in the Newtonian universe. Newton had seen time as linear, space as empty, matter as matter and energy as something else, but definitely not matter.

And Einstein turned what had been so clear and reliable inside out.

In discussing the velocity of light, the question seemed to be "Does light behave like a bullet or like the sound of the gunshot?" I refer you to Robert H. March's *Physics for Poets*, for a more detailed explanation, but I'll present two analogies that might help you to picture the problem. The one explained by March goes as follows. Imagine a bullet fired off the front of a moving train. Because the train is moving too, the bullet moves even faster than it would if it were fired at a stand still. It acquires the velocity of the train in addition to its normal speed. As for the sound, however, that doesn't acquire the speed of the train, traveling instead through the air at its usual rate. If you were standing at the station and could measure these things, the sound would seem to you to be traveling normally, but the bullet would travel faster than usual. However, if you were on the train, you would have a different experience of the speed of both objects. Measuring them, you would find that the bullet travels at its normal speed, because you're in the train, moving with it, and the sound moves slower than normal forward, faster than normal backward. Marsh explains Einstein's postulate this way: "to the man on the train, light behaves like a bullet, while to the man on the ground it behaves like the sound of the shot!"

Put another way by a friend with infinite patience, let's say you're playing ping-pong on a train. You bounce the ball in place, and to you, it just moves up and down. But, if I were watching you from the station and saw you on the moving train bouncing the ball, it would look to me like it was going up and down **and** forward at the speed of the train.

One of the ways I understood this business of things being relative to the observer was by contemplating the constellation Orion in the sky. It's hard to believe that if you stood on Antares there would be no Orion, because it exists only from our point of view, but that is true. Those scattered stars make a picture to us on earth, but nothing like it to an observer standing elsewhere. Like beauty, everything is in the eye of the beholder.

However you think of it, if you think of it, the effect was that the observer had become part of the equation.

Right away, rules started flying out the window.

Newtonians had thought that waves were part of the ether but that particles were the building blocks of matter. Quantum physicians began studying small packets of energy and discovering that each way of describing being, as a wave or a particle, complements the other. And to get the whole picture, you need to piece it together from these independent clues.

Moreover, if they measured for a wave, they found a wave. If they measured for a particle, they found a particle. Sir William Bragg stated in ironic amazement: "Elementary particles seem to be waves on Mondays, Wednesdays and Fridays, and particles on Tuesdays, Thursdays and Saturdays."

When Heisenberg developed his Uncertainty Principle, the wave-or-particle question got sorted out in the kind of ambiguity for which this field had now become famous. It seemed that in order to fully isolate the answer, we need to be able to describe both the wave and particle function. But, we cannot measure both at the same time. We can either measure the exact position of an electron when it manifests itself as a particle, or we can measure its momentum (its speed) when it expresses itself as a wave. Waves express themselves in motion. Particles, when they choose to be particles or we choose to see them as particles can have position. We simply cannot measure the two aspects both at exactly the same time.

What is more, again the observer figures in. Heisenberg also realized that the act of observing something changes it, there was no way to avoid that. Physicist John Archibald Wheeler has written: "In some strange sense, this is a participatory universe. Beyond particles, beyond fields of force, beyond geometry, beyond space and time themselves, is the ultimate constituent [of all there is], the still more ethereal act of observer-participancy?"

By the time we began in vague ways to understand that all possibilities exist as wave functions and that reality occurs when a wave function collapses, Erwin Schrodinger demonstrated that, in a manner of speaking, reality happens when we observe it. Science had moved definitively away from an external, fixed, material universe.

In *The Common Sense of Science*, J. Bronowski sums it up this way: "Physics does not consist of events; it consists of observations, and between the event and us who observes it there must pass a signal—a ray of light perhaps, a wave or an impulse—which simply cannot be taken out of the observation....Event, signal and observer: that is the relationship which Einstein saw as the fundamental unit in physics. Relativity is the understanding of the world not as events but as relations."

Add to this the impossible complexity of String Theory which postulates 11 dimensions in which, ultimately, reality is a mass of infinitely small strings which are defined by their vibrations, and maybe nothing is as it appears.

So, let's stop and think about it. We're trying to find out why miracles happen against what we know, or thought we knew about science, matter, bodies, time, etc.

Well, if it is true, as some quantum theorists, such as Niels Bohr and Heisenberg, postulate, that "fundamental reality itself is essentially indeterminate, that there is no clear, fixed, underlying 'something' to our daily existence that can ever be known," then our assumptions have to change. "Everything about reality is and remains a matter of probabilities."

Heisenberg and David Bohm, two of the most important physicists of our time, are quoted in Dossey's *Recovering the Soul*: "Shortly before his death, Heisenberg published a paper which contained the proposal that certain fundamental, mechanistic, common-sense concepts such as 'being composed of' and 'having distinct and nameable parts' may be meaningless for the ultimates with which physics seeks to deal.

"And physicist Bohm expressed the same sentiment. 'Thus,' he said, 'one is led to a new notion of *unbroken wholeness* which denies the classical idea of analyzability of the world into separately and independently existent parts.'"

Some of the world's greatest thinkers have said in so many words that reality is not what we think it is. You may be glad to find out this is so, because it is infinitely more wondrous, more magical, infinitely more infinite than we've been led to believe by archaic, mechanistic thinking.

Every time you've "known" something that you "had no right to know," picked it up out of the astral plane, had a "hunch," gotten a "feeling," dreamed a prophetic dream, it has been that something more. Chopra says "Intuition is the non-local cosmic field of information that whispers to you in the silence between your thoughts.' It comes from somewhere else, and it is meant for you. Accept it with thanks.

My notes on "time" appeared in the Interchapter 3, but for now, if you just allow yourself to question whether what we believe about matter may not be objectively accurate (that we may never be able to know, objectively, what matter is), then follow along for the Holographic Universe, the most provocative, wonderful explanation of consciousness ever devised.

* * *

Part III. The Holographic Universe

> *"One can disintegrate the world by means of very strong light.*
> *For weak eyes the world becomes solid,*
> *for still weaker eyes it seems to develop fists,*
> *for eyes weaker still it becomes*
> *shamefaced and smashes anyone who dares to gaze upon it."*

—*Franz Kafka*

This astounding theory was put forward by two major scientists from two different disciplines, working independently, at first, to come to these conclusions, and then working in unison.

Karl Pribram, was a brain researcher-neurosurgeon from Stanford University studying the brains of mice to learn where in that organ they held memory. Much to his surprise, no matter how much brain he removed, there seemed to be traces, however faint, of remembering. David Bohm was a theoretical physicist at the University of London.

Both men have impeccable credentials, so when they proposed the theory of the holographic universe, the world of science had to listen.

I don't do it a favor by oversimplifying it, but here goes—the more easily digestible points of that theory:

1) The brain is a hologram, interpreting a holographic universe. It does this by interpreting frequencies from another dimension which is beyond time and space, a realm of meaningful, patterned primarily reality. From that realm, our brain mathematically constructs what we consider "concrete" reality.

2) Most importantly, what follows from that is that the individual brain is a mirror of, a piece of, the whole universe.

Why do they say the universe, and our brains, are holograms?

Holograms, as everyone who's ever been to Disneyland knows, are projections which seem three dimensionally suspended in space. The way that they work is as follows. A coherent light source, (a laser beam) is split into two parts. One part passes through a half-silvered mirror. That portion is called the reference beam and it goes directly to a photographic plate. The remaining portion of light is reflected by the mirror toward the object to be holographed.

When the reflection of the object hits the photographic plate, it interferes with the beam of coherent light already there. And at the place where the two beams interact, they make an interference pattern on the photographic plate to form the holographic plate. Some poetic writers of this phenomenon use the analogy of pebbles thrown into a still pond to illustrate the interference pattern. As the waves criss-cross against each other, in some places doubling up to make a higher wave, in others canceling each other out, a pattern is formed.

When a beam of coherent light is passed through the plate, the three dimensional, holographic vision appears, free floating. Out there.

What is uniquely wonderful about a hologram, besides the obvious thrill of its three-dimensional projection in air, is that the plate itself contains the image in a particularly unusual way. Instead of being fixed like a photographic negative, the information which generates the image is smeared across it in that interference pattern.

Cut up the holographic plate and you get not two halves of a hologram, but two whole holograms, each slightly fuzzier than the original but each the full picture in its entirety. Cut it up again and you get more and more, smaller and smaller, less refined pictures of the whole.

The Pribram-Bohm theory of a holographic universe comes from the unique fact that *any piece of this hologram contains the whole picture.* Just as the memory was smeared, however faintly, across the mice's brains.

And just so, say Bohm and Pribram, is the mind to the universe. A piece of the whole.

Just as the gene in any cell in the body is a piece of the entire whole and has the DNA information necessary to construct another the whole body, so the entire universe is contained in each of its parts.

Just as an atom and its electrons mirrors the solar system.

Just as ontogeny recapitulates phylogeny (I learned that in biology and always loved the sound of it: it means that the history of man's rise from a single cell, through fish, amphibian, and mammalian stages, is repeated by every single fetus (we even have gills at one point) until we become a person, ready to be born). Within our DNA we carry bits of codes for all other living things, insects, fish, plants, the whole spectrum of life.

Just as the percentage of salt in our blood is equivalent to the percentage of salt in the ocean.

As the song insists: you are everything and everything is you.

Each of us is a little universe.

This also takes us full circle to our senses and how we see. Dr. Brugh Joy writes, "With all of our deepening understanding of the modality of vision, we do not understand how light, entering the eye and being transmitted back to the visual cortex is manipulated to make objects appear outside our heads. [Think of it! Why don't we see in our brains where the information is translated?!] The holographic theory comes closest to a possible solution."

It does happen that these two extraordinary scientists traveled in circles which included Alan Watts, Krishnamurti and Einstein, so they were uniquely situated between the scientific world and the mystical to bring the two together.

There are many more mysteries which this theory explains. For example, in his book *The Holographic Universe*, Michael Talbot points out the wide array of "previously inexplicable phenomena" which this theory helped illuminate, including the work on near death experiences of Dr. Kenneth Ring, psychologist from the University of Connecticut, in which death can be seen not as an end, but as a "shifting of a person's consciousness from one level of the hologram of reality to another," as Talbot puts it. He discusses Dr. Stanislav Grof's work as chief of psychiatric research at the Maryland Psychiatric Research Center and at Johns Hopkins University as assistant professor of psychiatry, utilizing this theory to explain the collective unconscious and other altered states of consciousness. He points out that Fred Alan Wolf, physicist, used this model to explain lucid dreams (those which are so vivid, we can actually step out of them and affect their direction) as trips taken to parallel realities. In addition, Dr. F. David Peat's book *Synchronicity: The Bridge Between Matter and Mind* uses the holographic theory to explain why those coincidences which are so much more meaningful occur. He calls them "flaws in the fabric of reality," a sort of peek around corners we were not meant to turn.

It's also been speculated that everyday beta wavelength brain waves might be considered incoherent waves, as incandescent light from a light bulb is. In an altered state our brain waves could become "coherent," as the laser is the coherent light that allows a hologram to materialize. In his book, *Vibrational Medicine*, Richard Gerber, M.D., writes, "Long-term meditators attempting certain psychic feats...were found to have brain wave patterns of increased energetic coherence during psychic events." He also reports increased hemispheric synchronization which shows up when people are performing psychic functions, as well as movement toward the delta/theta range of brain wave frequencies.

The upshot of this theory, then, is that when we are in an altered state, probably when our brain waves are at Delta–which used to be thought of as the sleep state but now is speculated to be the "radar" state—we may be picking up messages from the universal hologram. The possibilities are not only astounding, they are glorious.

Why do we want to know all this? It confirms our awareness of our being infinite, allows us to reach beyond self-imposed limitations and allows us to experience greater understanding and connectedness with all there is.

And being in an altered state is natural to us. Every time you get "dreamy" and nobody knows where you are, not even you...that is where you are. When you are driving your car and manage to get home without having noticed one stop sign of light, you were in a "trance." When your significant other says "Are you asleep?" and you're not quite, and yet you cannot or do not want to break the spell by answering, you are in an altered state. And it is there that you receive the wisdom, the precognitions, the enlightenment that you cannot explain and do not talk about.

Another crucial reason to know this is because of what we have to gain if we can become in sync with the whole, with the universe with which we were meant to resonate, because it is us. As we recognize our relation to the universe we can experience love, joy, creativity, our hologram resonating with the universal hologram. Where we didn't resonate, we would recognize a sense of being fragmented, separate and apart from the wholeness, stuck in our fears, anxiety, doubts, and angers. We would recognize where we needed healing. Healing could occur on every level if we could just get to who and what we are and what we are meant to be, which is not separate and apart, but connected.

We were not meant to live in fear. Fear is a signal that something is wrong. We are meant to address it and move on in confidence. The fight-or-flight syndrome built into us was meant to be used when we had to escape a predator. We were supposed to have a spurt of adrenaline for the energy to run away from a man-eating lion in the jungle and, when safe, we were supposed to get the all-clear and have our bodies go back to a relaxed mode. But as we saw in Interchapter 1 on the Mind/Body relationship, there is no all-clear in modern life.

The work I do is meant to provide people with a carpet of calm. That carpet of calm, that underlying wholeness is harmony with the vibration of the earth, the song of the universe.

Once in a moment of quiet (the source of all true knowledge) these words came to me: "It is harder to live frightened than brave." Now is the time to be brave.

Chapter Thirty

The Next Wisdom?

"The 21st Century will be religious or spiritual or it will not be at all."

—*Andre Malraux*

"The fact that there is nothing but a spiritual world deprives us of hope and gives us certainty."

—*Franz Kafka*

Over the centuries, wisdom has been wisdom.

In the popular book *Conversations With God*, the universal truths are reiterated: Thought is creative; fear attracts its own kind; love is everything.

I am indulging myself with this chapter because I believe that I have something to add to the wisdom of the centuries.

While the wisdom doesn't change, I believe that it is presented to us in forms we are able to understand as we are ready for it. As we would explain things rudimentarily to a child and more sophisticatedly as the child grew, so I believe we have been given the wisdom we are capable of understanding.

As we become more evolved, we become able to accept more complicated concepts and see things anew. And I believe we are ready for the next, most intangible ideas.

273

Here is an example of the way in which the wisdom we receive has been parceled out to match our readiness to absorb it.

The Old Testament talks of an eye for an eye. (That actually has been misinterpreted to mean one is owed or must take an eye for an eye, while the true meaning is that one may not take **more** than an eye, may not take a hand, a foot and an ear as well as an eye in return for the loss of an eye. If you kill my child, I may kill yours, but not your wife, your brother and all of your animals.)

An eye for an eye regulated the urge for revenge, a primitive but very human emotion.

Then along came Jesus and the New Testament, thinking we were ready to hear it, with the concept of "Turn the other cheek." Everyone in the healing business knows that until one forgives, one hurts. Buddha said, "Resentment is like a hot rock you carry around in your hand in the hopes that you get to throw it at somebody."

We may or may not have been ready to understand that concept, moving up from revenge to forgiveness, but as soon as we understand that forgiving, not revenge, is the answer to anger, we will be able to move out of an-eye-for-an-eye justice. Obviously we still have secular hatreds, tribal in nature even in civilized countries; we make villains of those who are not like us and are often locked in the idea of the "right" to avenge injustice. The new message has come, so there is new wisdom in the world whenever we are ready to discard the hot rock and move on.

The following thoughts have been banging around inside my head and insist on being told, so I am presenting them as the next level of wisdom. I hope I can express this theory well enough so that others, seeing in it some promise, agree that even if we cannot yet live by it, it can be a star to which we can affix our sights and toward which we can move on our evolutionary climb.

Here's the message: That we must look to the meaning, not the specific details of our lives. That we must look to the metaphor, not the literal facts in the matter. That who and what we are is larger than what "happened" to us, and as we are able to transform the incidents into symbols, let go of the concrete "facts" and move on to the meaning, we will be different beings.

It seems to me that we reach points in life where it is time for us to shift gears and change, if we are to grow. So, often we resist these impulses and dig in to the familiar, even if it is not working for us. But because we are not in sync with the universe and our own unfolding, something has to happen to give us what my friend calls, "The cosmic frying pan over the head."

When Christopher Reeve became paralyzed—our Superman, suddenly in a useless body—we had to redefine who and what a person really is, because he was still Superman to us, a hero even in that blasted wheelchair. When Michael J. Fox showed us the face of ALS, and it was a face we loved, we became involved in the search for a cure. By their public suffering and courage, they draw us all closer and move us to new levels of compassion, which is not really about the disease or infirmity, but about something larger that we all share.

My good friend Judith Acosta worked with very brutalized children at Daytop Village. Their parents have abused them, battered them, they are drug addicts, themselves; they have had no childhood. When they ask her "Why me?" she offers them an answer that lifts them above the role of victim, if they choose to take it. Why did it happen to them? "So that you can be a hero," she says. And some go on to slay the dragons and prove her right.

Here's my point, and it is a wild one:

It doesn't matter what may be the specifics of the incident that makes us change, that turns us around, that makes us see everything differently. It could be an illness. It could be a loss. It could be an accident.

It sounds callous to say it doesn't matter. When someone gets cancer, loses a parent or child, is injured in a crash, these are tragic events. What I mean is that the specifics of the event are not what they are really about or what they are there for, off the page.

E. M. Forester, the author of *Howard's End* and *Room With A View* among other classic novels, described storytelling this way: "…the sense of a solid mass ahead, a mountain round or over or through which the story must somehow go, is most valuable and, for the novels I've tried to write, essential. There must be something, some major object towards which one is to approach."

If we could think of our lives as a story, then we would understand that our main character, **us**, cannot simply enjoy only the fruits and have it be an otherwise uneventful life. There is a good reason for this. We would never get to know the main character's *character*. How is this person when challenged? How brave? How wise? How sensitive? How thoughtful?

But the particular "mountain round or through" which the main character must go is variable and not the point. He/she could meet a giant, or a dragon or a wicked witch. Can you see that, while the specifics would be different in each case—does he behead the giant, slay the dragon, dissolve the witch?—it is about and for the character that this "obstacle" appears.

So it doesn't really matter, ultimately, what the challenge is, only how we respond to it.

In the Tao it is put this way:
When we know where we come from,
who we really are,
we naturally become more tolerant,
more disinterested, more amused.

We watch and allow. We let it be and see the sense in it as it plays out.

I believe that everything that happens to us is not so much so we can learn a "lesson," but to have an experience we can generalize from, symbolically.

If we can see our lives symbolically, metaphorically, we can see meaning. And I believe that we will come to understand that that is why we are here.

There's a Gerard Manly Hopkins poem in which he says
"What I do is *me. For this I came.*"
I see it in healing. When people give up the need to say, "And then my mother did this, and my father said this..," when they let go of the specifics but hold tight to who they really are—"I am the one who survived, who became the person here today full of unlimited potential"— they will have taken that next step up the evolutionary ladder.

Let me put it another way, again somewhat literary. What if we could understand that our lives were not about the subject matter, not about the story, but about the theme. When I ask my sister, the romance writer, what her new book is about, she will always say something like, "It's about a woman in the 1890s who lives on a farm and is poor and meets two men, one rich and powerful, but cruel and one is poor and has a dream about..."

That is the story line. When I ask her what her book is about, I don't mean the details. I mean the theme. In that case, she might say, "It's about the triumph of love over greed." Or, "It's about how we hurt each other and nothing goes right until we figure out how not to do that."

And even if we are not there yet, even if we need to stick to the "details," there are ways that we can shift the perception to use this theory. Let's say that we are meant to be on a particular path, meant to unfold in a way unique to us and in rhythm with the particles and waves or strings that surround us. And let's say that we are moving down the wrong path, way off for our own completion and wholeness. So, the universe gives us a whack upside the head.

We get cancer, or lose our mother or the house burns down.

The customary human response at the level at which we function now is to focus on the pain in the head. Hey! I just got hit in the head. See my bruise? Hey, it hurts. Instead of saying, Wait a second! What was that?

I have worked with people who have come to realize the message in their crisis and let go of the details. Yes, many will say, "I'm so unlucky. I got cancer. Why did this happen to me? I'm a good person. Now I have to have chemo. I'm going to be afraid for the rest of my life." Yet I have been honored to know others who say, "In a way the cancer brought me closer to the meaning in my life. I recognized the value of my life and those I love. Everything came to the point at which I finally had to stop and appreciate the gifts I had, which in my health and haste I had overlooked."

My dear friend, Toni, when she found out she had cancer and decided to go on a search for alternative therapies, would smile and say, "This is going to be interesting," whether she was infusing herself with ozone, eating raw meat, sucking raw eggs and drinking the Chinese tea she dubbed "rhinoceros piss," hearing a variety of doctors and experts telling her that her cancer had metastasized or taking "zaps" from an electromagnetic machine. As she lived in San Francisco and I in LA, we worked together night after night on the phone, in her case slowly reducing the size of the growth. But the most important aspect of her healing was that she meant it when she said it would be "interesting," that it would be quite an adventure. I have never seen a person experience a challenge with that much grace or wise "disinterest."

Similarly, most would say, "How could it happen that my mother/husband/wife would die and abandon me? I needed her/him. Every single day I'm going to miss her/him and feel deprived and like an orphan. It's not fair." And while that is true, it might also be valid to see it this way: "You know, I really miss my mother and I'm sorry she's no longer here to share my life with me. But, you know, since she passed, I've discovered some things about myself I never knew, interests I somehow hadn't pursued, ideas I didn't know were mine. It's all been quite a revelation."

You may have seen it for yourself in a story like Maggie's, when she lost her only son to a hit-and-run accident (Chapter Eight):

> **No matter how tragic our stories,**
> **when we see the meaning, we smile.**

Odd as it seems, that's the truth. When we move our stories up from the sad, specific details to a higher understanding ("Oh, I see. It's not the person, it's the love.") our bodies relax, our minds are at peace. And we smile.

* * *

Some people believe it will be through archetypes that we will understand ourselves and our lives metaphorically. That's fine. As long as the literal facts begin to dissolve.

And I also believe that the reason we are now deluged with "virtual" everythings is to prove to us that there no longer **are** any "facts." History, of course, has always been an art, rather than a science, presented through the eyes of those (usually the victorious) who recorded it. "History is the version of past events that people have decided to agree upon," Napoleon said. The moment that it is no longer the present, it is reconstructed through an observer and therefore no longer "factual." Yet another reminder that everything is relative to the observer.

Then, as all of our information becomes digital and therefore infinitely manipulatable—so that photographs and film can invent and "document" what never happened, audio can take five sounds tones of your voice and reconstruct sentences you never said—we are being made to give up the facts and go for the meaning.

While this hurts the part of us that wants to nail things down, it must begin to call to our creative side. It must begin to invite us to search for overarching themes, understanding beyond the facts into the wisdom.

Everything but this moment is fiction.

When we make up stories, we know they aren't "true." And yet, sometimes, the truest things we ever experience are fictional. Think of movie that explained the world to you, that made some mystery clear so that you could generalize and say I see what was really happening and I see how it works for my life.

That's your choice then. Some people believe that every time you raise your level of awareness, you raise your actual physical vibration. I've felt that power when I've done healing work. It is ours to reach out and touch, as soon as we grasp the idea.

Metaphors, stories, symbols, archetypes are the next step in understanding. The sooner we look for meaning and let go of resentments and petty details, the quicker we'll raise our stature as the most a human can be. And the easier it will be to smile.

Exercises

In this section you'll find some of the exercises and practices I've used that continue to help me open doors and examine my relationship to the world.

If you choose, you can use them to explore stepping out of yourself, how you experience time, your mind/body, finding guides, even the meaning of life.

Exercise: Stepping Out

Here's an exercise I use just to get into the mode of connecting with consciousness beyond my daily awareness. This is an important one, even though it may seem simple. In my mind, I simply "step out of myself," and then I "watch" myself as I do something. For example, I could do it if I were reading this book. All you have to do is step outside of yourself and watch yourself as you read this book and react to the ideas I'm presenting here. Just imagine a part of you, as if in the movies, moving away from your body and looking at yourself as you read these words. Become aware of the opinions, the thoughts, the feelings which inject themselves, some verbal, others like waves of emotion washing over that person you are now watching. Does it make you self-conscious? How do you feel about being watched?

* * *

Does it occur to you that maybe you are not your opinions, that your opinions are just habits? (The great Spanish writer, Miguel de Unamuno said, "To fall into a habit is to begin to cease to be.") Most significantly, can you think differently if you do not automatically react as you always have? You'll discover that you have choices when you step outside and watch.

The next time you automatically become angry, you might step back and say "I could become angry. If I want to. Or I could become sad. Or I could think about it. Or I could laugh at it. Or I could cry...' And you would see that the choice is yours at every moment.

Exercise: About Time I

"Two minutes is a short time when you're talking with a beautiful girl. It's a long time when you're sitting on a hot stove. That's relativity"

—*Albert Einstein*

Dr. Larry Dossey says that we as a culture suffer from "time sickness." Maybe we're just not having fun. But it is a fact that the way we perceive time can injure our health and actually change the way time moves.

When "Type A" personality people, known to be driven and intense, were tested to imagine how long a minute took, they regularly gave themselves only a fraction of the time. These are people for whom there is never enough time, and yet they perceived of a minute as only a fraction of what it actually is! And, of course, as a group they die sooner, having perceived of their life as half as short as it really might be.

So then, test a minute with your eyes closed when you're feeling under pressure, when the day is slipping by and there's too much to do to fit it all in. Take out one small minute, close your eyes, and see if you can discern how long a minute really is.

Then, test a minute with your eyes closed when you're feeling relaxed. Try it on a slow day, maybe even a day that drags.

Which comes closer to a minute on your watch?

You know how long a slow, boring day seems. You know how quickly a good party moves along. Time really is elastic and you can influence it.

Here's a simple exercise to test that theory for yourself. Sometime when you're really panicked and trying to fit a lot of stuff into a short period of time, slow down. Elastic time will move more slowly when you stretch it out like that. Picture it stretching out before you in long slow waves and see if it doesn't slow down when you need it to. You will have more time and accomplish more, just by slowing time down, which is really slowing down how you perceive it. Literally, actually move more slowly. Take slower breaths. Hesitate. Smile. My colleague Meridith Duncan says that when it seems that she's going to be late for an appointment, she looks at the clock or her watch and imagines the hands or the numbers moving more slowly. Somehow, that gives her more time to get there. If you're cynical about it, just try it, and remember, it doesn't have to make "sense" on this plane, it just has to work.

Time Out in Exercises About Time

The next exercise asks you to visualize something from your past. A lot of people immediately freeze up at such a suggestion, contending that they "cannot visualize." Of course, what they forget is that they dream, which is a form of visualizing. But, to some, it seems a momentous task to bring a picture to mind, so I would like to show you how easy it is.

First of all, even some of us who are "good" at it don't really see what we're imagining, we just remember it in a way that it comes to mind. So when I ask you to picture an apple, picture one with a leaf attached to the stem, even with a nice, juicy bite take out of it, if I were to ask you "what color is your apple," chances are good you would say, "red." If you said "yellow," you're way ahead on visualizing. But "red" will do for a first step.

How about the dishes you eat breakfast on in your house. What do they look like? Do they have flowers on them, are they a color, are they thick pottery or slender bone china? And your bedroom. Can you imagine your bedspread, or your favorite picture or poster on the wall? You don't have to really see it for it to come alive in your imagination.

Imagine those dishes again and imagine some pasta on them. Marinara sauce or pesto? Whatever you said, you're on your way. And if you "saw" nothing, the old hypnosis trick is to make it up, anyway. Whatever comes from you tells you more about yourself. Whatever you imagine could only come from you. So see what you make up and try the next exercise about time.

Exercise: About Time II

This exercise helps you take yourself out of the span of linear time. It enables you to break time down, much the same as you would do if you were to photograph a moving picture of an event and then cut that movie into single frames, still pictures you could hang in front of you and study.

First, imagine a recent event, it can be a significant negative event like a quarrel with a loved one, or it can be a significant positive event, like earning an honor or winning a prize. It can also be a commonplace event, like sitting on a porch swing and watching the sun go down. The span of time the event covers can be anywhere from a few minutes to a few hours; it even can be a series of linked events occurring over a span of days or months.

The important thing is to be able to visualize whatever event you chose as if it were a movie. Sit down, relax, close your eyes if that makes it easier for you to imagine things, and watch the movie. Watch it from start to finish, the pain and the pleasure, and the tedium.

Now, when the movie is over, imagine yourself going back to the projector and taking the reel of film out and then placing it into one of those machines film editors use. You know the kind. You slide the film into it, so that it runs by in a lighted viewer on your desk. There is a big crank you can crank to look at the entire film as it goes through. You can crank it fast; you can slow it down; you can stop it on a single frame, so that that frame appears to you as a photographic slide would appear in a viewer. You can even run the film backward by reversing the crank, so that you can go back to just the picture you want.

Now find a single frame from this movie, and stop the crank so you can study it alone. It can be a picture of you at a moment of heightened emotion. It can be a photograph of somebody else. It can be a photograph of conflict between you and somebody else. It can even be a photograph of the location itself without anybody in it.

Now that you've chosen a single frame, just sit back and look at it a few minutes. Don't think about it. Don't try to force memories to bloom it into context. Simply look at the single image that came from the movie that was a part of your life. If it is a person, study the expression on the face. If it is several people in ""action," try to see the signals each person is giving the other[s], through gestures or body language. If it is a scene, simply view the scene as if you were seeing it for the first time, as if nothing significant has ever happened there.

After a minute or two of "viewing" your chosen still-frame, notice how time, the ticking of seconds and minutes and hours that were necessary to string together your movie, has disappeared. The expression on the face you are studying takes you back instantly to the time you saw that face when the "movie" was made. The expression is in fact happening "now," not only for you as you "view" it, but even for the person you are viewing, even if the event you've been replaying happened long ago, even if the person you are viewing has long since passed beyond this life. It is as if the experience of the single frame had never ended, as if it is eternal.

What do I *mean* by this? I can't really explain it, but I am fairly certain you will understand if you are doing this exercise. Your single frame has come away from time and stands before you, as if it always had been, always shall be. It has come away from the necessary progression of frames that led to it and will lead away from it. You can, if you wish, cut that frame from the time-linear movie, hang it on your wall, splice it into another motion picture that comes to a different ending, or that explains this frame by coming from a different beginning. The single frame stands alone, and as you gaze at it, the notion of time for you disappears.

Doing this exercise does not imply that you will necessarily gain any special insight from stopping the movie and viewing the frame. You might. Insight often comes at the points within your experience when notions of time fall away. You might understand the person you are studying with a deeper wisdom than you were able to muster when the frame first whizzed past in its happening. You might remember the scene you are viewing with a deeper intensity. You might be caused to contemplate details or moods in an entirely different way.

But then again, none of this needs to happen. You also don't need to penetrate the frame and run the sequence back magically to a place you didn't have a chance to be, a place that led without you to the frame you have chosen to study and that now, without time, you have an opportunity to contemplate. None of this needs to happen, but it might.

What could happen as you allow the process to work in its own way is that by freezing the frame, you will come to sense down deep how unnecessary it is to factor time into the experience of a moment.

A sense of time was necessary in order to catalogue that frame and string it into the motion picture of a memory. A sense of time may be necessary for you to be able to find that moment, and later, when you are finished with it, to set that moment back into its place. But that is all time was really needed for. It is simply a card catalogue for the indexing of moments. Like books picked from the shelves of a library, the moments live a life by themselves.

The importance of this exercise is to help you learn to appreciate the timelessness of moments. Then, when you do, you will be able to use the freezing of frames to facilitate the gaining of insight.

Time is mutable. Its apparent motion, its duration, its relation to this moment. Play with it. You'll learn a lot.

Exercise: About Time III

Keep a diary of the synchronistic events that happen in your life. Don't let a single "coincidence" pass your keen eye. Ask for them. You'll be amazed at how license plates or slogans on signs or fortune cookies really seem to start to fit.

One night while I was early for one of the classes I taught, I stood idly reading a *Vanity Fair* magazine at an outdoor newsstand in Beverly Hills. An article about Marianne Williamson, discussing the dissension in her ranks since she became famous and appeared on television, caught my eye. I stood there thinking how glad I was not to have my healing energies distorted by celebrity, especially on television. How I wouldn't let television turn my head.

Just then, someone tapped me on the shoulder and I turned to see a man with a microphone, and behind him, a man with a television camera. "Excuse me," he said, "May I ask you a question?"

There it was, an immediate test, a pop quiz. Television was calling me. Actually, it was a person-in-the-street interview about Rodney King, but it proved pertinent in that it showed me something about myself. After I answered the question into the camera, I went to teach my class that evening. My students were writing well and I became so involved in the readings that I forgot that I might appear on the 11 o'clock local news. By the time I got home, it was after 11:30 and I never learned whether my somewhat aberrant answer had appeared on television. So, the high-point of my brush with fame was that I discovered that I was not off-course from my purpose and swept up with "celebrity."

This was a synchronicity that went right into my synchronicity diary. So did the one about "Amazing Grace" in the story of the Ghost (Chapter Eleven). Small ones count, too. Like thinking of someone and having them call. The more you notice, the more they will happen. It's as if the universe says, "She's listening." "He's paying attention." "We can give them more signs." Be subtle. It will change the way you think about time and our being stuck in it. You will discover the interconnectedness. You will begin to notice how, when you focus on something, it jells. And you'll begin to feel your own magic.

Exercise: The Mind/Body Connection I

This exercise was inspired by one suggested by Sandra Ingerman in her book, *Soul Retrieval: Mending the Fragmented Self.* This is my version of it.

You have inside your body neuropeptides which respond honestly and without your intellectual sensor to your true emotions and your instincts. We ignore these signals at our peril, but sometimes we don't know how to hear them.

This exercises is meant to awaken you to the feeling in your body when you are telling yourself the truth and when you are telling yourself a lie.

So, sit quietly for a while and concentrate on a feeling which is true for you. If there is someone you love unconditionally, if there is something that gives you unmitigated pleasure, concentrate on it and feel in your body how it feels to bring that cherished person or activity into your awareness. Where in your body do you feel it? What is the sensation? Is it warmth? Is it tingling? Is it melting, like the relaxing of tense muscles?

Then get a drink of water or walk around, do something which grounds you, rub your feet on the floor, back and forth.

Next, allow yourself to deny your love for that person or activity. Lie to yourself about it. "I hate my dog," or "I hate painting," whatever it is that you love. Feel the sense of the lie in your body. When you lie to yourself, that's how it feels, that's where you feel it. How does it feel? Like a knot? Like a panic?

Then think of something that upsets you. A danger to someone you love, perhaps. How does that feel? And where? That may be your intuition talking. It may also be your fears. That's a harder one to discern, but at least now you know where in your body you hold your fears.

Now cancel that thought that upset you. Picture your loved one safe and happy. Feel the difference.

Your body is talking to you every moment. And it is uncensored. Sometime when you want to know what you "really" feel, you could flip a coin and see if you say "two out of three," if the answer your unconscious wants does not pop up first. Or you could ask your body. Now you know where to look for answers.

Exercise: The Mind/Body Connection II

Hypnotic anesthesia is a field which holds a great deal of potential, but which is as yet not fully explored because the lure of pain killers has been so great. Yet there are ways of using our minds to relieve our suffering which you might try, because they give you more control over your mood as well as your body.

As a simple test of your powers, just begin thinking about an itch inside your left ear. Think of that itch deep inside that ear, too deep down inside to scratch. It actually begins as a sort of tingle. Or maybe it feels as if a little ant were crawling around in there. Or a centipede with hundreds of hairy little feet, crawling, creeping along in a circular motion, round and round inside your ear. You'd love to touch it, but you don't want to give in. So you try to ignore it. But now it really itches. Maybe it makes you swallow hard. See how long it takes you, focusing on that part of your body, to develop an itch you finally have to scratch.

Now, here are two more useful exercises. The first one will help you to numb a painful area, the other could help you dissolve a headache.

Glove anesthesia
Sit quietly and become aware of your breath. Breathe deeply, slowly as you can, a deep, long inhale and then a release. Then twice more.

Now, allow your right hand to become very heavy and still. Allow it to become like a block of wood, almost as if you couldn't move it, almost as if no blood is running through it. As if it weren't even your hand. Maybe there's a strange sensation in your wrist or up your arm to your elbow. Maybe your fingers are tingling or even throbbing as your hand grows so heavy it feels like an artificial limb. Take as long as you need to allow that hand to feel somewhat detached, deadened, heavy.

Now imagine that you've placed that hand into a freezing mountain stream or into a bucket of ice water. Make it numb. Make it so numb that if you stuck a pin in it, you wouldn't feel a thing. The icy water moves around it so vibrantly that it almost hurts, it is so cold. Keep it in that stream or bucket of ice until it is so numb, it is a frozen block of ice, itself.

Now actually place that block-of-ice hand on any other part of you, your cheek, your thigh, and transfer the numbness. That is how to anesthetize a painful part of your body. I have done this work with cancer patients and they have found relief without drugs for hours at a time.

Dissolving a Headache

Generally when we have pain like a headache, we spend our energy resisting it, which causes it to tighten up like a fist and get worse. I have had some success helping people do the following. Close your eyes, get comfortable and relaxed, count your in and out breaths slowly five times. Then imagine yourself being inside your head, where the hurt is. Imagine not fighting it, but being with it, calmly, gently, recognizing it, saying there you are. I'm sorry you're hurting.

Then begin to picture the headache as a tight red ball. With every breath that you inhale, imagine filling the ball with air and starting to dissolve it. You exhale and breathe out some of the atoms and particles that make up that tight red ball. You inhale and the ball begins to soften, become less red and hard, to break up into a mist. You exhale some of the gasses. You inhale again and dissolve it further, watch and feel it becoming filmier, more pink, more diffuse. You exhale and release more of the pink fog. Every time you inhale, your breath turns the ball of pain into a more diluted pink fog, exhaling it from your body easily and gently. This relaxing action may actually affect the capillaries carrying the blood to the area , evening out the flow of blood and perhaps releasing the headache. Inhale and dissolve, turning the headache into a fluffy pink cloud. Exhale the smoke and let it go.

Exercise: The Meaning of Life I

Green Light Meditation

When you want to expand your ability to love and to help someone else who may be hurting, try this simple exercise. Imagine a beam of green light coming from your heart. The person you want to relate to may be in front of you or may be out of sight, it doesn't matter. Imagine the beam of light going to his or her heart and then surrounding the person in a green glow.

It is important to ask their permission on this level to send them light or love. Sometimes you may detect that they reject the love. You should never force the issue, as it is their decision, even to harm themselves if they so choose. (See Chapter Twenty-One.) However, if you feel that their higher selves might hold it for them until they are ready for it, you could ask permission to do that. If granted, you could imagine leaving it in a green ball above their heads.

In the movie *Shadowlands*, the story of the author C.S. Lewis and his love for a woman dying of cancer, someone suggests to Lewis that he pray because God listens. Lewis answers something to the effect that he doesn't pray because it changes God, but because it changes **him**. This Green Light Meditation may well change **both** the person you are thinking of and you.

For those who don't pray, this is a form of prayer that is more concrete and direct, more immediately purposeful. For those who do pray, this is just an enhancement of a familiar reaching out.

When you do this exercise, you have something to do in situations in which there is nothing for you to do. In situations in which you have to wait for someone else to have a "change of heart" or "see the light." This is not to tell them to love you or to control their behavior. It is simply to send them love energy. What they make of it is their own business.

When you're practicing, it's really a stunning confirmation to discover that the other person, unbeknownst to them, has received the gift. Call them and just see if you can detect an uplifting of spirits after you meditate with green light on their well-being. My daughter knows this exercise well, and recently she called me from New York, ill with a cold and said, "Did you send me light at 10:30?" She was right, of course, because counting back put the time at 7:30 in L.A., when I'd just awakened for work, thought of her and done this exercise. "That was the first time I could breathe clearly all day," she said.

One day I was sitting in an airport alone, waiting for a plane. A woman came over and sat down a few seats away from me. Her face was worn and wrinkled with lines of care, and she held in her hand a crumpled tissue in such a way that I knew she **always** held a tissue like that in her hand. For support, for solace. Because there was so much to weep about.

I had the inclination to open my heart and send her green light. Her eyes were closed, so I closed mine, asked her permission, received it and directed that energy toward her. I felt her accept it. I sat patiently sending out as much love as was being absorbed. Minutes passed, maybe two, maybe five. Then I opened my eyes and looked at her. I could hardly believe it, even with the faith I bring to every encounter. Her face was calm, the lines smoothed out. She looked almost serene, not asleep, just peaceful.

Our eyes never met, we boarded separate planes and I never saw her again, but she did me the great favor of proving to me once again that we are all connected and as close as a thought.

Exercise: The Meaning of Life II

Try literally to see everything that happens to you as a metaphor. Try to see the meaning in it. If the drain in your kitchen sink is stopped up, ask yourself, what else is stopped up in my life?

Use your car's symptoms to mirror yours. If your brakes are not holding, what is the symbology for your journey down the road at this time? If your car is having trouble changing gears, how does that relate to how you're feeling?

As soon as you put it that way in your mind, two things happen. The first is that you smile, even when you're annoyed at the occurrence in the "outside world." The second is that you might have a valuable insight about your life at this exact moment.

Exercise: The Meaning of Life III

One technique Dr. Ronald Wong Jue has developed for healing and transformation is the transformational journey. By relaxing his patients with music and awareness of their breathing, he describes a journey which their imagination can follow, filling in the metaphors, symbols and experiences particular to them.

The parent you held in your mind and heart before this journey was not the man who was your father, or the woman who was your mother, but simply what your father seemed like to you. To another sibling, s/he might have been different. To his or her spouse, someone else. To the boss, someone else. To his/her own mother, someone else, not the person you carried around inside of you.

And that image can be changed. That's the magic of a transforming journey. Even if s/he is no longer here in three dimensions, you can hold him/her in your heart in a way that you didn't before, alive and functioning in your life. You can separate the dark and the light energy and take that which is reverent to you at this time and hold it in your heart.

The journey takes you to a place where you experience your parent differently from the way you have so far.

Try reading this journey to yourself on tape with soft music in the background or have a sympathetic friend read it to you as you sit or lie quietly, letting your imagination take you where you need to go.

You are walking along a beach on a beautiful day. The air is fresh, you can feel it against your skin. The sun is warm against your face. You hear the seagulls singing and the sound of the waves slapping against the shore. Your feet make perfect footprints in the sand and you enjoy the smell of the salt-sea air.

Suddenly, you come upon a beautiful, large bird. It is the bird of your imagination and it has been waiting for you. You pick up a piece of sea-weed and, using it as a harness, you get on its back and fly off into the clouds. The wind whispers against your ears as you move through the clouds and you stare in wonder at the beauty from that height. Before you know it, you arrive at a ruined castle perched in a cloud. The bird takes you closer, lands, and you dismount, walking toward the ruins.

On a pedestal is your father (or mother). He (she) does not see you, but stands there, looking out into the vast reaches of space. Out from behind him (her) steps his (her) inner child. You watch in awe. This child is in need of healing. And you go to this child, your father's (mother's) inner child, and provide what s/he needs to heal so that your father (mother) may heal into wholeness. What does he (she) need? How can you help him (her) to be complete?

The child hugs you and returns to your father (mother). Then the parts of him (her) which constituted the dark side begin to separate out, to congeal, and they are frozen into a false shape around him (her). Then the outer form begins to crack and shatter, falling off into a pile of empty pottery around him (her). And what is left is all the good that he (she) has left to offer you. Now your eyes meet and you see the good and the vulnerable in this person. Between your heart and his (hers) a beam of green light exchanges.

The bird reappears and calls to you, so you run off to mount it and head back. But you bring the new awareness back with you in your heart as you return to the beach and then back to your conscious aware-ness here in this room.

This is where the journey moves into the holographic, because it is fine if your mother or father have passed on. Dr. Jue shows us that even though the parent may be physically dead, we can hold the spirit within ourselves. Everything s/he's ever given to you, you can maintain and articulate in your life, he says. This is a hologram holding energy of the spirit of the person who has died. And when you see him/her in the healing light, you hold a different, more valuable parent inside of you.

Exercise: Finding Guides

It might be true that from the moment we are born, we are guided beings. Maybe even before. Babies often seem to see things we cannot see, smiling and staring in wonder, although they cannot say who else surrounds us, glowing.

There are audio tapes on the market that can help you find guides, or you can find one for yourself by going into an altered state (for example, right before you fall asleep, or perhaps relaxed in a bath, meditating or dreaming while out in nature) and envisioning a beautiful place: a garden or a forest or a beach, perhaps. Taking your time, and with no special expectations, you can ask for and await the arrival of a guide, a being who represents your higher wisdom or your connection with the infinite. Sometimes the first person we see is not the guide, but can lead us to the guide. Do not be discouraged, but persist. When you find someone whose energy seems right, ask if he or she is "from the light."

A real guide will state how he or she can help you. He or she will give you a gift (which you may later find in the "real" world) or a way you can signal and call for him or her to come to you.

Ask the guide for his or her name. Once you have a name and an image, this guide can be of great service, and a source of comfort.

* * *

A less metaphorical way to reach your inner wisdom is by using a pendulum. Anything on a string can act as a pendulum, including a safety pin or a tea bag. Hold it suspended in the air and think a strong "no," something you definitely feel "no" about. Watch the direction in which the pendulum moves (usually back and forth). Then think "yes," think of something you feel very positive about. Watch the direction (usually a circle) the pendulum moves. When you have your "yes" and "no" signals, ask yourself questions that can be answered by either of those words and you have a direct line to your unconscious.

Amulet Exercise

While I invite you to have an active spiritual life, there are ways that you can connect those feelings to the material world. One is through an amulet. My sister-in-law had been harmed by a team of prestigious physicians in Boston who refused to take any responsibility for the destruction they had caused in her eyes and her life. She suffered a depression as a result of having been not only mutilated but dismissed and could not go on with her life until she felt a sense of "justice." She decided to sue, which caused great havoc and seemed futile because there is such bedrock respect for doctors in that community. In a spiritual store, she had bought a green rock and invested it with her hopes. Somehow it had been misplaced during her first arbitration and she lost her suit against one of the physicians. The rock resurfaced during the trial of the second physician and it gave her such a sense of strength to hold it while she testified and they tried to defame her on the stand, that she made a very credible witness and the doctor settled the case, the first time in his career he acknowledged a wrong.

The story of the rock made me consider the value of an "amulet," a magic piece that connects us with blessings. Certainly major league baseball players have their lucky bat or their lucky socks; likely we've all had something we felt brought us luck at some time or other and then forgotten about it.

Recently, I offered a client the opportunity to select a rock from a collection I had assembled, some polished, some gemstones, some just delivered to the shore by the ocean off the coast of Los Angeles, some found in the forest in Prescott. She chose one and held it in her hand as I took her into trance.

Her presenting issue was that she felt that life was a struggle and she was not struggling enough; that she was failing in the race to material success; that there were things she should be doing and time was running out. It was old programming from her father, whom she adored, and who had passed away a year before, after having lived a life of struggle and continual work just to keep up.

In trance, she walked along the beach and I asked her to imagine a guide coming toward her. She saw one who seemed more like a light and was stationed behind her back. She did not want to turn to face him. "Ask him his name," I said, and she said, "Jesus."

As you know, if you've read this book, guides can be holy or they can be Tinkerbell or even a piece of fruit (the orange was a metaphor, if not a guide, in Chapter Fourteen).

I asked her to ask Jesus if she was worthy of his love, even if she did nothing to further her career or earning capabilities. She said, "Yes." I asked if there was anything she needed to do or be to be worthy of his love. She said, "No." I asked if he would enfold her and surround her with his love and light and then it occurred to me that her father should be here, too, so I asked that he come and be part of this experience with Jesus, finding out that just by being, without having to do anything, one is whole and worthy. Tears streamed down her cheeks as she stood in the circle of love.

"What are you feeling?" I said.

"I'm so glad to be able to give this to my father," she said.

Then, after we further clarified the experience, I asked her to ask Jesus to fill the rock in her hand with the light, which was done, and then let the light go up her arm and fill her body and beam out through her aura so that everyone might see it and see her worthy. She did. And to see herself in the future, feeling worthy and loved and shining. And she did.

When she left, she took the rock with her, knowing that by simply holding it she could go back to that feeling of wholeness.

That's an amulet.

If you want one, first find one. In can be from a store, from a friend, one you find at the beach, in the woods, on the street, in the attic, it doesn't matter. Then experience in any way that works for you, the love of God or the rich, bright fullness of the universe. You could go to some place in nature to find both the rock and the experience. Or simply take some time for yourself, being so quiet and still that you notice yourself feeling tingly or light or heavy or somehow infused with a different kind of energy. When that happens, become aware of the rock in your hands and fill it with that energy. Move it up your arm, through your body, and out your aura. Sit quietly in that glow. You are worthy, just for having been born into this life. There is nothing you have to do or be to be whole, but know it.

Mantra Exercise

I discovered one day several years ago that a thought seemed to fly 'round and 'round above my head as if it were suspended there for me to notice all the time, like sky writing. That year, the thought was "impeccable integrity," a concept given coin by Carlos Casteneda in the Don Juan books. It meant that everything I did had to be completely honest and honorable. I remember saying to my boss one day, "I'm taking this paperclip home," and having her look at me in confusion, but I felt I could do nothing that was not completely above-board.

The next year, the word that came to me was "faith." I guessed I was lacking in the appropriate amount, so I held that thought lightly and constantly in my mind.

It was interesting that, once a thought had its run and I had lived with it, it became completely incorporated in my being. I can't say I have perfect integrity or faith today, only that awareness of them have led me to make those choices much more often.

The particular words came to me by themselves, but because I "asked" for them. You might try it for yourself and see what concept or idea might best serve you to work on at this time.

Yet another little mantra exercise was given to me by a friend. He said if you say something seventy times for seven days, and then let it go, it could manifest. I must say, I enjoyed the process of selecting my week's mantra and of incorporating it into my life. The saying, "be careful what you wish for, you might get it," weighs heavily on you as you craft your mantras.

What all this is about, of course, is consciousness. Connecting with the universal and being aware of it. Practicing this conscious choice brings magic into your life, whether you actually "get" what you ask for or not. Add to this the idea of "being aware of God" (See Chapter Twenty-Seven) and life can be transformed.

And remember, too, that we are not necessarily smart enough to see what is best for us from here. Sometimes the incident that seems the most unfortunate becomes the very impetus for our greatest change.

Next Steps: Finding Your Strengths
"Getting Unstuck without Coming Unglued"

In 1998, I wrote a proposal for a book entitled *Getting Unstuck Without Coming Unglued.* The ideal condition, as defined by a restatement of the title, would be to be both "unstuck" and "glued." That means that, while you are not hindered by past failures (stuck), you also do not deny your essential being and purpose (you're not unglued), that you do not have to abandon the most valued parts of yourself in order to let go of those that no longer serve you. You are glued to your strengths and carry them with you into the future.

How does that process work? Since I believe that metaphors and stories illuminate our understanding, here are four brief scenarios help set the scene.

* * *

I. There is an organic farm in Arizona that grows acre upon acre of alfalfa and barley of exceptionally nutritious protein, vitamin and mineral content. The soil is tended with care and bathed in mineral supplements. When you look across the field, you notice something wonderful. There are no weeds. There are no bugs. And yet, no pesticides are being used. How can this be, when down the road, and across the country, farmers contend they have to use pesticides and poisonous weed killers on food products to bring them to market?

The answer is in the soil. Some 80 percent of our national topsoil has been eroded, denuded of elements and minerals that used to nourish the plants. Today, plants grown in this environment cannot be strong, cannot even be nutritious because, while plants can make vitamins, they don't create minerals but have to absorb them from the soil. While we look to vegetables for minerals, today, you might say that they have become unglued.

In fact, in 1945, when Popeye told us to eat our spinach to get iron, he had a good point. At that time, a cup of spinach contained 159 milligrams of iron per 100 grams. By 1965, a cup of spinach contained about 27 mg of iron. Today, when you tell your kids to eat their spinach for iron to build their blood, they get barely over 2 mg per cup; not enough to make it worth the scene they would likely cause. (Today, that is, it would take 75 cups to get the equivalent of iron supplied in the same dish fifty years ago, and not even Popeye's up for that).

The barley and alfalfa on the organic farm have been bathed in minerals and they are of such high quality, so strong, that bugs and weeds cannot compete and/or attack.

II. Along the same lines of strength in wholeness is the Ancient Chinese system of health. The way they saw it, it was the job of the physician to keep the emperor, and by extension all of his patients, healthy. (The incentive 5,000 years ago to do so was simple: when the emperor died, his physicians were buried with him.) It did not occur to those physicians that they should be patching people up when something went wrong. Their job was to keep them in perfect running condition with the appropriate herbal foods, all the while monitoring the body's balance through pulse and tongue. If a patient had symptoms, the physician had already failed (and didn't deserve to get paid). Making and keeping the body whole, so invaders have no entree—that is, calling on the body's own strength rather than treating a specific symptom with a specific drug—is another way of looking at health.

III. In the jungles of Central America there is a tribe of aboriginals who have an unusual way of disciplining those among them who misbehave.

They ask the "criminal" (let's say it's a young man) to sit in the center of their community circle and listen to them as they retell the good that he has done in the past!

"Don't you remember?" they might say, "when my horse ran away, and you were the one who found him?"

"And when I fell down from the tree, you ran for help."

"And you loaned me your knife when mine broke."

And he sits there, having now done something which violates the social standard, and hears about who he **really** is. And he remembers how to be.

IV. The last example of this approach is validated in the creative writing class Harry and I teach in the UCLA Writers' Program. There, we never harp on our students' weaknesses. We never tell them what they are doing "wrong." Instead, we focus on what they are doing well. We reinforce their talents, and, as a result, in the writing of each story, so do they. They begin to gain their own voice from the awareness of their greatest abilities. They begin to notice improvements in each other's and their own writing efforts, in a safe, nurturing environment. They begin to soar, their work being uniquely theirs, coming from parts of them that they had not even acknowledged. They begin to write from what the great writer and teacher John Gardner called "the fictive dream," instead of being more concerned with commas and criticism.

What do all of these examples have in common? Each thing that thrived was allowed to come from its strength. Each used what was inherent in it to build into wholeness and to repel that which was not good, simply by being complete, not open to attack.

* * *

A Few Fallacies to Overcome

One study of creativity found that the most creative people are not those who have had the most training, the best opportunities, the highest IQs, but simply those who THINK they are creative. They believe that there are answers, and that they can find them.

If a creative person is one who thinks he/she is creative, is a stuck person one who thinks he/she is stuck?

If you buy into any of the following fallacies, you might want to trade them in on a new model of thinking.

Do you believe:

1) that negative elements of your individual history are fixed and permanent, like gall stones that have to be removed or pulverized or endured? That you **are** those qualities you and others have identified with you, those labels like *lazy* or *stubborn* or *non-creative*?

2) that your ability to overcome and avert obstacles is restricted by the limitations your past has imposed upon you?

3) that you are entirely free simply to cast off and forget about everything that got you to the point where you find yourself so bereft?

The first two fallacies are the causes of our becoming STUCK; the third is what causes us to become UNGLUED.

∗ ∗ ∗

"Find out what you are and be it on purpose." Dolly Parton

Some of the answers lie in the past; some in the present; some in transcendence. Ultimately, the goal is to resonate with your place in the universe based on who you are and who you are here to become.

The goal is to learn how to identify your unique strengths and lean into them.

Nikos Kazantzakis, the profound author of *Zorba the Greek*, stated our spiritual task this way: he felt we had to plunge far enough into our own souls to find—and free—"the endangered spirit of God.' Each of us, he insisted, must consider ourselves solely responsible for the salvation of the world! Therefore, we were charged with finding out what we are here for and what we can uniquely do for humanity, so that we can accomplish it before we die and that gift is lost.

* * *

Find the metaphors and images that connect with your strengths. Animals, role models, symbols all can "impress" us, help guide us into the courage we need. Remember the strengths of the past (see Chapter Fifteen, Annie Oakley). Find guides to commune with. If it helps, remember the biblical call to be "wise as serpents, gentle as doves." In the Tao, my favorite image is being "kindhearted as a grandmother; dignified as a king."

When my sister-in law was mutilated by that doctor (see Amulet Exercise), I mentioned to her that she reminded me of Jacqueline Kennedy at the funeral of JFK, and she so warmed to that image that she became it, carrying herself through the painful trial with an air of elegance and self-possession that superceded all the ugliness of the proceedings.

You were born with a power to repel that which does not suit you and a power to build upon that which you were given.

While it is desirable to be unstuck, you'll want to be glued to that perhaps-yet-unidentified mission. You won't find the answers in the outside, material world. It is inner wisdom and our connection with it that must guide us in this process. Metaphors, moving into Alternity, can help you with the work of identifying it. It is truly a lifetime's work, but accomplishing it allows you to be free to live it, uniquely, as only you can and as you were born to do.

About the Author

Judith Simon Prager, Ph.D., is a practicing clinical hypnotherapist and clinical homeopath. As a consultant to Cedars-Sinai Medical Center in Los Angles, she has written a series of pre-intra-and post-operative and ICU creative imagery CDs which are being used in a pilot program in the Cardio-thoracic Surgery unit. She has also trained firefighters, emergency medical personnel, nurses and Cedars' pediatricians in hypnotic language for pain and stress relief in emergencies and magical interactions with children.

A best-selling novelist, TV writer, columnist, creative director of major New York and Los Angeles advertising agencies and an instructor with her husband, Harry Youtt, in the UCLA Writers' Program, she believes that all consciousness is one and sees creativity as our connection with our wisdom, each other and the infinite.

Printed in the United States
22612LVS00003B/184-192